"Heffner and Cowan have offered the field a well-written and well-conceptualized guide for the practice of clinical supervision. The workbook covers a lot of ground in a highly accessible and helpful manner. The content will not only ground new as well as experienced supervisors but will help to make supervision more transparent to trainees as well."

Janine M. Bernard, PhD, LMHC, *Professor Emeritus Syracuse University*

"This book is an excellent resource! The authors provide comprehensive guidelines for ethical supervision, as well as practical guidance and worksheets. The book is based in a thorough review of the supervision literature, with an emphasis on strength-based feedback and the supervisory relationship. Highly recommended for both supervisors and therapists training to become supervisors."

Tony Rousmaniere, PsyD, *Clinical Faculty, University of Washington; coauthor of* The Cycle of Excellence: Using Deliberate Practice to Improve Supervision and Training

"A unique aspect of this workbook are the concrete and practical activities that encourage supervisor–supervisee communication around key issues, such as giving and receiving feedback. These activities can foster genuine collaboration around the growth and development of both supervisor and supervisee."

L. DiAnne Borders, PhD, ACS, LMHC, NCC, *Editor,* The Clinical Supervisor; *Co-Founder, Clinical Supervision Research Collaborative; Excellence Professor, Department of Counseling and Educational Development, The University of North Carolina at Greensboro*

"I am very impressed with *The Strength-based Clinical Supervision Workbook*, as it is a much needed practitioner's guide to supervision from the perspective of both the supervisor and the supervisee's training. The integration of evidence-based practice throughout this work makes it an excellent and practical resource for training programs and supervisor development. I highly recommend this user-friendly guide to supervision."

Amy Wasserbauer, PhD, *Assistant Director, ASU Counseling Services*

THE STRENGTH-BASED CLINICAL SUPERVISION WORKBOOK

Supervision is the cornerstone of clinical training across all types of mental health providers. It facilitates the growth of mental health trainees and maintains the integrity of the field of mental health services by ensuring the competency of clinicians. However, the process can be complex and potentially confusing for both supervisors and trainees at any stage of their development or post-licensure career. Utilizing strength-based approaches is crucial to the success of supervision. This workbook facilitates a collaborative and strength-based approach to clinical supervision that both supervisors and trainees can use during the entire course of supervision, or for specific goals related to supervision. Each chapter of this workbook contains information and activities specific to both the trainee and supervisor to facilitate dialogue about individual and combined strengths, areas for growth, and goals for collaborative work.

This is an essential start-to-finish guide addressing the entire supervision process, from preparing for the first session to conducting the last session, and everything in between.

Christopher L. Heffner, PsyD, PhD, is a Licensed Psychologist and Core Faculty member in the Clinical PsyD Program at Antioch University Seattle (AUS) where he teaches Solution-Focused Interventions, Clinical Supervision, Consultation, and Community Psychology, and serves as Faculty Director of the Positive Psychology Lab. He has a bachelor's degree with a dual major in Psychology and Business Administration, an MS and PsyD in Clinical Psychology, and a PhD in Organization and Management, focused on leadership development. He completed the Certification for Solution-Focused Interventions from the Institute for Solution-Focused Therapy at Framingham University and the Positive Psychology Specialization through the University of Pennsylvania. Dr. Heffner founded and directs AllPsych.com, a psychology education website.

Jessica A. Cowan, PsyD, is a Licensed Clinical Psychologist in Washington and Arizona. She is currently in private practice and is also a clinical supervisor for the University of Washington's Department of Psychology. During the writing of this book, she completed her pre-doctoral internship and postdoctoral fellowship both of which contributed heavily to the supervisee perspective that she contributed to the development of the workbook's content and activities. Dr. Cowan completed her bachelor's degree in applied psychology with an emphasis on child and adolescent psychology from Seattle City University. She earned a doctorate in Clinical Psychology from Antioch University Seattle. Dr. Cowan is a member of the American Psychological Association (APA) and the Academy for Eating Disorders (AED). Her clinical and research interests are centered on clinical supervision and the treatment of eating disorders.

THE STRENGTH-BASED CLINICAL SUPERVISION WORKBOOK

A Complete Guide for Mental Health Trainees and Supervisors

Christopher L. Heffner and Jessica A. Cowan

Routledge
Taylor & Francis Group
NEW YORK AND LONDON

Cover image: © Getty Images

First published 2023
by Routledge
605 Third Avenue, New York, NY 10158

and by Routledge
4 Park Square, Milton Park, Abingdon, Oxon, OX14 4RN

Routledge is an imprint of the Taylor & Francis Group, an informa business

Library of Congress Cataloging-in-Publication Data
A catalog record for this title has been requested

ISBN: 978-0-367-43936-1 (hbk)
ISBN: 978-0-367-43935-4 (pbk)
ISBN: 978-1-003-00655-8 (ebk)

DOI: 10.4324/9781003006558

Typeset in Stone Serif
by KnowledgeWorks Global Ltd.

Access the Support Material: https://www.routledge.com/9780367439354

CONTENTS

Acknowledgments ix

SECTION I Foundation and Framework for Strength-Based Supervision 1

CHAPTER 1 Historical and Theoretical Foundations of Clinical Supervision: How Where We've Been Informs Where We Are 3

CHAPTER 2 Does Supervision Matter? What the Evidence Suggests in Support of Supervision and Best Practices 19

CHAPTER 3 How We Can, Not Why We Can't: Theory and Techniques of Strength-Based Clinical Supervision 45

SECTION II The First Supervision Session 57

CHAPTER 4 Preparing for the First Session: Identifying What You Bring Individually to the Supervision Process 59

CHAPTER 5 The Role of Cultural Competence and Social Justice in Effective Strength-Based Supervision 84

CHAPTER 6 We Need to Talk: The Relationship as a Foundation for Effective Strength-Based Supervision 91

CHAPTER 7 Start with the End in Mind: Developing Strength-Based Supervision Goals 99

SECTION III Moving Forward: Building on Strengths in Ongoing and Final Supervision Sessions 119

CHAPTER 8 It's a Journey and a Destination: Essential Tasks and Goals of Ongoing Supervision Sessions 121

CHAPTER 9 What You See Is What You Get: Monitoring and Observing Clinical Work 134

CHAPTER 10 Effective Feedback: Best Practices for Giving Trainees More of What They Want (Hint: Feedback) 152

CHAPTER 11 A Focus on Solutions: Addressing Obstacles through Strength-Based Remediation and Rupture Repair 172

CHAPTER 12 Ending Well: The Final Supervision Sessions and Stepping Into the Future 185

Conclusion 200

References 202

Index 210

ACKNOWLEDGMENTS

Many people contributed to this workbook, both directly and indirectly, and we would like to acknowledge their work and thank them for helping in our effort to advance clinical supervision and strength-based interventions in the mental health professions.

First, we would like to thank our spouses ... Shawn DeGraw and CJ Cowan, for their encouragement, patience, and tireless tech support. You finally get to stop asking us "is the book done yet?"

We would like to thank Ashley Turner, MSW, who reviewed the text through the lens of both an advanced doctoral student in clinical psychology and a practicing Social Worker. Her feedback, especially her critique of positive psychology and its integration into strength-based clinical supervision, was invaluable. Lizz Keiper served as a teaching assistant for Dr. Heffner's Consultation and Supervision course at AUS. She assisted with in-class roleplays that both demonstrated and helped to refine many of the skills discussed in this workbook. The prior year Dr. Cowan, Dr. Heffner's coauthor, founded this role and helped to integrate the voice of the trainee into the Consultation and Supervision course.

Thanks to Tony Rousmaniere, PsyD for our discussions on clinical supervision and deliberate practice and for his trainings with our students and faculty on these topics. He helped us broaden how we look at training and the roles that trainees play in their clinical development. We would like to share our appreciation for Dr. Bill Heusler's advice, who, as a colleague and fellow supervisor, shared his experiences as both a trainee and a supervisor. We hope this workbook has enough pizzaz.

We would also like to thank the interns at the Antioch University Seattle Community Psychology Clinic, including Elizabeth Schmitz-Binnall, Jennifer Hutchinson, and Patricia Hastings, as well as Dr. Cowan's fellow interns at Arizona State University, Dr. Madison Martins and Dr. Jennifer Holzapfel, for reviewing and providing feedback on many of the handouts and worksheets used in this workbook.

Dr. Heffner would like to thank both Anne Bodmer Lutz, MD and Yvonne Dolan, MS who developed and facilitated the SFT Certification program and inspired him to become a **Solution-focused** practitioner. The program changed his professional direction and added skills to support his strength-based orientation and interest in positive psychology. He would also like to thank Dr. Cowan who brought the trainees voice to this workbook and her firsthand experience transitioning from trainee to psychologist to clinical supervisor. I continue to learn a lot from you – thank you for your dedication to the field, to your clients and trainees, and for your work to continually move us forward as a profession. I am a better psychologist and supervisor because of you.

Dr. Cowan would like to thank her clinical supervisors, Dr. Shannon Albert, Dr. Dan Dodd, Dr. Michael Sakuma, Dr. Nina Parker-Cohen, and Dr. Shirley Yang. She is grateful to each of them for generously sharing their time, wisdom, and mentorship - and for exemplifying the kind of supervisor she aspires to be. Their contributions to this book are countless. She would also like to thank Dr. Amy Wasserbauer—her internship supervisor-of-supervision—whose enthusiasm for supervision and training effective supervisors is boundless, and whose feedback helped shape many of the elements of this workbook. Dr. Cowan would also like to thank her co-author, Dr. Heffner for inviting her as a 3rd year clinical psychology student to assist him in providing a continuing education course on supervision, leading to countless discussions of "there should be a workbook for this ..." which is now a reality.

SECTION I

FOUNDATION AND FRAMEWORK FOR STRENGTH-BASED SUPERVISION

Introduction & How to Use This Workbook

Supervision is the cornerstone of clinical training across all types of mental health providers. It facilitates the growth of mental health trainees, and it maintains the integrity of the field of mental health services by ensuring the competency of clinicians and thus protecting the interests of the public. It is no wonder, then, that this process can be so complex and potentially confusing for both supervisors and trainees at any stage of their development or post-licensure career.

Despite supervision's longstanding history and seemingly permanent place in the training and development of mental health professionals, it is not without complications that can potentially confuse and confound trainees and supervisors alike. We have witnessed, and experienced first-hand, confusion about how to prioritize the multiple "hats" (teacher, coach, administrator ...) worn by a supervisor; of wanting to see your trainees succeed while also balancing your ethical and clinical priorities; of being unsure how to approach, versus avoid, obstacles in supervision. From a trainee's perspective, we know that supervision is often an abstract and wildly varied process that leaves many trainees wondering what is supervision, how can they be a more active participant, and how do they know that they're getting what they need? We have also witnessed and experienced the powerful potential of supervision to promote positive change in our trainees, ourselves, and our clients. We wanted to do something to help all supervisors and trainees have these positive experiences.

In our work and training (one of us was on internship during most of the writing of this book), we also noticed that most supervision texts were heavily weighted toward academic and conceptual material. This doesn't go far enough in helping supervisors and trainees understand how to apply the material in their practice of supervision and how to adapt evidence-based practices to meet their individual or programmatic needs.

Finally, we've learned, and the evidence supports, that utilizing **strength-based** approaches is crucial to the success of supervision. Many of us can recall a moment when one or more of our strengths were recognized by someone we respected, admired, and/or trusted, and how that motivated our desire to continue improving our work; to work even harder toward all our goals (even those that felt out of reach); and to value even more highly the positive and constructive feedback we receive. It is for all of the reasons listed above that we developed this workbook. We hope it will serve as a tool, as a guide, and as inspiration for supervisors and trainees to get the most out of their work together, and to lead and inspire each other toward ultimately enhancing their clinical competency and the competency of those whom they go on to supervise.

DOI: 10.4324/9781003006558-1

Ways to Use This Workbook

We've designed this workbook to facilitate a collaborative and **strength-based** approach to clinical supervision that both supervisors and trainees can use during the entire course of supervision, or for specific goals related to supervision. We offer the following considerations for how you might use this workbook, together or separately, to meet your supervision goals:

- A start-to-finish guide addressing the entire supervision process, from preparing for your first session to conducting the last session, and everything in between.
- A guide for addressing specific challenges within supervision, including remediation of problems, providing feedback to one another, and/or repairing ruptures in the supervision relationship.
- An informational tool to help set expectations for supervisors and trainees who are new to one another, or new to their role as supervisor or trainee, who might be wondering, *What is supervision? What is my role within supervision, and how do I know that I'm doing it well?*
- A way to enhance collaboration between supervisor and trainee. Each chapter of this workbook contains information and activities specific to both the trainee and supervisor to facilitate a dialogue about your individual and combined strengths, areas for growth, and goals for your work together. For example: supervisors, you might ask your trainee(s) to complete certain activities before supervision meetings so that you can review and discuss them in supervision together. You might also use activities during supervision sessions, such as reviewing case examples, to learn more about each other and facilitate clinical growth.
- In addition to standalone activities, we have also included activities that are designed to contribute sequentially to the development of your own approach to supervision including setting the foundation and framework of supervision, preparing for the first session, managing ongoing sessions, overcoming obstacles, and ending supervision with reflection and goals for ongoing deliberate practice. For trainees, these activities will facilitate an understanding of their individual approach to supervision to enhance dialogue with their supervisor about individual similarities and differences.

CHAPTER 1

HISTORICAL AND THEORETICAL FOUNDATIONS OF CLINICAL SUPERVISION

How Where We've Been Informs Where We Are

INFORM	ENGAGE
• Understand the historical context of how supervision came to be • Learn the theoretical basis for how supervision has evolved since its inception • Understand the basics of supervision models and the developmental and process-based approaches to clinical supervision	• Reflect on your approach to supervision in the context of existing models and supervision frameworks • Consider which supervision processes are strengths or areas for growth

In this chapter we'll introduce you to foundational elements of effective supervision, including its historical context (spoiler: it starts with Freud) and more recent efforts to increase evidence-based practices in supervision. We're going to give you a lot of information. Some of it may be redundant depending on your level of familiarity with supervision, and if that's the case we encourage you to consider an à la carte approach by reading (or skimming—our feelings won't be hurt) the information that's most helpful to you at this or other points in your supervision journey. We'll also share a lot of evidence-based practices and approaches to conducting and engaging in supervision. Take a deep breath—you don't need to use all these approaches all of the time. Our goal is to give you enough information, skills, and tools that you can tailor supervision to your needs and the needs of your trainee or supervisor. Because supervision is an art *and* a science, we encourage flexibility and improvisation, and we recognize that this workbook is just one of many tools in your supervision kit.

DOI: 10.4324/9781003006558-2

History of Clinical Supervision and Training in Mental Health Professions

Clinical supervision is the primary pedagogy of the mental health professions, including Health Service Psychology, Clinical Mental Health Counseling, Marriage and Family (or Couples and Family) Therapy, Clinical Social Work, and related professions. Just like grand rounds allow medical students to practice under the guidance of a licensed physician, clinical supervision provides the process for mental health trainees to practice under the guidance of a licensed mental health provider. Clinical supervision looks very similar across mental health professions, which share a common history.

Sigmund Freud is considered the father of psychology, but most do not associate him with clinical supervision. As the developer of the first approach to talk therapy and the first teacher of that approach, Freud was also the first clinical supervisor. When he published *The Interpretation of Dreams* in 1899, Freud theorized that much of what drives us is buried in our unconscious. He proposed the idea that these drives manifest themselves in our dream world when we can let down our defenses that shield us in the real world. This idea gave rise to psychoanalytic theory and psychoanalysis, which included interventions such as dream analysis. Psychoanalysis also focused on the importance of the therapist–client relationship, as well as the impact and use of transference and countertransference. When Freud taught others his approach, he would often discuss the feelings the therapist had for the client, or about dreams the trainee had about clients or others. Psychoanalytic clinical supervision began as an extension of therapy but the lines between psychoanalytic supervision and psychoanalytic therapy were blurred at best, and supervision often looked remarkably similar to therapy.

We now recognize that supervision and therapy are distinct practices. But Freud was right on several fronts. First, he identified key components of therapy that are necessary for success, including the importance of the therapist–client relationship. Second, he used the same theory about human behavior in both therapy and supervision, allowing for powerful tools such as modeling and role-play. Third, he considered the impacts of past experiences on current behavior, suggesting we develop in a linear and scaffolded manner. Finally, he stressed the importance of process within therapy and the necessity of drives or motivators.

Freud contributed many things to the supervision processes we still use today, including:

- Emphasis on the relationship
- Modeling and role-playing
- Sequential process of clinical development
- Integrating internal and external processes

Clinical Supervision has changed a lot in the last century, but these four concepts are still important. Models of supervision are often broken down using these ideas: relationship, theory, development, and process, all of which will be discussed throughout this workbook. We'll dive into the models of supervision next and also explore integrated approaches to supervision.

Supervision Approaches: Models, Theories, and Integrations

Just as clinicians seek to define and refine their theoretical orientation—as a way to stay grounded and consistent in their conceptualizations and application of interventions—supervisors also benefit from having a conceptual framework from which they operate. We're going to cover several different frameworks that have emerged since Freud's earliest work on supervision. You'll notice that some of them are called *models*, some are referred to as *theories*, and some are labeled more simply as *approaches to supervision*. In application, these terms are largely interchangeable.

Supervision models help to create a collaborative relationship featuring a common language and shared goals and expectations. Often, supervisors integrate established supervision approaches with processes and techniques that emphasize their individual values and strengths as supervisors—in essence developing their own model of supervision. Developing your individual model provides the structure and framework for supervision that fits you best. As you review the approaches in this chapter, you may decide to incorporate other theories or techniques into your approach to supervision, some of which may fit nicely in a strength-based model and some of which may feel more counterintuitive.

Developmental Approaches to Supervision

Like stage theories, **developmental models** of supervision assume that trainees pass through stages as they develop as therapists. The models often include aspects of training or areas of focus at each of the developmental stages. For example, the APA sees training as a developmental undertaking that is "sequential, cumulative, and graded in complexity" (Commission on Accreditation (CoA), 2015, p.6). This means that competence is developed in a specific order; that knowledge, skills, and attitudes or beliefs (**KSAs**) build upon each other; and that this process becomes more complex as we progress.

The **Integrated Developmental Model** (IDM; Stoltenberg & McNeill, 2011) is one of the most widely used developmental models of supervision. Although it identifies four developmental stages, the model also includes processes as well as **domains** or areas of focus. The four states, or levels, of **trainee development** are simply named 1, 2, 3, and 3i, where the *i* refers to *integration* across domains. We'll discuss the IDM in more detail later.

Developmental theories of supervision such as the IDM provide a framework for our work with trainees. They help us understand where the trainee is and where they are headed across multiple domains. In this sense, conceptualizing within a developmental frame can focus supervision and facilitate evaluation. Additionally, trainees can move up and down the developmental stages within each structure and/or domain—for instance, when new clients bring new issues to the forefront, and when new research and techniques add to the trainee's knowledge and skill set. And finally, the approaches supervisors use can vary greatly, resulting in the supervisor wearing many hats that represent each of the roles they play in the relationship.

As a trainee-focused model, the biggest criticism of the IDM is that it fails to incorporate theory. Integrating and modeling a therapeutic approach in supervision can be a useful tool for teaching a therapeutic approach, as it provides a way to discuss the approach and its application with clients. It is generic enough, in our opinion, to integrate with a wide variety of theoretical approaches and allows supervisors to wear various hats to provide both effective client treatment and sufficient trainee development. As it is one of the most popular **supervision models** used today, we will discuss the IDM in greater detail later in this chapter, as well as later in this text, as it relates to assessment, goal-setting, remediation, and evaluation.

Process-Based Approaches

Most professionals agree that attending to the developmental progression of skill acquisition in supervision is important. As psychotherapists and psychotherapists-in-training, our work is often focused on the end result, the outcome. But this misses two important means to this end: the supervision relationship and the journey or processes that keep us moving forward. We discussed the relationship and its importance earlier, but the process of supervision has often been minimized or even ignored.

Process models break down each **domain** into functional areas that improve or mature as a student develops knowledge, skills, and attitudes within a specific domain. A popular **process-based model** is the Loganbill, Hardy, and Delworth (1982) model that proposes eight functional areas or processes that would apply to every training domain. **Domains** include areas of focus such as relationship building, therapy/counseling, evaluation/assessment, consultation, and even supervision. The processes in the Logan et al. (1982) model include:

1. Competence
2. Emotional Awareness
3. Autonomy
4. Professional Identity
5. Respect for Individual Differences
6. Purpose and Direction
7. Personal Motivation
8. Professional Ethics.

If we focused on the domain of counseling as an example, the supervisor and trainee would want to work together to evaluate the trainee's current level of knowledge, skills, and or attitudes about counseling as they relate to each of the eight processes. Questions might include the following, respective to the numbered processes above:

1. Competence: Is the trainee demonstrating competence in counseling skills at a level consistent with their development?
2. Emotional Awareness: Is the trainee aware of their own and others' emotions, and can they navigate these in a respectful and effective manner?
3. Autonomy: Has the trainee developed an appropriate balance between autonomy and seeking guidance at their current level of development?
4. Professional Identity: Has the trainee developed a sense of professional identity appropriate for their developmental level?
5. Respect for Individual Differences: Does the trainee demonstrate cultural awareness, respect for individual differences, and a regard for social justice at a depth appropriate for their developmental level?
6. Purpose and Direction: Does the trainee demonstrate an appropriate drive to increase their KSAs and engage in behaviors that bring them closer to their next developmental milestone?

7. Personal Motivation: Does the trainee demonstrate motivation and **grit**, and do they derive meaning from their work with clients and their clinical training?
8. Professional Ethics: Does the trainee demonstrate an understanding of, appreciation for, and adherence to ethical and legal requirements?

Reflection Question

What processes within clinical supervision stand out to you as important to your development as a trainee or your work as a supervisor? These might be processes outlined in this chapter, as well as other processes that you find important in clinical supervision.

Reflection Question

For Trainees: Consider your strengths as a clinician. In which of the processes do you feel more confident and competent across various domains? Why are these strengths for you? How could you build on these strengths while developing more skill with all processes?

Reflection Question

For Supervisors: Consider your strengths as a supervisor. In which of the processes do you feel more confident and competent? Why are these strengths for you? How could you build on these strengths while developing more knowledge and skill with all processes?

Loganbill et al. (1982) also describe three stages or developmental levels, including **stagnation** (or lack of awareness), **confusion** (or awareness without answers), and **integration** (or awareness, answers, and integration). Those in stage one, stagnation, are often unaware of what they don't know and therefore may not know what questions to ask regarding a specific domain. At stage two, confusion, trainees begin to understand the various aspects of their work and questions begin to form. Finally, in stage three, integration begins as trainees begin to find answers and integrate them into their work. Logan et al. (1982) includes developmental levels and process, but it lacks domains. For this reason, it is often integrated with other approaches, like the IDM.

Process + Developmental Approaches: The Integrative Developmental Model (IDM)

Like counseling and psychotherapy, supervision has become more integrated than it was a decade or two ago; it has certainly become more ethically stringent and research-based than it was when Freud first started training others in psychoanalysis. Through integration, supervisors can best meet the needs of their trainees and clients while still adhering to an evidence-based practice. **Integrative Supervision** does not mean merely picking interventions and ideas from various models that you like or that meet a need in the moment. Integration refers to the creation of a purposeful and symbiotic model of supervision that is individualized to fit the supervisor, their trainees, and their clients.

The **Integrated Developmental Model (IDM)** is one of the most widely used models of supervision, likely because it creates a structure that can be used as is or modified to fit the unique needs of most supervisors, trainees, and clinical training placements. The model lacks a specific grounding theory, which some see as a weakness, but it can be easily adapted to any theoretical orientation. We see its flexibility as a strength. In fact, we will use the IDM in this text as the model to build on as you consider your own model or approach of clinical supervision.

IDM identifies eight **domains** of professional functioning according to Stoltenberg and McNeill (2010), including: (1) Intervention, (2) Assessment, (3) Interpersonal Assessment, (4) Client Conceptualization, (5) Individual Differences, (6) Theoretical Orientation, (7) Treatment Planning, and (8) Professional Ethics. These domains are interrelated, so a weakness in one can create issues in any of the others. We therefore often see trainees progressing through them at a somewhat consistent pace. Trainees will certainly have both strengths and weaknesses and will even fluctuate in their development as they work with more challenging client issues or expand the diversity of their clinical work.

Developmental models of supervision focus specifically on clinical training. Bernard and Goodyear (2019) discuss three structures important to trainee development within IDM and four stages, or levels, of trainee development. The three structures include motivation, autonomy, and awareness. Motivation refers to the trainee's drive, which represents the desirable attitude to learn and develop as a trainee. Autonomy refers to the trainee's level of independence and competence in their skills. Awareness reflects the trainee's self-awareness of their own strengths and weaknesses. The idea is that a competent practitioner needs to be motivated to continually learn and improve, must be skilled at their work, and must be open to self-reflection and continuous self-improvement.

The four stages of the IDM are labeled 1, 2, 3, and 3i. According to Bernard and Goodyear (2019), trainees at Stage 1 have very limited experience within each of the three structures. They are often motivated by anxiety and a strong desire to learn the best way to help their clients. They are dependent upon their supervisor and require direct feedback. Stage 1 trainees are often very focused on themselves as beginner therapists and have limited awareness of their own skills and how to work with clients.

Stage 2 trainees are beginning to develop a sense of competence in their skills. They are moving from high dependence to some independence and are gaining an awareness of their role in the supervision triad. Stage 2 trainees may need less authoritative supervision and will likely benefit from a slightly more facilitative approach. This stage could be compared to the teen years in human development because the trainee might take risks and push back against the authority of the supervisor. Supervisors will do well to be flexible and recognize the push-and-pull associated with this developmental level. Bernard and Goodyear (2019) indicate trainees reach this level after about a year of clinical training.

Stage 3 trainees show increased confidence and a more developed sense of their own strengths and weaknesses. They are increasingly autonomous, and the relationship between the trainee and the supervisor becomes less authoritative and much more facilitative. Trainees will likely be working within this stage by the end of their clinical training experiences.

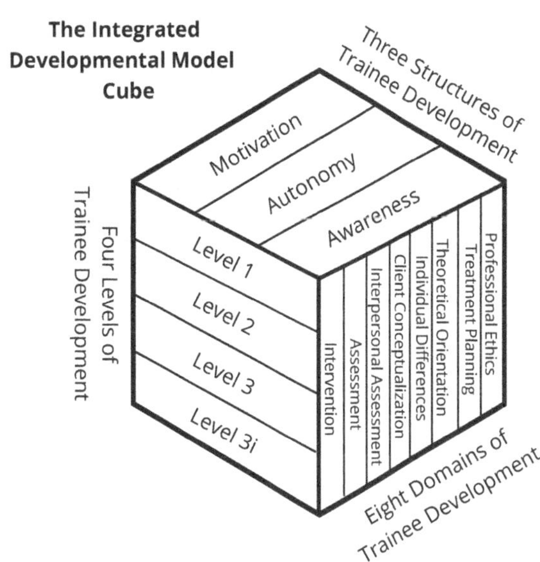

The *i* in the final stage, 3i, refers to integrating. It suggests that the trainee has successfully navigated the first three stages across all three structures and has begun the career-long process of integrating their training and developing a sense of who they are as a mental health practitioner. Beginning this integrative process would be an appropriate goal for the advanced trainee. In total, IDM has three structures, four stages, and eight domains, resulting in 96 smaller cubes of focus within the larger IDM cube.

The following worksheet can be used to determine where the trainee is on the various domains across the three structures of trainee development. Page two of the worksheet provides an overview and definitions of terms.

SUPERVISION IDM EVALUATION WORKSHEET

Trainee:

Date:

Supervisor:

DOMAIN	PROCESS	1	2	3	4	NOTES
Professional Ethics	Motivation					
	Autonomy					
	Awareness					
Treatment Planning	Motivation					
	Autonomy					
	Awareness					
Theoretical Orientation	Motivation					
	Autonomy					
	Awareness					
Individual Differences	Motivation					
	Autonomy					
	Awareness					
Client Conceptualization	Motivation					
	Autonomy					
	Awareness					
Interpersonal Assessment	Motivation					
	Autonomy					
	Awareness					
Assessment	Motivation					
	Autonomy					
	Awareness					
Interventions	Motivation					
	Autonomy					
	Awareness					

Additional / General Notes:

DEFINITIONS FOR IDM TRAINEE ASSESSMENT

DOMAINS

Professional Ethics Trainee demonstrates an understanding of and adherence to ethical and professional standards.

Treatment Planning Includes KSAs related to the last two treatment planning questions: (3) Where should the client be? and (4) How does the client get there?

Theoretical Orientation Includes the level of complexity and sophistication of the trainee's understanding and application of theory.

Individual Differences Trainee's understanding of individual differences, including ethnic and cultural issues.

Client Conceptualization Includes KSAs related to the first two treatment planning questions: (1) How is the client now? and (2) How did the client get here?

Interpersonal Assessment Awareness of the self and the role it plays in the trainee's interactions and work with others.

Assessment KSAs related to psychological testing and assessment.

Interventions KSAs related to psychological interventions, including psychotherapy, supervision, and consultation.

PROCESSES (STRUCTURES)

Motivation Trainee's interest, investment, and effort in supervision and therapy.

Autonomy Trainee's degree of independence in delivering competent evidence-based client interventions.

Awareness Trainee's perception of and responsiveness to the thoughts, behaviors, emotions, and motivations of the self and of others, including the client and supervisor.

LEVELS

1 A score of 1 would indicate a readiness to begin practicum training. Use Notes column to provide details.

2 A score of 2 indicates a readiness to begin pre-internship training. Use Notes column to provide details.

3 A score of 3 indicates a readiness to begin pre-doctoral internship training. Use Notes column to provide details.

3i A score of 3i indicates a readiness to begin independent practice, including continued integration of all professional activities and a commitment to lifelong learning.

SUBLEVELS (NOT PART OF THE IDM)

New learning or novel situations often include a cycle of stagnation, confusion, and integration within each level. Use the Notes column to indicate or provide details on these sublevels.

Stagnation A lack of awareness. Trainee does not know what questions to ask.
Confusion Awareness with appropriate but mostly unanswered questions.
Integration Appropriate questions and increasingly integrated answers.

Supervision Approaches Based on Clinical Theory

Here we will review the predominant clinical theories that have traditionally informed clinical supervision and variations in supervision approaches. These theories include psychodynamic, humanistic, cognitive behavioral, feminist, narrative, and **solution-focused** therapy. All of these are described in the following pages except for **solution-focused** therapy which we review in greater detail throughout the following chapters because it gives action to strength-based supervision.

Psychodynamic Supervision

We briefly discussed psychoanalytic supervision as the first model of supervision. It remains a popular approach to clinical supervision, especially when taken more broadly to include psychodynamic approaches that stemmed from Freud's original ideas. According to Bernard and Goodyear (2019), **psychodynamic supervision** promotes (1) the ability to be in a relationship with clients and supervisors; (2) the ability to self-reflect; (3) assessment and diagnosis from a dynamic framework; and (4) interventions consistent with psychodynamic theory. In this sense, psychodynamic supervisors often incorporate affective reactions, defense mechanisms, transference, and countertransference (Smith, 2009).

Using a psychodynamic approach in supervision involves focusing on the client's processes (Wade & Jones, 2015). There are three broad categories when using this approach: patient-centered, trainee-centered, and supervisory-matrix-centered (Callifronas et al., 2017; Wade & Jones, 2015).

In the patient-centered category, the focus is on the client's presentations and concerns (Norberg et al., 2016). Within supervision, it is assumed that the trainee has an innate ability and the resources to develop as a therapist. The task of the supervisor is to help the trainee understand the client's content and dynamics (Norberg et al., 2016; Wade & Jones, 2015). Within the trainee-centered category, the focus is on the content and processes of the trainee's experience and is more experiential than didactic.

The supervisory-matrix-centered category, which is a relationally based model, creates a **parallel process** by analyzing the supervisor–trainee relationship. A **parallel process** means the focus is on the trainee's interactions with the supervisor as they parallel the client's behavior with the therapist–trainee. There is also an emphasis on the power differential between the supervisor and trainee. This power differential is recognized, acknowledged, and conceptualized as "shared power"; it is similar to the power differential seen in a therapist–client relationship. In supervision, this shared power appears through the agreement or disagreement between the supervisor and trainee (Norberg et al., 2016). The supervisor and trainee further process, reflect, and discuss aspects of their supervisory relationship together, which helps the trainee become more skilled in discussing and sharing aspects of the therapeutic relationship with their clients (Thomas, 2010).

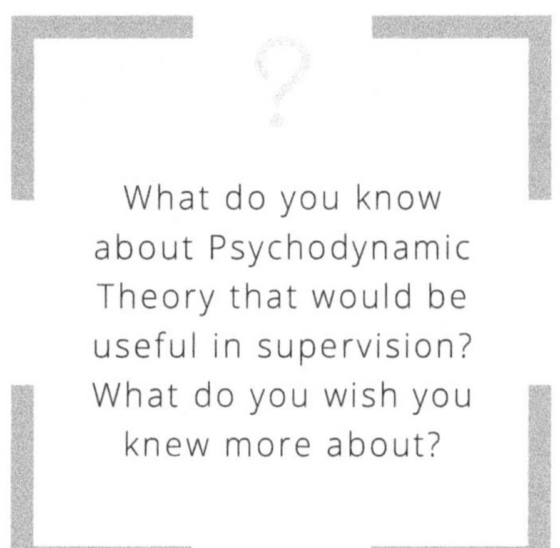

Humanistic Supervision

The central theme of the **Humanistic Model** is relationships across the supervision triad. It often uses concepts from Roger's person-centered therapy as the foundation, wherein the humanistic supervisor serves more as a collaborator than expert (Smith, 2009). Rogers saw client and therapist as equal and argued that the relationship alone is both necessary and sufficient. The idea of sufficiency may conflict with the evaluative and teaching roles of the supervisor, but few argue against the importance of the relationship. The idea of congruence and working toward an ideal self (or ideal counselor or therapist, in our case) remains consistent across person-centered models of therapy and supervision.

Within a **person-centered approach**, one important supervisor's goal is to work on the personal and professional development of their trainee, identify their internal resources, and help them build relationships with their clients (Callifronas et al., 2017; Wade & Jones, 2015). The supervisor creates an environment that offers a trainee empathy, respect, genuineness, and mutual acceptance and responsibility for shared practices and task-planning (Callifronas et al., 2017; Talley & Jones, 2019; Peters & Rivas, 2018; Thomas, 2010). Creating this environment for the trainee is fundamental in the process of becoming a professional. In such an environment, the supervisor can structure their supervision around the trainee's experiences with their clients to explore their uncertainties and concerns, discuss their relationships with clients, and learn to manage situations more effectively (Callifronas et al., 2017; Talley & Jones, 2019; Wade & Jones, 2015).

This approach also focuses on the trainee's process of examining their self and experiences so they can grow their self-awareness, self-confidence, and understanding of the therapeutic process, thus entering the therapeutic relationship more congruently (Talley & Jones, 2019). More specifically, therapists bring to therapy whatever is within their own personhood that could potentially interfere with their client's processes. Through increased self-awareness, therapists (or trainees) can explore their internal processes and better serve their clients' processes (Talley & Jones, 2019).

> ?
>
> What do you know about Humanistic Theory or Person-Centered Therapy that would be useful in supervision? What do you wish you knew more about?

One concern of this approach is that it can often resemble therapy. However, in therapy, a client can explore any processes and experience, but in supervision, the focus is on the trainee's experience only as they relate to their therapeutic relationship with a client (Talley & Jones, 2019). This is an important distinction for all theory-based supervision models that should be clear for both supervisor and trainee at the start of the supervision process.

Cognitive-Behavioral Supervision

Cognitive-behavioral theory (CBT) is applied to supervision just as it is applied to psychotherapy or counseling. Aimed at goal achievement, it provides a common language and a set of beliefs about learning. Like most theory-based models, there is some overlap (or **parallel processes**) that occurs between supervision and therapy. In fact, according to the Beck Institute,

?

What do you know about Cognitive-Behavioral Theory that would be useful in supervision? What do you wish you knew more about?

"CBT supervision is most effective and efficient when the supervisor uses processes that parallel CBT therapy" (Sudak et al., 2016, para. 5). These **parallel processes** include having a safe enough relationship for the trainee to be honest and to be able to hear and incorporate constructive feedback; the use of Socratic questions to inspire learning, discussion, and self-reflection; and action plans (or homework) between sessions (Sudak et al., 2016). The approach allows the trainee to learn from the supervisor, practice with the supervisor's guidance, and then apply the approach with their client. The CBT mantra is "see one, do one, teach one," which parallels the processes and the use of CBT supervision with a trainee who is also learning how to perform CBT therapy.

Cummings, Ballantyne, and Scallion (2015) add agenda-setting and problem-solving skills to the list of **parallel processes** between cognitive-behavioral therapy and cognitive-behavioral supervision. Setting an agenda serves two main purposes: it helps organize the supervision session for more effective time management, and it provides for collaboration across the supervision dyad that encourages problem-solving skills, self-assessment, and self-development (Cummings et al., 2015). As an example, a supervisor may use Socratic questioning to help the trainee assess their current skill level in a specific domain, such as relationship building, then they may set goals for their work together to build on these skills and meet the next level of competency. Goal-setting should be collaborative, but this approach teaches skills in self-assessment and goal-setting that are crucial to the trainee's development and their continued **deliberate practice** once they are licensed to practice independently.

Additional interventions that are commonly used in CBT can also be applied in supervision, with adjustments to ensure supervision does not cross the line into therapy. For example, a supervisor might investigate irrational thinking for a trainee who is unable to see their strengths; they might use thought records to record the trainee's reactions to clients and to encourage self-reflection (Sudak et al., 2016). Again, these exercises provide a **parallel process** for the trainee, allowing them to learn how to perform the task with their supervisor, practice the task, and then teach a client the task, all under the guidance and expertise of the clinical supervisor.

Feminist Supervision

Feminist theory focuses on the individual and relational impacts of the attitudes and values of greater society as they relate to gender, class, ethnicity, sexuality, and other diversity variables (Brown, 2016; Smith, 2009). Likewise, feminist approaches to clinical supervision emphasize awareness and exploration of these factors within the supervision relationship dyad, and within the triad of supervisor, trainee, and client, with a goal of individual empowerment (Brown, 2016). Within the supervision dyad this most often means explicitly

?

What do you know about Feminist Theory that would be useful in supervision? What do you wish you knew more about?

inviting and modeling transparency and open dialogue regarding diversity variables, social justice opportunities, individual and systemic attitudes and values, and the innate hierarchical, evaluative nature of the relationship between supervisor and trainee (Brown, 2016; Fickling & Tangen, 2017). The evaluative hierarchy is perhaps in the most conflict with other models of supervision, and perhaps with the role of supervision entirely, in that feminist supervision attempts to discourage and disassemble power differentials toward a collaborative and egalitarian relationship within the dyad and clinical triad (Brown, 2016; Fickling & Tangen, 2017). This conflict also represents one of the strengths of feminist supervision: by emphasizing collaboration, transparency, and empowerment, it naturally orients itself toward one of the core elements of supervision: a positive working alliance (Brown, 2016; Tsong & Goodyear, 2014).

Examples of feminist supervision practices might include a strong emphasis on informed consent within supervision; collaboratively developing the supervision contract; routine discussion of diversity and social justice factors as they relate to the supervisor, trainee, and/or client; and a routine discussion of power dynamics and empowerment interventions within the supervisory and trainee–client relationships.

Narrative Supervision

Narrative supervision shares some interventions with **solution-focused** therapy, as both are considered strength-based postmodern approaches. A narrative approach focuses on the direct reflection on the trainee's immediate work as a therapist, such as competency, accountability, reflections of their therapeutic process, or their development of their therapist identity and confidence (Neuger, 2015; Shachar et al., 2012). Much like a narrative approach in therapy, this approach to supervision focuses on how the stories we tell ourselves and others shape our sense of self and our work as clinicians.

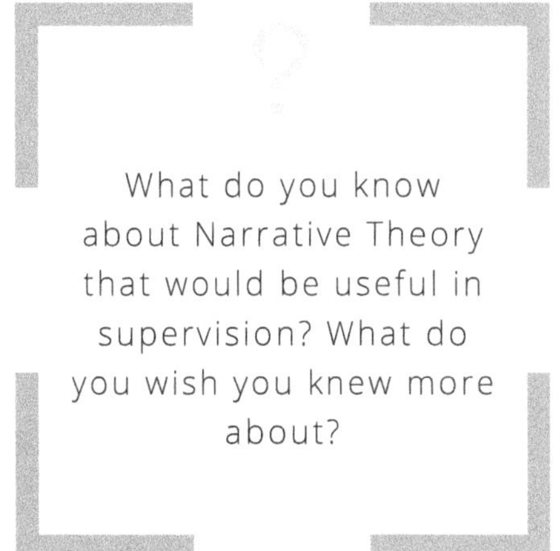

The supervisor and trainee work together to examine the possible stories and then practice separating the trainee from the problem so other perspectives and explanations can emerge (Neuger, 2015; Shachar, 2012). In this sense,

> the supervisor needs to work against the tendency to take on the problem story as their focus or to be drawn into the narrative the problem story expects. The notion of double listening applies here, where the supervisor listens to the problem story [as told by the trainee] but at the same time listens for the other stories (exceptions, unique outcomes) that are hidden by the problem story.
>
> (Neuger, 2015, p. 16)

We have summarized the primary clinical theories that inform supervision approaches in the following graphic.

THEORY-BASED CLINICAL SUPERVISION MODELS

PSYCHOLOGICAL THEORY	THEORY OVERVIEW	EXAMPLES OF TECHNIQUES OR ACTIVITIES	RESOURCES
Psychodynamic	Human behavior is rooted in the unconscious and moderated by often conflicting internal drives. Psychodynamic therapies focus on both uncovering the unconscious and processing it, relationally, in the here and now. Psychodynamic supervision is often centered on one of three areas: patient-centered, supervisee-centered, or supervisory-matrix-centered.	***Patient-Centered*** Didactic approach designed to facilitate the trainee's understanding of the patient and how to treat the patient ***Supervisee-Centered*** Experiential focus that examines the supervisee's process and experiences as a trainee and clinician such as transference, countertransference, resistance, and anxiety. ***Supervisory-Matrix-Centered*** Relational approach that focuses on the patient, the trainee, and the relationship between the trainee and supervisor. Techniques include exploring parallel process and bi-directional processing of supervision experiences.	• Sarnat, J. E. (2016). *Supervision essentials for psychodynamic psychotherapies.* American Psychological Association. • Bomba, J. (2011). *Psychotherapy supervision as viewed from psychodynamic standpoint. Archives of Psychiatry and Psychotherapy*, 4(4), 45–49. • Norberg, J., Axelsson, H., Barkman, N., Hamrin, M., & Carlsson, J. (2016). *What psychodynamic supervisors say about supervision: Freedom within limits. The Clinical Supervisor*, 35(2), 268–286.
Person-Centered / Humanistic	Individuals are independently capable of resolving their concerns and reaching their goals. The role of the therapist is to facilitate the client's self-efficacy via collaborative, egalitarian facilitation. Person-Centered supervision likewise assumes that the trainee is capable of reaching their goals and that the supervisor's role is to hold the space for the trainee to learn and grow and have new experiences.	Unconditional Positive Regard: accepting the trainee and trusting in their potential and the process while still maintaining the responsibility of the supervisor. This is different from a person-centered therapy in that supervision includes an evaluative component that cannot be overlooked; as such, there are conditions in place related to specific behaviors. Genuine Curiosity: seeking to understand a trainee's unique perspective, experiences, and wisdom.	• Dollarhide, C. T., & Granello, D. H. (2012). *Humanistic perspectives on counselor education and supervision. Humanistic perspectives on contemporary counseling issues*, 277–303. • Lambers, E. (2007). *A person-centred perspective on supervision.* In M. Cooper, M. O'Hara, P. F. Schmid, & G. Wyatt (Eds.), *The handbook of person-centred psychotherapy and counselling* (p. 366–378). Palgrave Macmillan. • Talley, L. P., & Jones, L. (2019). *Person-Centered Supervision: A Realistic Approach to Practice Within Counselor Education. Teaching and Supervision in Counseling*, 1(2), 2.

THEORY-BASED CLINICAL SUPERVISION MODELS

PSYCHOLOGICAL THEORY	THEORY OVERVIEW	EXAMPLES OF TECHNIQUES OR ACTIVITIES	RESOURCES
Cognitive-Behavioral	Cognitive behavioral supervision utilizes similar processes to cognitive behavioral therapies, including checking in, connecting to the last supervision session, collaborative agenda setting, summarizing, providing and eliciting feedback, and assigning next steps or homework.	Socratic questions: "is that based on evidence or emotion?" Action plans (homework, next steps) Collaborative agenda setting: prioritizing supervision content and developmental needs Handouts and worksheets Countering faulty or unhelpful thinking	• Cummings, J. A., Ballantyne, E. C., & Scallion, L. M. (2015). *Essential processes for cognitive behavioral clinical supervision: Agenda setting, problem-solving, and formative feedback.* Psychotherapy, 52(2), 158. • Liese, B. S., & Beck, J. S. (1997). *Cognitive therapy supervision.* In C. E. Watkins, Jr. (Ed.), *Handbook of psychotherapy supervision.* Hoboken, NJ, US: John Wiley & Sons Inc.
Feminist	The central theme of feminist supervision is to empower the trainee while heightening awareness and analysis of power differentials within the supervision relationship, the trainee-client relationship, and in broader society/culture. It also encourages trainees to consider how mental health practices serve to mitigate or promote oppression.	Focus on an egalitarian relationship in supervision: both supervisor and trainee bring important knowledge and expertise. Supervisors seek to enhance the egalitarian relationship as supervision progresses. Integration and emphasis on multicultural factors and competency related to clients, trainees, and the supervisor. Encourages advocacy for self and others. Provides education and increased awareness of political and social issues Analyzing institutionalized attitudes and values	• Brown, L. S. (2016). *Supervision essentials for the feminist psychotherapy model of supervision.* American Psychological Association. • Szymanski, D. M. (2003). *The feminist supervision scale: A rational/theoretical approach.* Psychology of Women Quarterly, 27(3), 221–232.
Solution-Focused	A strength-based intervention focused on future successes rather than on past problems.	Scaling goals - e.g. 1-10 Imagined future or miracle question - *If you woke up tomorrow and internship was over...* Starting with the end in mind Looking for Exceptions Flagging the Minefield	• Marek, L. I., Sandifer, D. M., Beach, A., Coward, R. L., & Protinsky, H. O. (1994). *Supervision without the problem: A model of solution-focused supervision.* Journal of Family Psychotherapy • Lutz, A. B. (2013). *Learning solution-focused therapy: An illustrated guide.* American Psychiatric Pub.
Narrative	A strengths-based intervention focused on retelling stories to find hidden meaning.	Use of stories, characters and titles Understanding therapist identity through self-reflection and narrative Externalizing to separate the problem from the trainee	• danyainstitute.org/clinical-supervision/ • Neal, J. H. (1996). *Narrative therapy training and supervision.* Journal of Systemic Therapies, 15(1), 63–78.

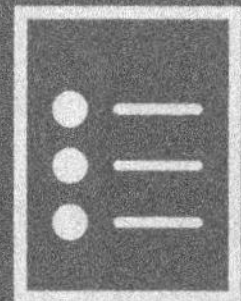

CHAPTER 1 TAKEAWAYS AND RESOURCES

TAKEAWAYS

- Clinical supervision originated with Freud, who used supervision to teach his students his approach to psychoanalysis
- Freud's work as a supervisor paved the way toward understanding several key components of supervision including the importance of relationships
- Although supervision originated in psychoanalysis, it has since expanded into several different approaches to supervision which are broadly categorized as the relationship, theory, trainee development, and supervision process.
- Most clinical supervisors use an integrated approach to supervision, combining aspects of various models.

RESOURCES

- (Eds. Watkins & Milne, 2014) *The Wiley International Handbook Of Clinical Supervision.*
- Stoltenberg, C. D., & McNeill, B. W. (1997). *Clinical supervision from a developmental perspective: Research and practice.* In C. E. Watkins, Jr. (Ed.), *Handbook of psychotherapy supervision* (p. 184–202). John Wiley & Sons Inc.
- Bernard, J., & Goodyear, R. (2019). *Fundamentals of Clinical Supervision* (6th ed.). Pearson.

What are your top 3 takeaways from this chapter?

1. ____________________
2. ____________________
3. ____________________

What do you wish you would have learned and how can you learn this?

- ____________________
- ____________________
- ____________________

What is one thing that you want to do differently moving forward and how will you do this?

____

____

____

____

CHAPTER 2

DOES SUPERVISION MATTER?

What the Evidence Suggests in Support of Supervision and Best Practices

CHAPTER 2 GOALS

INFORM	ENGAGE
• Learn the evidence base for supervision including why supervision matters for trainee and client outcomes. • Understand the evidence-based practices that contribute to successful supervision outcomes. • Understand supervision competencies for supervisors and trainees.	• Reflect on assumptions and experiences related to the impacts and importance of supervision. • Use self-assessment to measure your competence related to supervision as either a trainee or supervisor. • Explore how to integrate best-practices into your work in supervision.

In this chapter we'll discuss the evolving **evidence base** of clinical supervision, including the evidence supporting the use of supervision, evidence-based best practices, and supervision competencies. Many of these areas are still under debate regarding their empirical support. It is important to consider that in contrast to the abundance of research on psychological interventions, relatively little research exists on **clinical supervision** even though it has been utilized and identified as a core component of mental health training for decades (Simpson-Southward et al., 2017). As we present information on the evidence for supervision as a whole, or on specific components and best practices of supervision, we do so with an awareness that research

DOI: 10.4324/9781003006558-3

on this important topic in mental health professional training is still emerging. Before we jump into the information on the evidence for supervision, take a moment to consider the following questions.

Does Supervision Matter?
What do you think, based on your assumptions, experiences, or observations?
And who does it matter to—is it only for trainees?

Does supervision matter? The field of mental health professional training has only recently begun to try to answer this question, and the answers tend toward "yes," "no," and "it depends." What research that exists offers conflicting evidence for the utility and applications of supervision. Some researchers argue that supervision has little impact on either **client or trainee outcomes**, based on (1) the absence of a statistical relationship between client outcomes and the presence or quality of supervision, and (2) evidence suggesting that, based on client outcomes, trainees' improvement during training and supervision is variable (Miller et al., 2018; Owen et al., 2016; Rousmaniere et al., 2016). Others assert that supervision has marginal to significant positive impacts on client and training outcomes. They find that supervision can improve important treatment factors (like the therapeutic relationship) or mitigate others (such as premature termination) (Owen et al., 2016).

So where does this leave us? Supervision is still considered a foundational element of mental health professional training, and it seems it's here to stay. The general consensus is that supervision *does* matter; that further research is needed to continue to improve and understand supervision practices; and that we should engage in supervision with the attitude that it matters to clients, trainees, and our professions at large (Simpson-Southward et al., 2017). So for now let's shift our focus to some of what we currently know about the evidence of supervision's impacts on trainees and clients:

- Supervision plays a large role in facilitating the positive growth and development of trainees, but it can be harmful when it's inadequate, unethical, or missing key

components (Holt et al., 2015; Wilson et al., 2016).
- Supervision serves an important **gatekeeping** function that can protect the **integrity** of the field and the interests of the populations served by mental health professionals (Ellis et al., 2015; Gray et al., 2001; Holt et al., 2015; Wilson et al., 2016).
- Effective supervision leads to enhanced trainee **self-awareness**, **clinical knowledge**, and **self-efficacy**.
- Supervision facilitates trainee **skill acquisition** and utilization of evidence-based practices.
- When the working alliance within supervision is positive, supervision is correlated to a strengthened trainee–client **relationship/working alliance.**
- Supervision can account for as much as 12% of variance in **client outcomes** even when we control for complexities and individual factors, including symptom severity. Supervision has also been correlated to specific client outcomes including lower symptom severity, higher satisfaction with treatment, better relationships with their therapist–trainee, and lower rates of premature termination (Owen et al., 2016; Rousmaniere et al., 2016; Wrape et al., 2015).

Supervision has been correlated to specific client outcomes including lower symptom severity, higher satisfaction with treatment, better relationships with their therapist-trainee, and lower rates of premature termination from treatment.

As you consider this evidence for why supervision matters and how it can impact trainees and clients, contemplate how it aligns with your initial attitude and assumptions when you answered the question *Does supervision matter?* Consider how you might use these insights as you develop your goals and practices for supervision in subsequent chapters.

What Makes Supervision Effective: Evidence-Based Best Practices and Supervision Competence

Now that we have an idea of the evidence supporting supervision and its role in training, we can explore what the evidence suggests concerning **best practices** within the supervision process, including core components, behaviors, skills, and techniques that have been correlated to **effective supervision** outcomes. This will serve as an introductory overview of these key components; several (feedback, for example) will be covered in greater detail in subsequent chapters as we move into preparing for the first session and engaging in specific practices of supervision. Before we review, take a moment to reflect on your assumptions and experiences related to supervision best practices.

EVIDENCE-BASED BEST PRACTICES IN SUPERVISION

Based on your experiences and what you've read or heard about supervision, what best practices do you think are important in order for supervision to be successful?

1. ____________________
2. ____________________
3. ____________________
4. ____________________
5. ____________________
6. ____________________
7. ____________________
8. ____________________
9. ____________________
10. ____________________

As you review the evidence-based practices introduced in this section, consider how they compare to your list and how you might use these to shape your goals and development as a trainee or supervisor. Write your thoughts below.

COMMON FACTORS IN EFFECTIVE SUPERVISION

There are many factors that can influence supervision outcomes, including individual characteristics of the trainee and supervisor, the clinical setting, and client or patient population, just to name a few. Researchers have identified the following factors (sometimes referred to as common factors) as being correlated to effective supervision:

Relationship

Strong *working alliance* and positive *relationship* between supervisor and trainee (Enlow et al., 2019; Falender & Shafranske, 2014; Holt et al., 2015; Rieck et al., 2015; Staples-Bradley et al., 2019).

Fidelity to Ethical and Regulatory Requirements

Supervisors' adherence to and *modeling* of *ethical guidelines* and standards as they relate to *dual relationships, protection of clients,* and *gatekeeping* (Barnett & Molzon, 2014).

Multicultural Competence

Cultivating openness, transparency, and routine attention to *multicultural factors,* including trainee and supervisor's individual factors within supervision, as well as multicultural factors among the trainee's clients (Falender & Shafranske, 2014; Pettifor et al., 2014; Tsong & Goodyear, 2014).

Observation and Monitoring

Effective supervisors engage in *monitoring* and *assessment* of trainee's actual clinical work, including live, video, or audio *observation*. Effective supervisors also routinely incorporate treatment progress or outcome measure data into supervision (Amerikaner & Rose, 2012; Barrett et al., 2019; Falender & Shafranske, 2014; Kangos et al., 2018; D. L. Milne et al., 2011).

Emphasis on Teaching Evidence-Based Practices

Modeling and *role-playing* the utilization of *evidence-based clinical practices* during supervision, in addition to *discussion* of evidence-based practices (D. L. Milne et al., 2011).

Having a Plan that Includes Appropriate and Attainable Goals

Having an agreed-upon *plan* (formal or informal) that outlines training needs and learning methods. The plan can be included as a part of the supervision contract, or it can be a separate document co-created by trainee and supervisor that can be adapted as necessary. The plan should include *specific goals* that are appropriate for the trainees' development that are attainable and congruent within the trainee's *developmental level*, training *setting,* and the supervisors' *clinical competency* (Borders, 2014; Kangos et al., 2018; Tangen et al., 2019; Watkins, 2017).

Frequent Feedback

Routine, frequent, *strength-based feedback* from supervisor to trainee that is *behaviorally anchored* and applicable to trainee's developmental level and training goals (Borders et al., 2017; Falender & Shafranske, 2014; Holt et al., 2015; Kangos et al., 2018; Milne et al., 2011; Milne & Reiser, 2012; Wade & Jones, 2014).

Clearly-Defined Roles and Expectations

Establishing clear *expectations,* including *defining supervisor and trainee roles;* clarifying expected behaviors from supervisors and trainees in supervision (e.g., expectations for preparation, monitoring and observation, administrative tasks, administration of progress measures, evaluation, and other components); and setting the scope and *limitations of supervision* (e.g., overall goals of supervision, dual roles, *limits of confidentiality*) (Barnett & Molzon, 2014; Falender, 2018; Falender & Shafranske, 2014; Lu et al., 2019; Martin et al., 2014).

Strength-Based Approach

Last but certainly not least, the best available evidence concerning supervision also tells us that supervision should be predominantly *strength-based* (Falender & Shafranske, 2012; Fialkov & Haddad, 2012; Wade & Jones, 2015). Having a strength-based approach to supervision doesn't mean ignoring or minimizing weaknesses or areas for growth, but rather eliciting and amplifying strengths to overcome or compensate for deficiencies. Using strength-based approaches also helps shift our generally problem-focused perspective to intentionally look at what's going well. Strength-based approaches, which are illustrated throughout this workbook, have been correlated to a *positive working alliance*, increased trainee *motivation*, positive training outcomes, and improved *competency* of trainees in clinical supervision (Falender et al., 2004; Wade & Jones, 2015).

We also believe that strength-based supervision facilitates a more positive experience for supervisors, particularly those who are more anxious about providing feedback on their trainees' areas for growth, by reinforcing their focus on utilizing strengths even when addressing weaknesses. Because it's so vital to both supervisors and trainees, serves as a model for strength-based counseling, we will continue to utilize, and emphasize, strength-based supervision approaches throughout this workbook.

Characteristics and Behaviors of Effective Supervisors and Trainees: What the Evidence Suggests

We mentioned earlier that effective supervision is moderated by individual and contextual variables. Individual variables are generally related to the supervisor, trainee, and the trainee's client(s). Research on client variables is limited; however, studies have identified several characteristics and behaviors of effective supervisors and trainees. You'll notice that all of these characteristics are tied primarily to their influence on the supervisory relationship (Bright & Evans, 2019; Bucky et al., 2010; Kangos et al., 2018; Kemer et al., 2019; Norem et al., 2006; Rogers et al., 2019; Stark, et al., 2017; Vespia et al., 2002).

In the worksheets on the following pages, we've summarized those characteristics and behaviors to allow you to consider which ones you feel are your strengths and your areas of growth. You can use those strengths and aspirations to shape and meet your goals as a trainee or supervisor. Consider how they will integrate into other areas of supervision, such as providing or receiving feedback. You'll also notice that many of these characteristics and behaviors are correlated to **strength-based approaches** to interpersonal interactions in supervision—again highlighting the importance of both the supervisory relationship and strength-based approaches in effective supervision.

CHARACTERISTICS & BEHAVIORS OF EFFECTIVE SUPERVISORS WORKSHEET

Review the following characteristics and behaviors of effective supervisors and note which of these you feel are Strengths (S) or Areas for Improvement (I)

CHARACTERISTICS OF EFFECTIVE SUPERVISORS

____ Empathetic, genuine, and open-minded
____ Appreciate and respect their responsibilities to clients and trainees
____ Value their own learning and growth
____ Value and respect evidence-based practices
____ Have a positive attitude towards supervision and their roles as supervisors
____ View themselves as positive role models within the training process
____ Cultivate awareness of how their personal values, beliefs, and experiences impact supervision
____ Personally and professionally mature
____ Value supervision as a "protected time"
____ Have a good sense of humor and humility
____ Value exploration and amplification of strengths as well as remediation of deficits

BEHAVIORS OF EFFECTIVE SUPERVISORS

____ Communicate directly and effectively
____ Strive to develop trust and rapport
____ Accessible and available beyond designated supervision times
____ Directly observe trainee's clinical work
____ Discuss their own individual contributions (values, beliefs, experiences, etc.)
____ Provide developmentally appropriate and intentional challenges
____ Strive to be as collaborative as possible
____ Provide transparency and clarity related to supervision roles and processes
____ Active, engaged, and focused in supervision sessions
____ Model and lead by example
____ Routinely offer formative feedback that is clear, goal-oriented, and strength-based
____ Encourage trainees' exploration, experimentation, and relevant self-disclosure
____ Routinely solicits feedback on training and supervision experiences
____ Maintains clear professional boundaries
____ Models and promotes the use of evidence-based practices

Of these strengths and areas for improvement, which do you feel are most important for you to focus on at this time?

1. ______________________________
2. ______________________________
3. ______________________________
4. ______________________________

CHARACTERISTICS & BEHAVIORS OF EFFECTIVE TRAINEES WORKSHEET

Review the following characteristics and behaviors of effective trainees and note which of these you feel are Strengths (S) or Areas for Improvement (I)

CHARACTERISTICS OF EFFECTIVE TRAINEES

___ Empathetic, genuine, and open-minded
___ Have a growth-oriented mindset committed to learning
___ Respect and value their clients and the nature of their work with clients
___ Have a good sense of humor and humility
___ Emotionally mature and self-aware
___ Self-confident (but not arrogant)
___ Self-motivated
___ Honest and appropriately self-disclosing
___ Sets, maintains, and respects boundaries

BEHAVIORS OF EFFECTIVE TRAINEES

___ Proactively engages in self-reflection, including evaluation of attitudes, biases, and experiences
___ Actively participates in supervision (before, during, after)
___ Integrates feedback into clinical practice
___ Demonstrates responsibility and accountability
___ Complies with agreed-upon expectations or direct instructions from supervisor
___ Takes appropriate behavioral risks (e.g., trying new skills)
___ Proactively identifies and discusses their strengths and weaknesses
___ Expresses conflicting opinions, values, etc. in a collegial and respectful way
___ Maintains and respects appropriate boundaries
___ Seeks out or accepts appropriate developmental challenges
___ Acts non-judgmentally toward clients
___ Engages in appropriately autonomous and self-directed behavior
___ Seeks additional supervision or consultation when needed

Of these strengths and areas for improvement, which do you feel are most important for you to focus on at this time?

1. ______________________________
2. ______________________________
3. ______________________________
4. ______________________________

Evidence-Based Supervision: The Role of Clinical Supervision Competency

Defining Competence

There are many different and yet synonymous ways that competence has been defined as it relates to the training of mental health professionals. According to the American Psychological Association, competence is

> one's developed repertoire of skills, especially as it is applied to a task or set of tasks. A distinction is sometimes made between competence and performance, which is the extent to which competence is realized in one's actual work on a problem or set of problems.
> (APA Dictionary of Psychology)

When you think about the word "competence" what thoughts, assumptions, or descriptors come to mind?

Others have defined competence for therapists and other mental health professionals as "the extent to which a therapist has the knowledge and skill required to deliver a treatment to the standard needed for it to achieve its expected effects" (Fairburn & Cooper, 2011).

Conceptually, we might expect that competent clinical supervision thus encompasses the effective utilization of a supervisor's **knowledge**, **skills**, and **attitudes** (**KSAs**) toward the delivery of supervision that results in enhanced development of the trainee and fulfillment of the supervisor's primary duties (training, protection of the public, etc.). And as is often the case in developmental processes, a supervisor's competence may vary across contexts and KSAs: for example, a supervisor may feel that they are competent in their knowledge, skills, and attitudes related to ethical problem-solving in supervision, or alternatively that they have adequate attitudes and knowledge but are working to develop their *skills* in this area of competence.

Competence to Provide Supervision

While each level of practice or licensure has specific competency requirements or guidelines for supervisors, the majority are universal across the fields of psychology, therapy, counseling, and social work. They often include provisions pertaining to the roles and priorities of supervisors as both facilitators of trainees' growth and protectors of public/client welfare. Additionally, they often include expectations that supervisors will practice within their scope of clinical competence and to adhere to regulatory, accreditation, or program/setting standards for supervision processes and resolution of problems.

There are some universal elements of competence to provide supervision across all mental health professions including: protecting the interest of the clients and the public and supervising within your scope of *clinical* competence.

The following is a summary list of the major areas of competency for supervisors; resources for obtaining more detailed information are included at the end of this section. As you review, consider how each of these areas of competence might be represented in **knowledge**, **skills**, and **attitudes**:

1. Supervisors should have (and continue to receive) training and education on supervision and how to be effective supervisors (e.g., evidence-based practices).
2. Supervisors should have clinical experience and training in the areas that they'll be supervising.
3. Supervisors' interpersonal skills should allow them to effectively establish rapport, provide feedback, set boundaries, and create an environment where trainees can feel supported and appropriately challenged.
4. Supervisors must be aware of the basic processes in supervision (informed consent, gatekeeping, evaluation, and feedback, etc.) and also be able to flexibly utilize or adapt processes to their trainee's individual, program, or setting needs.
5. Supervisors should be competent to fulfill each of the core roles of supervisors, including gatekeeper, teacher, mentor, and coach; supervisors should also be able to identify which role(s) are needed and when.
6. Supervisors should be proactive and confident in conducting observation of their trainee's clinical work, providing developmentally appropriate evaluation, and offering routine feedback.
7. Supervisors should have up-to-date knowledge of all applicable legal, ethical, and professional regulations and guidelines within their field, including those that apply to supervision processes and documentation.
8. Supervisors should be able to competently facilitate their trainee's growth and empowerment through modeling different practices, including clinical skills, multicultural competence, consultation with other professionals, and ethical problem-solving.
9. Supervisors should be able to confidently utilize technology in supervision, including understanding the applications, limitations, and regulations concerning video/audio recording, remote supervision, and telecare services.

What other competencies do you think should be added to this list, for supervision in general, or for your own standards of supervision competence?

It's Not Just Supervisors ... Trainees Have Competencies in Supervision, Too

At this point we've talked a lot about the different responsibilities and tasks of *supervisors*, and a little about the responsibilities and tasks of trainees. As mental health professions increasingly shift toward emphasizing clinical competencies (supervision included) for licensed clinicians and supervisors, we're also starting to think more about the competencies that trainees need in order to get the most out of their training and supervision experiences. If we have our way, gone are the days of trainees being passive recipients of supervision. Ahead are the days where trainees are actively engaged in supervision—and are perhaps even more responsible for ensuring the quality of supervision that they (and thus their clients) receive.

Just as supervisors are expected to demonstrate competence in their ability to provide supervision, trainees might consider their various stages of competence in their engagement in supervision. Kangos et al. (2018) explored this in a review paper that encourages trainees to contextualize their supervision competence in parallel to the expectations placed on their supervisors. For example, trainees can demonstrate competence in being supervised by taking steps to understand their supervisor's training and experience in supervision (e.g., their supervisor's competence to supervise). Trainees' competence can also be related to their knowledge, skills, and attitudes across various domains of supervision. A trainee may have a positive *attitude* toward the importance of verifying their supervisor's training and experience, but they may feel that they lack the *skills* to verify that information. These variations are expected, developmentally speaking, and can provide robust opportunities for trainees to grow as professionals and consumers of supervision throughout their training experiences.

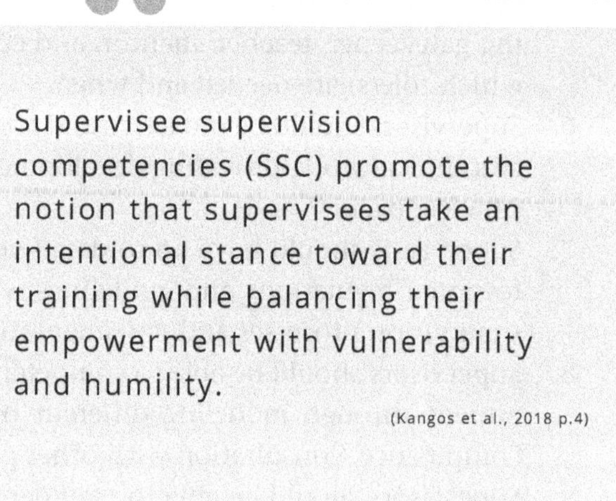

Self-Assessment of Supervision Competencies for Supervisors and Trainees

To consider these competencies in more real-world and individual terms, we suggest that supervisors take a moment to review the supervisor and trainee competence self-assessment tools below. Each tool breaks down competencies for both roles, incorporates the primary domains of competence for most mental health professions, and invites you to consider your knowledge, skills, and attitudes related to each competency within the context of supervision. It's important not to just review your own competencies, but also consider those that you can expect from your trainee or supervisor.

Appendix
Supervisor Competency Self-Assessment

This supervisor competency roadmap is intended to help you to identify both your strengths as a supervisor as well as those areas in which you can develop greater supervisor competence through continued professional learning and practice. Please rate each item using the scale below.

How characteristic of your own behavior is this competency description?

Not at all/slightly	Somewhat	Moderately	Mostly	Very
0	1	2	3	4

Domain A – Supervisor competence		
1. I'm competent in the areas of clinical practice that I supervise. When I supervise a case outside my area of expertise, I work to develop my own knowledge, skills, and attitudes in this new area.	K/S/A	
2. I'm committed to learning more and getting better at providing supervision.	K/S/A	
3. I communicate and coordinate with colleagues who are also involved in the training of my supervisee.	S	
4. I learn about the diversity of populations and settings that my supervisees encounter.	K	
5. When (if) I employ technology in the supervisions that I conduct, I'm competent in its use.	K/S	
Domain B – Diversity		
6. I pay attention to my own diversity competence, strive to keep my knowledge, skills, and attitudes up in this area of practice, and serve as a good role model of a self-aware psychologist vis-à-vis diversity issues.	K/S/A	
7. I make efforts to be sensitive to individual differences and diversity in the interest of establishing positive relationships with all of my supervisees, inclusive of their background or individual characteristics.	K/S/A	
8. I pursue learning opportunities that increase my competence in diversity.	K	
9. I'm knowledgeable about the effects of bias, prejudice, stereotyping, and other forms of institutional or structural discrimination that may impact my supervisees and/or their clients/patients.	K	
10. I'm familiar with the literature regarding the impact of diversity in supervision, including the importance of navigating conflicts between personal values and professional practice in the supervision of supervisees (e.g., assisting a client/patient with an issue that conflicts with one's religious beliefs).	K/S	
Domain C – Supervisory relationship		
11. I create and maintain a collaborative relationship with my supervisees.	K/S/A	
12. At the outset of a new supervisory relationship with a supervisee, I discuss the responsibilities and expectations for each of us.	S	
13. I regularly revisit the progress of supervision with my supervisee, the effectiveness of our relationship, and address characteristic interpersonal styles that may affect the supervisory relationship and process.	S	

Domain D—Professionalism		
14. I'm professional in my interactions with supervisees, and help them learn how to similarly conduct themselves as professionals.	S	
15. I provide my supervisees with on-going (e.g., formative) as well as summative feedback about their progress in developing professional behavior.	S	
Domain E—Providing assessment, evaluation & feedback		
16. I am straightforward and sensitive in providing feedback that is linked to the supervisee's learning goals.	S	
17. I'm careful to observe and monitor my supervisee's clinical performance, so that my evaluation is based on accurate information.	S	
18. My feedback is clear, direct and timely. It is behaviorally-anchored so that my supervisees know explicitly what they do well and how they could improve. I monitor the impact of my feedback on our relationship.	S	
19. I help my own supervisees to get better at accurate self-assessment, and incorporate their self-assessment in my evaluation of them.	S	
20. I seek feedback from my supervisees about the quality of supervision I provide to them, and use it to improve my own competence as a supervisor.	K/S	
21. When dealing with supervisee performance problems, I address them directly and in accordance with relevant policies and procedures of my setting, institution and jurisdiction.	S	
Domain F—Managing professional competence problems		
22. If I see a performance problem, I identify and address it promptly with my supervisee, so that they have reasonable time to improve.	S	
23. I am able to develop and implement a formal remediation plan to address performance problems.	S	
24. I understand that supervisors have an obligation to protect the public from harmful actions by supervisees, and take seriously my role as a gatekeeper to the profession.	K/S/A	
Domain G—Ethics, legal and regulatory considerations		
25. I serve as a positive role model to my supervisees by conducting myself in accordance with professional standards, ethics and laws related to the practice of psychology.	K/S/A	
26. My primary obligation as a supervisor is to protect the welfare of my supervisee's clients. This remains at the forefront of my supervision.	K/A	
27. I provide clear information to my supervisees about what is expected of them in supervision.	K/S	
28. I maintain timely and accurate documentation of my supervisee's performance.	S	

Note. K = knowledge, S = skill, A = attitude

Scoring: Now that you've completed this self-assessment, please take a quick scan at the lowest-rated items. These are areas in which you can focus (and model) your own competency development. If you find that low rated items cluster in any particular domain, you might consider directed reading, peer consultation and/or continuing education in this area.

Reprinted with Permission From: Falender, C. A., Grus, C. A., McCutcheon, S., Goodyear, R. K., Ellis, M. V., Doll, B., Miville, M., Rey-Casserly, C., Kaslow, N. J. (2016). Guidelines for clinical supervision in health service psychology: Evidence and implementation strategies. Psychotherapy Bulletin, 51(3), 6-16. http://societyforpsychotherapy.org/guidelines-clinical-supervision-health-service-psychology/.

SUPERVISOR SUPERVISION COMPETENCE SELF-ASSESSMENT WORKSHEET

What areas stand out as your strengths?

1. ______
2. ______
3. ______
4. ______
5. ______

What 3 areas would you like to focus on improving during this term?

Example: Providing more clarity in regard to informed consent in supervision.

1. ______
2. ______
3. ______

Using a 0 (Not at All) to 5 (Very Much) scale, where are you now and where would you like to be at the end of the term for each goal.

Example: Knowledge about how to evaluate a trainee's competence = 4; Skill of utilizing informed consent at the start of supervision = 2

1. Now: ______ Goal: ______
2. Now: ______ Goal: ______
3. Now: ______ Goal: ______

What information, resources, or activities will help you grow in these areas?

Example: Establish routine consultation with other clinical supervisors.

1. ______
2. ______
3. ______

How will you know when you've reached your goal?

Example: I'll feel confident in articulating delivering all of the essential elements of informed consent in the first supervision session and I'll be able to answer any questions that my trainee has.

1. ______
2. ______
3. ______

TRAINEE SUPERVISION COMPETENCE SELF-ASSESSMENT

The goal of this assessment is to help you identify your strengths and where you would like to focus on improving as it relates to your utilization of supervision. Keep in mind that utilization of supervision is a developmental process—your knowledge (information), skills (application), and attitudes (assumptions, values, biases) will shift throughout your training experiences.

Please indicate how well the following statements describe your
Knowledge, Skills, and Attitudes Related to Clinical Supervision Supervision

0 = Not at All *1* *2* *3* *4* *5 = Very Much*

UNDERSTANDING OF SUPERVISION AND SUPERVISOR COMPETENCE	K	S	A
I understand how to verify my supervisor's credentials, training, experience and competence to provide supervision and to oversee my clinical work including specific presenting concerns, populations, or treatment modalities			
I pay attention to and seek to understand my supervisor's strengths and rationale for their supervisory and clinical methods/approaches			
I am able to express concerns, utilize consultation, and work collaboratively to remedy concerns associated with my supervisor's competence or supervision methods including understanding what resources and supports are available if I am uncomfortable talking to my supervisor directly			
I understand that my supervisor is ultimately responsible for quality of client care			
I am able to assess the quality of the supervision I receive and to advocate for myself if supervision is inadequate or harmful			
I pay attention to my understanding and utilization of supervision and seek to enhance my use of supervision as a part of my growth and development			
MULTICULTURAL COMPETENCE AND SOCIAL JUSTICE IN SUPERVISION	**K**	**S**	**A**
I understand the importance of multicultural competence and social justice in supervision and all other areas of my clinical training and competence			
I am proactive in monitoring my multicultural competence and discussing my strengths and limitations in supervision			
I make efforts to be sensitive to individual differences and diversity in supervision and in all other areas of my clinical training			
I'm knowledgeable about the effects of bias, prejudice, stereotyping, and other forms of institutional or structural discrimination and I seek to promote social justice within and outside supervision and my training program/setting			
I'm familiar with the impact of diversity in supervision, including the importance of navigating conflicts between the personal values of supervisors and supervisees			
I feel comfortable consulting with peers, trusted professionals, and/or training directors about negotiating diversity-related challenges occurring in supervision, and requesting support or advocacy on my behalf if needed			
THE SUPERVISION RELATIONSHIP/WORKING ALLIANCE			
I understand the importance of the supervisory relationship and strive to maintain a positive and authentic relationship with my supervisor			
I seek clarity and collaboration in understanding mutual responsibilities and expectations within the supervision relationship			
I routinely seek feedback on my engagement in and utilization of supervision including my contributions to the supervision relationship			
I understand the importance of being authentic and honest in supervision including the use of relevant self-disclosure including discussion of anxiety I may have related to training			

TRAINEE SUPERVISION COMPETENCE SELF-ASSESSMENT

Please indicate how well the following statements describe your Knowledge, Skills, and Attitudes Related to Clinical Supervision Supervision

0 = Not at All *1* *2* *3* *4* *5 = Very Much*

PROFESSIONALISM & SELF-CARE IN SUPERVISION	K	S	A
I strive to be professional in supervision including engaging in ways that are respectful, collegial, and demonstrate my aspirations as a professional in the field			
I pay attention to what professionalism standards are applicable in my setting or field and strive to uphold and discuss those standards in supervision			
I strive to maintain professionalism in all forums (in person, social media, etc.) when discussing experiences or interactions related to supervision or my clinical work/training			
I appreciate and understand how to monitor my overall functioning and seek guidance through supervision on the development of sustainable self-care practices			
EVALUATION AND FEEDBACK IN SUPERVISION	**K**	**S**	**A**
I proactively seek out feedback on my strengths and areas for growth and strive to remain receptive, open, non-defensive, and ready to implement the feedback that I receive			
I understand the criteria, processes, and measures that my supervisor will use to evaluate and provide feedback on my strengths and areas for improvement regarding my development and competence			
If I am unclear about the feedback that I receive, or how to implement it, I ask for clarification from my supervisor			
I understand the importance of my supervisor observing my clinical work and am proactive in ensuring that my supervisor and I routinely utilize live, video, or audio observation			
I provide feedback on my assessment of, or experiences related to, supervision and strive to point out strengths and collaboratively address areas of concern			
PERFORMANCE PROBLEMS AND REMEDIATION	**K**	**S**	**A**
I understand my rights and the processes for documentation, evaluation, and remediation if problems with my performance are identified			
If a problem with my performance is identified I feel confident in my ability to seek out or advocate for clarification, information, or resources that I need in order to correct the issue			
ETHICAL, LEGAL AND REGULATORY ISSUES IN SUPERVISION	**K**	**S**	**A**
If not otherwise provided, I require a supervision contract and I pay attention to the supervision contract to ensure that all essential elements are present and that I fully understand each element and its application to my training and clinical work.			
I strive to know and uphold the applicable site/setting, regulatory/legal, and ethical guidelines and requirements pertaining to supervision and clinical work. I seek consultation and supervision related to ethical problem-solving and defer to my supervisor or other appropriate authority figure at my site/training program.			

References:

Supervisor Competency Self-Assessment:

Falender, C. A., Grus, C. A., McCutcheon, S., Goodyear, R. K., Ellis, M. V., Doll, B., Miville, M., ReyCasserly, C., Kaslow, N. J. (2016). Guidelines for clinical supervision in health service psychology: Evidence and implementation strategies. Psychotherapy Bulletin (Division 29), 51(3), 6–18. http://societyforpsychotherapy.org/guidelines-clinical-supervision-health-service-psychology/

In-Depth Information on the Supervision Process and Supervisee Best Practices:

Falender, C. A., & Shafranske, E. P. (2012). Getting the most out of clinical training and supervision: A guide for practicum students and interns. American Psychological Association.

Supervisee Supervision Competency Framework:

Kangos, K. A., Ellis, M. V., Berger, L., Corp, D. A., Hutman, H., Gibson, A., & Nicolas, A. I. (2018). American Psychological Association Guidelines for Clinical Supervision: Competency-Based Implications for Supervisees. The Counseling Psychologist, 46(7), 821-845.

TRAINEE SUPERVISION COMPETENCE SELF-ASSESSMENT WORKSHEET

What areas stand out as your strengths?

1. ______
2. ______
3. ______
4. ______
5. ______

What 3 areas would you like to focus on improving during this term?

Example: Knowledge about assessing my supervisor's competence; Skills for advocating for others

1. ______
2. ______
3. ______

Using a 0 (Not at All) to 5 (Very Much) scale, where are you now and where would you like to be at the end of the term for each goal.

Example: Knowledge about assessing my supervisor's competence = 2; Skills for advocating for others = 1

1. Now: ______ Goal: ______
2. Now: ______ Goal: ______
3. Now: ______ Goal: ______

What information, resources, or activities will help you grow in these areas?

Example: Review my licensing board's requirements and consult with my program's training director about how they select and vet supervisors.

1. ______
2. ______
3. ______

How will you know when you've reached your goal?

Example: I'll feel confident in articulating the general supervision competencies that are required by supervisors in my region.

1. ______
2. ______
3. ______

Clinical Competencies: How Distinct Professions Define Clinical Competence for Supervision and Beyond

Supervision competencies, while distinct in many ways, are not mutually exclusive from other clinical competencies. For example, a supervisor who is inexperienced in providing family therapy (a specific type of intervention competency) may not be competent to supervise a trainee who is providing family therapy despite the supervisor's general competence as a *supervisor*. It is for this reason that we have outlined the respective clinical competencies for counselors, social workers, psychologists, and therapists in the table on p. 33–36. You will also find additional resources for details on these and supervision competencies at the end of this section.

	COUNSELING (CACREP)	SOCIAL WORK (NASW)	PSYCHOLOGY (APA)	MARRIAGE AND FAMILY THERAPY (AAMFT)
Clinical Competencies	Professional Counseling and Ethical Practice	Competency 1: Demonstrate Ethical and Professional Behavior	Professionalism: values and attitudes; individual and cultural diversity; ethical legal standards and policy; reflective practice/self-assessment/self-care.	Each competency includes Conceptual, Perceptual, Executive, Evaluative, and/or Professional Skills or Knowledge components relative to each domain.
	Social and Cultural Diversity	Competency 2: Engage Diversity and Difference in Practice	Relationships	Admission to Treatment
	Human Growth and Development	Competency 3: Advance Human Rights and Social, Economic, and Environmental Justice	Science: Scientific Knowledge and Methods; Evidence-Based Practice	Assessment & Diagnosis
	Counseling and Helping Relationships	Competency 4: Engage In Practice-informed Research and Research-informed Practice	Application: Assessment Intervention Consultation	Treatment Planning & Case Management
	Group Counseling and Group Work	Competency 5: Engage in Policy Practice	Education: Teaching Supervision	Therapeutic Interventions
	Assessment and Testing	Competency 6: Engage with Individuals, Families, Groups, Organizations, and Communities	Systems: Interdisciplinary systems, management and administration, advocacy.	Legal Issues, Ethics, and Standards
	Research and Program Evaluation	Competency 7: Assess Individuals, Families, Groups, Organizations, and Communities		Research and Program Evaluation
		Competency 8: Intervene with Individuals, Families, Groups, Organizations, and Communities		
		Competency 9: Evaluate Practice with Individuals, Families, Groups, Organizations, and Communities		

Ethical and Regulatory Considerations for Clinical Supervision: Connecting Competencies to Ethical Adherence and Problem-Solving

> It is imperative that supervisors and trainees *both* enter into the supervision relationship with a clear understanding of ethical and regulatory necessities that inform and direct their interactions.

Ethical and regulatory considerations play a vital role in supervision. They relate to supervisors' competence and responsibility to protect the public by monitoring, assessing, and facilitating the competence of their trainees. This is no small task, given that supervisors are also tasked with cultivating collaborative and positive working alliances with their trainees, a goal that can seem counterproductive when issues of competency and ethical dilemmas arise (Barnett & Molzon, 2014). It is thus imperative that supervisors and trainees both enter into the supervision relationship with a clear understanding of ethical and regulatory necessities that inform—and in some instances direct—their interactions (Falender, 2018; Lu et al., 2019; Tangen et al., 2019).

Ethical issues in supervision often mirror the ethical issues that psychologists face in working with clients, including setting and maintaining appropriate boundaries, attending to dual or multiple role considerations, keeping accurate documentation and records, integrating multicultural factors, and practicing within the clinician's area(s) of competence, just to name a few (Barnett & Molzon, 2014; Falender, 2018; Kangos et al., 2018). Ethical dilemmas in clinical work and in supervision are often centered on evaluating what is best for the client and/or trainee while factoring in responsibilities, individual rights, values, and best interests. For the purposes of this workbook, we will briefly address the core ethical responsibilities that supervisors have towards trainees and trainees' clients. Then, we will expand on these practices as they relate to the processes of supervision detailed in subsequent chapters.

Of all the ethical and regulatory responsibilities that supervisors and trainees have, their primary responsibility is to protect the public (Barnett & Molzon, 2014). This is accomplished through monitoring, observation, and formal evaluation of clinical work throughout training and supervision. In addition, supervisors and trainees should be attentive to the following:

> Monitoring and observing a trainee's *actual clinical work* is an ethical requirement as a part of a supervisor's duty to protect the client and the public.

- **Principle ethics**, or the laws, standards, and codes that govern our fields. Beneficence versus non-maleficence is one example of established norms in our field that guide us to what we *should* do based on those norms or previously established rules. **Virtue ethics** can be more abstract in nature, encompassing individual, contextual, and cultural factors that influence moral values and decision-making—in essence, virtue ethics are concerned with determining the *most appropriate* decision based on all of the influencing factors, which may also include principles (Meara et al., 1996).

- **Informed consent** within supervision in the form of the written supervision contract, as well as routine discussion concerning the nature and processes of supervision, the **limits of confidentiality**, and the expectations and responsibilities for both supervisor and trainee within the relationship.
- **Dual relationships** as many supervisors serve multiple roles in their or their trainees' programs, such as providing supervision, teaching, acting as the clinical training director, etc. In small communities, supervisors may also encounter trainees and their clients in a variety of settings (e.g., at the supermarket or PTA meeting) that can add complexity to the supervisor relationship (Remley & Herlihy, 2014).
- **Liability standards** and implications in the supervisor and trainee's jurisdiction. Both roles should be familiar with the liabilities that supervisors face when their trainees provide services under the supervisor's license. A term that should be familiar is the **strict liability** standard, which in essence can make supervisors responsible for adverse outcomes regardless of the appropriateness or inappropriateness of the trainee's actions (Polychronis & Brown, 2016).
- **Documentation** is another important ethical component of supervision regarding documenting supervision session content, evaluation, and feedback. For example, licensing boards may audit training programs to ensure that weekly supervision logs reflect the supervision required for a particular trainee at a particular developmental level.
- Awareness of applicable variations in **ethical rules and guidelines** depending on the jurisdiction, credentialing organization, or accrediting body (Henriksen et al., 2019).
- Awareness, utilization, and modeling for **ethical problem-solving** based on the expectations or guidelines of their fields. For example, APA asks that psychologists discuss ethical concerns directly with one another as a first step in ethical problem-solving, and that ethical issues should only be elevated to the level of the program or licensing board if unresolved or if direct intervention is not feasible or successful.
- Incorporating **discussion of ethical/legal issues** in case conceptualization and treatment planning to increase trainee ethical/legal competence and model ethical decision-making. According to Barnett and Molzon (2014), supervisors and trainees are encouraged to use the following questions to explore ethical decision-making in supervision:
  - *Will engaging in this behavior be in my client's best interest?*
  - *Will acting in this way be consistent with my obligations to this individual?*
  - *Will this action possibly result in harm to this or other individual(s)?*
- Providing a supervision environment that encourages respectful and professional interactions to promote growth/learning and encourage transparency.

This chapter covers a broad range of topics—all of which could merit a book in their own right—and so we have summarized the key takeaways and resources by topic area starting with evidence-based supervision on the following page.

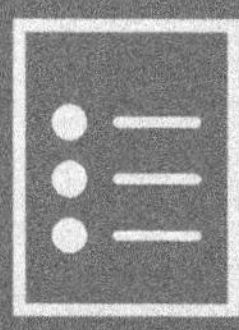

CHAPTER 2 TAKEAWAYS AND RESOURCES: EVIDENCE-BASED SUPERVISION

TAKEAWAYS

- Researchers have only recently begun to fully assess the impacts and best practices of supervision.
- The best available evidence supports the importance of supervision as a cornerstone of clinical training. The evidence also suggests that supervision can positively impact both trainee and client outcomes.
- Effective supervision encompasses several key components, including a positive working relationship; routine/frequent feedback; clear roles, expectations, and objectives; and an overall use of strength-based approaches.
- Supervision success relies on characteristics and behaviors of both the supervisor and trainee. Each bring their own unique skills and attitudes to the process: many characteristics and behaviors (such as supervisor communication style and trainee receptiveness to feedback) have been identified as being strongly correlated to positive outcomes.

RESOURCES

- Bearman, S. K., Schneiderman, R. L., & Zoloth, E. (2017). Building an evidence base for effective supervision practices: An analogue experiment of supervision to increase EBT fidelity. *Administration and Policy in Mental Health and Mental Health Services Research, 44*(2), 293–307.
- Borders, L. D. (2014). Best practices in clinical supervision: Another step in delineating effective supervision practice. *American Journal of Psychotherapy, 68*(2), 151–162.
- Holt, H., Beutler, L. E., Kimpara, S., Macias, S., Haug, N. A., Shiloff, N., & Stein, M. (2015). Evidence-based supervision: Tracking outcome and teaching principles of change in clinical supervision to bring science to integrative practice. *Psychotherapy, 52*(2), 185.
- Wrape, E. R., Callahan, J. L., Ruggero, C. J., & Edward Watkins, C. (2015). An exploration of faculty supervisor variables and their impact on client outcomes. *Training and Education in Professional Psychology, 9*(1), 35–43.
- Watkins, C. E., Jr. (2017). Convergence in Psychotherapy Supervision: A Common Factors, Common Processes, Common Practices Perspective. *Journal of Psychotherapy Integration, 27*(2), 140–152.

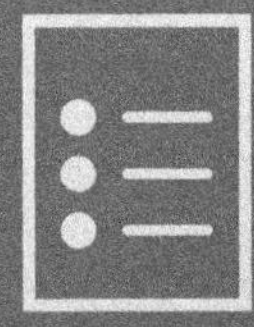

CHAPTER 2 TAKEAWAYS AND RESOURCES: ETHICAL AND REGULATORY CONSIDERATIONS

TAKEAWAYS

- The supervisor's primary responsibility in supervision is to protect the public, including the trainee's clients/patients.
- Supervisors and trainees are both responsible for understanding and adhering to the ethical and regulatory guidelines and laws pertaining to their field and training.
- Supervisors are encouraged to model and teach ethical decision-making and problem-solving approaches throughout the course of supervision.

RESOURCES

- Kangos, K. A., Ellis, M. V., Berger, L., Corp, D. A., Hutman, H., Gibson, A., & Nicolas, A. I. (2018). American Psychological Association Guidelines for Clinical Supervision: Competency-Based Implications for Trainees. *The Counseling Psychologist, 46*(7), 821–845.
- State Requirements of Continuing Education for Psychologists : customce.com/psychologists-continuing-education-requirements-by-state/ *(authors' disclosure - website is owned and managed by Dr. Chris Heffner)*
- Barnett, J. E., & Molzon, C. H. (2014). Clinical supervision of psychotherapy: Essential ethics issues for supervisors and trainees. *Journal of clinical psychology, 70*(11), 1051–1061.
- Cottone, R., & Claus, R. (2000). Ethical decision-making models: A review of the literature. *Journal of Counseling & Development, 78*(3), 275–283.
- Marson, S. M., & McKinney, R. E., Jr. (2019). *The Routledge Handbook of Social Work Ethics and Values*. Routledge.
- Meara, N. M., Schmidt, L. D., & Day, J. D. (1996). Principles and virtues: A foundation for ethical decisions, policies, and character. *The Counseling Psychologist, 24*(1), 4–77.

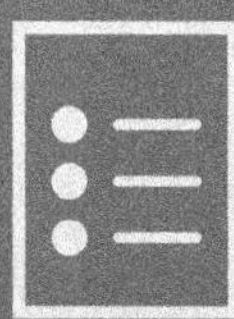

CHAPTER 2 TAKEAWAYS AND RESOURCES: COMPETENCY IN SUPERVISION

TAKEAWAYS

- Mental health provider competencies vary across fields but commonly include expectations for competence pertaining to interventions, assessment, multicultural and diversity factors, professional development, supervision and consultation, and ethical and regulatory factors.
- Supervisors are expected to maintain competency as both clinicians and supervisors. These competencies often overlap and inform one another (e.g., competence in family therapy may indicate competence to supervise family therapy, etc.).
- Supervisors and trainees should understand what competencies are required for their fields, and how those competencies can be measured and achieved within supervision.

RESOURCES

Social Work

- Counsel on Social Work Education—*Social Work Competencies* National Association of Social Workers—Social Work Supervision
- Munson, C. (2012). *Handbook of clinical social work supervision*. Routledge.
- Schmidt, G., & Kariuki, A. (2019). Pathways to social work supervision. *Journal of Human Behavior in the Social Environment, 29*(3), 321–332.

Counseling and Therapy

- Council for Accreditation of Counseling and Related Educational Programs—*Standards* Authors' note: CACREP has established specific competencies and standards for counseling specialties including substance use. We encourage readers to utilize Google Scholar or their program's library database to identify many of the recent peer-reviewed articles pertaining to counseling specialty competencies.
- American Association for Marriage and Family Therapies—*Marriage and Family Therapy Core Competencies*
- Counselor Competencies Scale (CCS)

Health Service Psychology

- American Psychological Association—*Supervision Guidelines*
- Association of State and Provincial Psychology Boards—*Competencies Expected of Psychologists at Licensure*
- Association of State and Provincial Psychology Boards—*Supervision Guidelines for Education and Training Leading to Licensure as a General Applied Provider*
- Falender, C. A., & Shafranske, E. P. (2017). *Supervision essentials for the practice of competency-based supervision*. American Psychological Association.

CHAPTER 2 TAKEAWAYS AND RESOURCES

What are your top 3 takeaways from this chapter?

1. ____________________
2. ____________________
3. ____________________

What do you wish you would have learned and how can you learn this?

- ____________________
- ____________________
- ____________________

What is one thing that you want to do differently moving forward and how will you do this?

CHAPTER 3

HOW WE CAN, NOT WHY WE CAN'T

Theory and Techniques of Strength-Based Clinical Supervision

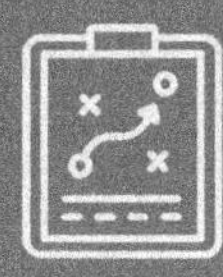

CHAPTER 3 GOALS

INFORM	ENGAGE
• Understand the foundation of Strength-Based Clinical Supervision (SBCS). • Learn about the importance of operating from a strength-based perspective to facilitate optimal development. • Learn about positive psychology and its components, such as flow, grit, psychological capital, and strengths to provide a framework for SBCS. • Begin to explore how solution-focused interventions give action to SBCS.	• Reflect on your own views on what it means to be deficit-based and strength-based in your work with others. • Consider how you are already integrating strength-based approaches and positive psychology into your work as a supervisor or trainee.

Just as evidence-based best practices, awareness of culture, and social justice form a foundation for clinical supervision, the theory and techniques of strength-based supervision provide the structure and framework that hold everything together. In fact, utilizing strength-based practices in supervision is also a component of both evidence- and competency-based practices as explored in the previous chapter. So, what does it mean to be strength-based?

DOI: 10.4324/9781003006558-4

Working through a strength-based lens complements the more traditional deficit-based lens that allows us to diagnose mental illness and create assessments that measure treatment progress. Taken together we are able to look at the full person—not just what's wrong, but also what's right. Strength-based approaches do not ignore deficits, but rather identify and activate or amplify strengths to reduce deficits and increase resources. They bring about a desired solution, or what **solution-focused** therapists call the **preferred future** (De Shazer & Dolan, 2012). In **strength-based clinical supervision (SBCS)**, we are more focused on the present and future than on the past. We work proactively toward solutions rather than focusing only reactively on problems.

Utilizing strength-based practices in supervision is a component of both evidence - and competency-based best practices.

SBCS carries this positive lens throughout the supervision process. It may be most apparent during the process of goal-setting, but it is important to purposefully attend to the concepts associated with SBCS throughout the supervision process. This includes during supervision sessions, audio or video review, live observations, note review, case discussion, goal-setting, and formative and summative evaluations. We are advocates for using a strength-based approach not only during clinical supervision, but also psychotherapy, counseling, assessment, consultation, teaching, advocacy, and any other roles we play as mental health professionals and treatment providers. Strength-based theory and practice is easily integrated into other approaches, including the models we discussed previously. We recommend that supervisors take advantage of modeling SBCS to help trainees develop competency in strength-based interventions outside of supervision.

This chapter begins with a discussion of strength-based theory and techniques, including Positive Psychology and **solution-focused** interventions, and continues with a discussion of strength-based clinical supervision as an integrative approach that allows easy incorporation of other theories and techniques. At the end, we ask you to consider your own model of clinical supervision and how you will integrate a strength-based perspective.

Theories and Techniques of Strength-Based Clinical Supervision

Strength-based interventions, including strength-based clinical supervision (SBCS), are inherently integrative. SBCS is congruent with just about any theoretical model of supervision, several of which are detailed in Chapter 4. SBCS pulls from a variety of strength-based theories, like Positive Psychology and feminist theory, and from strength-based approaches like **solution-focused** interventions, narrative therapy, and motivational interviewing. To provide a foundation for what strength-based clinical supervision builds on and draws from, we will dedicate some time here to talk about Positive Psychology and **solution-focused** Interventions. Positive Psychology provides us with a science-based framework and common terminology to identify and amplify an individual's strengths. **Solution-focused** interventions, like

What do the concepts of 'deficit-based' and 'strength-based' mean to you in your work with others? What can you do to help ensure that you see the entire person(s)—both problems and solutions?

other strength-based approaches, give action to theory by providing a set of tools aimed specifically at bringing about positive change.

Positive Psychology: A Framework for Strength-Based Interventions

Positive Psychology provides a framework in which to create a strength-based **supervision model**. Some have argued that Positive Psychology represents the fourth wave of psychology, following (1) the Disease Model, (2) Behaviorism, and (3) Humanism and Existential Psychology (positivepsychology.com, n.d.).

The disease model, a deficit-based model, is used in the medical field where the clinician's primary purpose is to identify what is wrong and work to minimize or eliminate it. This model is still prominent today, and for important reasons. It allows us to identify and diagnose mental illness based on common features, which in turn helps us develop and research treatments. Assessments allow us to measure mental illness and track our clients' progress. The disease model also provides us with a common language to discuss mental illness and allows for third-party reimbursement for mental health treatment. This model was given to us by Dr. Freud himself and continues to be a vital component of our work as mental health professionals.

Behaviorism was pushed as an alternative to Freud's psychodynamic theory, which was predominant but very difficult to measure and operationalize. Concepts such as operant and classical conditioning led to a better understanding of how pathology develops and how it is reinforced. The idea that our thoughts impact both our behaviors and our emotions resulted in the merging of Behaviorism with cognitive approaches. Cognitive-behavioral theory (CBT) has since become one of the most prominent approaches, some argue because of its ease of measurement and fit with evidence-based practice. For mental health practitioners, behavioral approaches and CBT are traditionally focused on identifying and repairing what is wrong, holding that faulty behaviors and irrational beliefs cause or help maintain mental disorders. This second wave also empowered clients more since it focused on conscious thoughts and behaviors that the client had direct control over.

Humanism and Existentialism came about as a response to these deficit models that focus on eliminating problems. Its proponents, such as Carl Rogers, Abraham Maslow, and others, argued that radical acceptance is the first step in change and that we are inherently good. Overcoming deficits was replaced with building relationships and becoming genuine or congruent with who we want to be (Rogers & Skinner, 1956). The Positive Psychology model includes a lot of what Rogers believed was important in relationships and in moving toward positive change.

As the fourth wave, Positive Psychology represents another paradigm shift in the understanding and treatment of mental health issues. Positive Psychology can be traced back to at least 1954 when Abraham Maslow used the term in his book *Motivation and Personality* (Al Taher, 2021). However, Martin Seligman and Mihaly Csikszentmihalyi are typically considered the founders of Positive Psychology. To illustrate the old and new models, Seligman (2004) used the metaphor of a rose garden. He argues that traditional mental health treatment involves understanding the past, how the past led to the present, and then eliminating or minimizing the deficits. In the garden metaphor, this is akin to weeding the garden and tilling the soil. There is nothing wrong with this—in fact, it's a necessary step if one wants to grow roses.

> What aspects of Positive Psychology or strength-based approaches do you already incorporate into your life and work? What stands out and what do you want to learn more about?

The problem is that if we stop there, nothing will grow. We need to plant the seeds and nurture them as they grow. We are great at weeding and tilling, but we have a way to go still with our planting and nurturing skills.

So, traditionally our minimum goal is to get our clients to a neutral status—an absence of problems. In supervision, we might see neutral as achieving minimum competence with no areas in need of remediation. Applying Positive Psychology principles means that we use our strengths to get to neutral but we don't stop at neutral—we work with our clients (and our trainees) to help them to move beyond the absence of problems. Competency, like neutral, is not the end; it is the baseline, the starting place for growth. Strength-based supervision follows this mantra and Positive Psychology provides the science and theory that builds the framework for strength-based interventions.

Consider strength-based models and deficit-based models as two sides of the same coin. Below we share a few major contributions from Positive Psychology that provide us with the framework and common language for strength-based supervision. These include the constructs of flow and grit, character strengths and virtues, happiness and well-being, and psychological capital, which includes the additional constructs of hope, self-efficacy, resilience, and optimism.

Flow and Grit

In his now-famous Beeper Study, Mihaly Csikszentmihalyi (1990) gave pagers to high school kids and then paged them at random times throughout the day. They were asked to record their thoughts and feelings at the time. What he found was that most of the time these teenagers were unhappy or experiencing negative emotions. But there was an interesting exception. When these teenagers focused their energies on tasks that were challenging, their mood was more upbeat. Following a strength-based approach, Csikszentmihalyi focused not on the negative emotions, but rather on the exception to the negative emotions.

This formed the basis for his work on the concept of **flow**. **Flow** is the opposite of apathy. It is a state in which people are so involved in an activity that nothing else seems to matter: the experience is so enjoyable that people will continue to do it, even at great cost, merely for the sake of doing it. In between apathy and **flow**, according to Csikszentmihalyi, are various states that correspond to our abilities and challenges in any given moment.

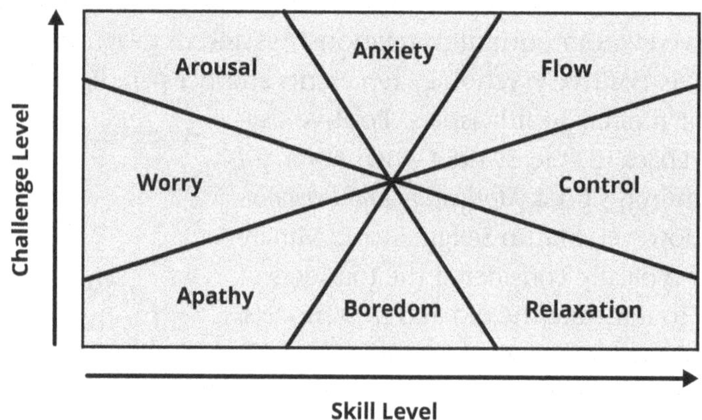

Flow occurs when our strengths are aligned with our activity and our goals. This causes a gestalt of sorts, wherein the sum of our efforts is multiplied because of how smoothly everything is working together. Regarding clinical supervision, it is important to understand your own skill level relative to the tasks. Practicing at a highly challenging level without the necessary preparation and skill can lead to anxiety and burnout. Practicing at a level that provides relatively little challenge results in boredom, as the Beeper Study revealed. Based on his work on **flow**, Csikszentmihalyi concluded: "The best moments in our lives are not the passive, receptive, relaxing times .... The best moments usually occur if a person's body or mind is stretched to its limits in a voluntary effort to accomplish something difficult and worthwhile" (1990). The same can be said for clinical training and strength-based supervision—the best moments occur when trainees develop new knowledge and skills necessary to take on challenging tasks that allow them to grow.

Clinical supervision varies between states of flow, where we are exercising our strengths effectively, and grit, where we are pushing ourselves to the next level.

More recently, Duckworth (2016) introduced us to her conceptualization of **Grit** as the drive that moves us forward, especially when tasks become more challenging. She describes grit as the combination of passion and perseverance and says it becomes most obvious, and more important, when obstacles are placed in our way. Passion refers to our drive or our motivation to achieve something that matches our values and goals. Perseverance refers to our stick-to-it-iveness or our ability to use our strengths and other resources to press forward despite challenges. In the best circumstances, we carry on and grow because of these challenges. Being in **flow** represents full engagement. Stepping out of **flow** (or being knocked out of flow) and activating strengths in pursuit of the next level is an exercise in grit. In this sense, the practice of clinical supervision varies between states of flow, where we are exercising our strengths effectively, and grit, where we are pushing ourselves to the next level. We'll talk more about flow and grit when we discuss supervision goals later in this workbook.

Character Strengths

Positive Psychology differentiates strengths from more innate abilities such as aptitude or talent, arguing that the innate abilities represent starting points, but do not dictate our direction or our destination.

When we think of strengths, we typically think of things that we are good at. However, Positive Psychology differentiates strengths from more innate abilities such as aptitude or talent, arguing that the innate abilities represent starting points, but do not dictate our direction or our destination. Strengths, from a Positive Psychology perspective, refer more to how we use what we have to move forward toward our goals or to improve our well-being. They take into consideration our values, interests, and what brings us joy or meaning. Strengths are internal resources that allow us to maximize our aptitude and talents to move forward toward our goals.

Peterson and Seligman (2004) identified 24 character strengths that fit into six virtues (a list and brief description of the character strengths and virtues can be found on p. 50). For a more detailed description, or to take the Values in Action Strengths Survey, which ranks your strengths from most prominent to least prominent, we recommend you review the website: viacharacter.org/character-strengths. There is a fee if you want more detailed information about your survey results, but the initial ranking is free.

CHARACTER STRENGTHS & VIRTUES

Positive Psychology

Peterson and Seligman (2004) identified 24 character strengths within six virtues, as well as an assessment instrument that uses traditional psychological testing theory and approaches. Rather than identifying psychopathology or abnormal behavior, their instrument, known as the VIA Character Strengths Survey (viacharacter.org), measures positive aspects of normal behavior. This sheet summarizes the six virtues and the character strengths that fall within each.

THE VIRTUE OF WISDOM

Creativity • Curiosity • Love of Learning • Judgement • Perspective

People high in WISDOM enjoy and value cognitive aspects of life. They consider how information can be used to impact themselves and the world.

- Creativity - looking for new ideas or approaches
- Curiosity - interested in gaining knowledge
- Love of Learning - motivated to learn
- Judgement (Open-Mindedness) - search for evidence
- Perspective - understanding and advice-giving

THE VIRTUE OF COURAGE

Bravery • Honesty • Perseverance • Zest

People high in COURAGE enjoy and value the exertion of effort when faced with difficulty.

- Bravery - standing strong
- Honesty (Authenticity) - being true to the self
- Perseverance (Persistence) - following through
- Zest - jumping in with both feet

THE VIRTUE OF HUMANITY

Kindness • Love • Social Intelligence

People high in HUMANITY value and enjoy caring relationships with others.

- Kindness - being helpful to others
- Love - mutual caring and sharing
- Social Intelligence - intrapersonal skills

THE VIRTUE OF JUSTICE

Fairness • Leadership • Teamwork

People high in JUSTICE enjoy and value social justice in their community.

- Fairness - treating everyone equally
- Leadership - helping others be productive
- Teamwork - doing your part and being team oriented

THE VIRTUE OF TEMPERANCE

Forgiveness • Humanity • Prudence • Self-Regulation

People high in TEMPERANCE enjoy and value balance and the avoidance of harmful extremes.

- Forgiveness - counters hatred and negative emotions toward others
- Humility - counters arrogance
- Prudence - counters excessive risk taking
- Self-Regulation - self-discipline

THE VIRTUE OF TRANSCENDENCE

Appreciation • Gratitude • Hope • Humor • Spirituality

People high in TRANSCENDENCE enjoy and value connection to the world and finding meaning in life.

- Forgiveness - counters hatred and negative emotions toward othersAppreciation of Beauty and Excellence - mindful and appreciative of the world around you
- Gratitude - thankful for the good things; expressions of thanks
- Hope - believing the future will be good
- Humor - seeing the lighter side of life
- Spirituality - having a higher purpose

Well-Being and Happiness

When we spoke of strengths, we acknowledged that aptitude and talent set a starting place for us, but our strengths carry us forward from there. Similarly, happiness has been operationalized as the sum of genetics, circumstances, and actions (Lyubomirsky, Sheldon, & Schkade, 2005). Happiness is a positive emotion and is part of the concept of well-being, but according to Seligman it is just *one* positive emotion within the five pillars of well-being. It is an important positive emotion, but it is not the only path to well-being. Seligman argues for five pathways to well-being, represented by the acronym PERMA (Positive Emotions, Engagement, Positive Relationships, Meaning, and Accomplishment). According to this theory, we can flourish in any or all of these areas—and the more we do, the more we flourish (Heffner, 2021b).

The first pathway is Positive Emotions. Happiness would fit into this category, but so would joy, contentment, amusement, pride, inspiration, gratitude, satisfaction, relief, love, awe, and especially hope. The second, Engagement, concerns our activities. How do we spend our time, what do we focus on? Csikszentmihalyi's research on **flow** fits here as the ultimate engagement (Csikszentmihalyi, 1997). If you have experienced **flow**, then you have been able to successfully focus your values, strengths, and goals into a single activity that has monopolized your concentration.

Positive Relationships refers to our connections with others. Research has overwhelmingly demonstrated the importance of relationships to our mental health functioning and overall life satisfaction. The fourth pathway, Meaning, represents a focus or dedication to something bigger than ourselves. Finding meaning allows us to feel a part of something larger and gives our lives purpose. Meaning can be religious or spiritual; it can be about social justice, or family, or giving back to the community. Seligman's fifth and final pathway is Achievement or Accomplishment. This is the sense of forward movement and productivity that we feel when we get something done, contribute to something, or feel we have created something important or meaningful. Having a sense of pride in what we do supports well-being and improves overall life satisfaction. Accomplishment is amplified by Angela Duckworth's (2016) concept of **grit**, although **grit** can be beneficial in any of the five pillars.

Psychological Capital

Psychological capital is a personal reserve that allows us to engage in the world more effectively and more efficiently. Some have referred to it as our psychological bank that we can withdraw from when needed and invest in when things are going well. As our psychological capital increases, our ability to flourish is increased. Psychological capital includes four components: **Hope**, **Self-Efficacy**, **Resilience**, and **Optimism** (often abbreviated with the acronym **HERO**). Together the four components allow us to move toward psychological well-being.

As our psychological capital increases, our ability to flourish is increased.

Hope is the possession of the willpower (agency and goal directed energy) and waypower (pathway) to achieve positive change (Snyder et al., 1991). When we can imagine our preferred future (our goal), a way to get there, and are driven to bring about this future, hope is born (Heffner, 2021a). Self-efficacy is the belief that one can bring about positive change. The concept was developed by Albert

Bandura as part of his social learning theory, which argues that we learn about ourselves, the world, and our effectiveness in the world through our social interactions. In this sense, social learning takes on a cognitive component as we work to make sense of our experiences and a behavioral component as we act upon our environment (Rumjaun & Narod, 2020).

According to the American Psychological Association (2012), resilience is "the process of adapting well in the face of adversity, trauma, tragedy, threats, or significant sources of stress—such as family and relationship problems, serious health problems, or workplace and financial stressors." Resilience allows us to bounce back more quickly and more effectively and may help us avoid difficulty altogether.

Optimism is the belief that positive change can occur, given the current resources and environment (Heffner, 2021a). Research with parents of children with depression or anxiety found that parents who were more optimistic tended to experience a lesser amount of strain than their counterparts who took a more pessimistic stance (Gross, 2020). Optimism has also been found to counter distress associated with chronic medical diagnoses, such as cancer (Carver et al., 2010). It has been linked to positive parenting practices and overall better physical health (Scheier & Carver, 1987; Taylor et al., 2010) and is often associated with increased resiliency to distressing life challenges (Carver et al., 2010).

Solution-focused Interventions: Tools to Add Action to Theory

Solution-focused brief therapy (SFBT), as it was originally named, is based on the idea that we should look more toward future solutions and spend less time focused on past deficits or problems. SFBT is "theory light," in that it developed out of a desire to do what works, regardless of why it works. Steve de Shazer, one of the founders of SFBT along with Insoo Kim Berg, famously advised: if it is working, do more of it; if it isn't working, do something different. In this sense, **solution-focused** interventions give action to the ideas of Positive Psychology.

> Insoo Kim Berg famously advised: if it is working, do more of it; if it isn't working, do something different.

Lutz (2013) describes **solution-focused supervision (SF)** as a three-stage process that includes (1) identifying trainee's strengths and goal negotiation; (2) patient-focused supervision; and (3) feedback, education, and homework. Like the humanistic approach to therapy, SF models see the client and therapist as equals and assume that the client is internally motivated to do well. SF models of supervision, however, recognize that "supervision entails promoting professional development and ensuring patient safety" (Lutz, 2013, p.182), thus acknowledging that supervision is an inescapably hierarchical and evaluative process. Like its therapy approach, SF supervision appears more conversational. It emphasizes asking the right questions rather than offering the right answers.

Lutz (2014), Dewane (2015), O'Connell and Jones (1997), Fowler, Fenton, and Riley (2007) and others list specific **solution-focused** interventions that can be applied in supervision. These include the "**miracle question**," best hopes, scaling, focusing on what works, looking for exceptions, and identifying and activating (or amplifying) resources. The "**miracle question**" asks the trainee (or the supervisor) to envision a future time when a skill has been mastered or a competency achieved, and to discuss what that would look like. This envisioning of the future, much like asking about best hopes, provides a means to set aspirational goals for the trainee, the supervisor, their relationship, and their work together.

Once goals are set, scaling can be used to evaluate current levels of competency and to help identify tasks that will move the trainee or supervisor closer to their goals. Looking for exceptions is one of the few times a **solution-focused** practitioner would look backward. It refers to a brief review of the past to identify times when an identified problem did not occur, or when it occurred with less frequency or intensity. For example, a supervisor may ask a trainee who is frustrated with his client's lack of progress to think about a time when this client was making good progress, then to consider how they can replicate that success in the current moment.

Finally, identifying and activating (or amplifying) resources is a common practice among strength-based interventions. It refers to the focus on the trainee's (or supervisor's) strengths rather than their deficits in order to reinforce the strengths and move the trainee (or supervisor) toward their goals. **Solution-focused** techniques are discussed more throughout this workbook as you begin to learn how to practice strength-based clinical supervision.

Conceptualizing Your Own Model of Clinical Supervision

Now that you have reviewed the various approaches to supervision, including the IDM and strength-based clinical supervision, we invite you to end this section by considering which of these approaches, combined with your own strengths and values as a clinician and supervisor, can be integrated into your individual model or approach of supervision using the following worksheet.

For trainees, consider this activity to start reflecting on the kind of supervision you want to provide one day. You might notice that your ideal approach to supervision varies across your development and experience. Starting this work now can make your supervision-training process, in whatever context it occurs, even more robust.

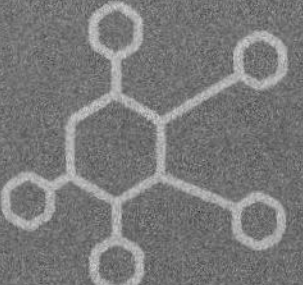

CONCEPTUALIZING YOUR MODEL OF SUPERVISION

What are some evidence-based best practices or other processes that you find particularly important to your role in supervision? Consider the summary list below and also adding additional elements based on your experiences.

- Positive working alliance
- Adherence and modeling of ethical guidelines and standards
- Routine attention to multicultural factors
- Monitoring and observation of clinical work
- Modeling and role-playing evidence-based practices
- Collaboratively establishing goals that are developmentally appropriate
- Providing routine feedback
- Using a strengths-based approach
- Establishing clear expectations for supervision and supervisor and trainee roles

- ____________________
- ____________________
- ____________________
- ____________________
- ____________________
- ____________________

Integrating Your Theoretical Orientation

Your Theoretical Orientation

____

Theory and Skills from Your Orientation that You Want to Integrate into Supervision

____

Summarizing Your Approach to Supervision

Use this space to develop a brief summary - like an elevator pitch - of how you might introduce someone to your supervision approach.

____

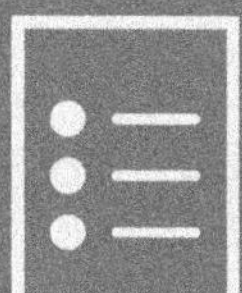

CHAPTER 3 TAKEAWAYS AND RESOURCES

TAKEAWAYS

- Strength-based approaches, including supervision, don't ignore what's wrong; rather, they add a new lens that also focuses on what's right. SBCS uses an individual's strengths to work toward solutions. SBCS focuses on how we can achieve our goals by amplifying our strengths and resources. It does not ignore deficits, but rather than categorizing deficits as problems to be fixed, it casts them as obstacles to overcome.
- Positive Psychology is the study of what helps us thrive. Incorporating this approach and its related research into clinical supervision provides for its strength-based foundation.
- Solution-focused interventions give action to strength-based clinical supervision by providing interviewing tools focused on identifying goals and working toward solutions.

RESOURCES

- Peterson, C. & Seligman, M. E. P. (2004). *Character Strengths and Virtues: A handbook and classification*. New York, NY: Oxford University Press.
- Lutz, A. B. (2013). *Learning solution-focused therapy: An illustrated guide*. American Psychiatric Pub.
- Duckworth, A. (2016). *Grit: The power of passion and perseverance*. Scribner.
- Csikszentmihalyi, M. (1990). *Flow: The psychology of optimal experience*. Harper & Row.

What are your top 3 takeaways from this chapter?

1. ____________________
2. ____________________
3. ____________________

What do you wish you would have learned and how can you learn this?

- ____________________
- ____________________
- ____________________

What is one thing that you want to do differently moving forward and how will you do this?

____

____

____

____

SECTION II

THE FIRST SUPERVISION SESSION

Introduction to Section II

In the previous section we provided an overview of clinical supervision, its historical context, evidence base, and best practices. We also covered the foundation of strength-based interventions, including clinical supervision. To review:

- Supervision is a distinct practice that is different from consultation or therapy. Supervisors have multiple responsibilities, including protecting the public and facilitating developmentally appropriate growth and competence of trainees.
- Supervision is also generally broken down into different approaches, or models of supervision, which include developmental, process-based, and psychotherapy-based models. These models are frequently integrated.
- Supervision started with Freud, who initially conceptualized supervision to promote adherence to his model of psychoanalysis.
- The best available evidence tells us that supervision is most effective when there is a positive working alliance (i.e., one that is transparent, collaborative, and strength-based) between supervisor and trainee, and that supervision processes are related to successful outcomes for both trainees and clients.
- Positive Psychology provides a framework and common language, including concepts such as grit, flow, character strengths, and well-being.
- Skills related to **solution-focused** and other strength-based interventions give action to the strength-based approach to clinical supervision.

Building from this foundation, Section II shifts our focus into specific steps for preparing for the first supervision session and emphasizes these three essential tasks for the first session:

- Establishing a positive working alliance (remember, it's all about the relationship);
- Providing informed consent and finalizing the supervision contract; and
- Establishing strength-based training goals and identifying and building on strengths, learning styles, and best hopes.

Each chapter in this section is linked to accomplishing these three tasks which, while distinct in many ways, work synergistically with one another. For example, providing **informed consent** and introducing the **supervision contract** are two of many ways to promote a

DOI: 10.4324/9781003006558-5

positive working alliance. Likewise, promoting a positive working alliance is essential to **identifying strengths** and **setting appropriate goals**.

It's a lot to ask of a first session, which often takes place over the course of only 1–2 hours. Our goal is to help you enter into the first session feeling prepared and ready to focus on collaborating with your supervisor or trainee to establish a solid foundation together.

CHAPTER 4

PREPARING FOR THE FIRST SESSION

Identifying What You Bring Individually to the Supervision Process

CHAPTER 4 GOALS

INFORM	ENGAGE
• Understand the importance of individual and collaborative supervision preparation processes to get the relationship off to a positive start • Learn how individual attitudes, strengths, and learning styles can be assessed and integrated into supervision • Understand what the essential tasks are for the first session in order to prioritize your time and tasks in and outside of that session	• Reflect on your attitudes and experiences related to supervision • Collaborate to set expectations for the first session and to get the relationship off to a positive start • Practice introductions to provide context for your experiences and approaches in providing, or receiving, supervision • Consider questions and topics that will help you get to know your supervisor or trainee and to establish expectations within a solid working alliance

Just as preparing for a first session with a client is essential, preparing for the first supervision session is also a crucial component of setting the process up for success for both supervisor and trainees (Tangen et al., 2019). In fact, supervisors and trainees both report *planning, organization, and intentionality* of sessions as among the most helpful supervision qualities—and when these elements are absent, supervision can feel inadequate or even harmful (Fickling & Tangen, 2017).

In our first session with clients we want to feel confident and prepared with the information we need to provide to them as well as the information we need to gather from them; we must also be prepared to adapt our skills and competencies to fit their individual needs and goals, and to answer questions they may have about us or the process. It's a lot to think about!

DOI: 10.4324/9781003006558-6

We also typically spend a significant amount of time prior to that first session exploring the internal and external resources that have shaped our experiences, values, and attitudes about our identity and work as clinicians so that we can remain aware of how our individual experiences impact our work and what strengths we can bring to the process.

Supervisors and trainees report that planning, organization, and intentionality of sessions are among the most helpful qualities of supervision.

The first supervision session is no different. In this chapter we'll guide you through strategies for preparing for that first session by increasing your awareness of what you bring to the process. Our method includes:

- Reflecting on your **best hopes** for this first session
- Reflecting on your **attitudes** and **beliefs** about supervision
- Identifying your strengths and learning style.

Our goal is for you to step into that first supervision session feeling confident, competent, and ready to build a successful and collaborative process together. It all starts with knowing yourself in your role as supervisor or trainee.

Research has shown that the development of supervisors—and of trainees who will become supervisors—includes both the development of competence *and* an ongoing awareness of their own strengths, biases, values, and attitudes (Goodyear et al., 2014; Bennett-Levy, 2019). For this reason, this chapter focuses on individual processes for both supervisors and trainees to cultivate their awareness of what they bring to the process.

> Reflection is the means by which self-awareness can be developed...being a supervisor requires one to extend these skills to a new and more complex domain.
>
> (Goodyear et al., 2014, p. 1046)

As you work through the activities in this chapter—activities that will help you identify your internal resources for supervision including your attitudes, strengths, and learning styles—we'd like to begin with the **solution-oriented** technique of *starting with the end in mind* and reflecting on your **best hopes** for this first session. Starting with our ideal outcome in mind helps keep our attitudes, thoughts, and behaviors focused on what is most important, which is particularly helpful in supervision—a process that involves competing, and sometimes unexpected, tasks and responsibilities.

Best Hopes for the First Session

As you consider your first supervision session, what are some idea outcomes or **best hopes** that come to mind? These may be general outcomes, or specific outcomes related to you and your trainee. We've provided some examples in the worksheet on the next page to help get you started.

YOUR BEST HOPES FOR THE FIRST SUPERVISION SESSION

WHAT ARE YOUR OVERALL BEST HOPES FOR THIS FIRST SESSION?

Example: I hope that this first session feels collaborative and energizing.

WHAT DO YOU HOPE TO WALK AWAY WITH FROM THIS FIRST SESSION?

Examples: I hope to walk away feeling excited and enthusiastic about working with my new supervisor; I hope to walk away feeling confident in my new role as a supervisor

1: ____

2: ____

3: ____

WHAT DO YOU HOPE YOUR SUPERVISOR OR TRAINEE WILL WALK AWAY WITH?

Examples: Feeling optimistic about training; Knowing how committed I am to meeting my training goals; Understanding what supervision is and my role in the training process

1: ____

2: ____

3: ____

Attitudes and Beliefs about Supervision

Attitudes and beliefs are important factors to consider in supervision and are often shaped by our experiences in supervision (whether as a trainee or as a supervisor) and what we've heard or learned about supervision from others. Some beliefs and attitudes about supervision are inaccurate and pervasive, including the ten myths about supervision listed below.

SUPERVISION MYTHS

Campbell (2006) identified ten common myths about supervision that are listed below. Which of these myths reflect some of your own attitudes or beliefs about supervision?

1. If I am an experienced counselor or psychotherapist, I can be successful and effective as a supervisor.
2. True clinical supervision is strictly for the review of cases. If you give handouts or teach, that's training, not supervision.
3. If supervision is not going well, it's the supervisee's fault.
4. Supervision is only needed for beginners or the inexperienced. If you have to be supervised, then you must be deficient or incompetent.
5. Because supervisors are professionals, diversity issues do not have to be addressed.
6. The best feedback is direct. Tell it as you see it. There is no need to coddle supervisees.
7. A supervisee's thoughts and feelings are not relevant to learning.
8. Supervisors are experts, so it is important to make that clear and never admit to mistakes or that you don't know something.
9. Because supervisors are totally responsible for the actions of their supervisees, the supervisor's directions should not be questioned.
10. In order to avoid a dual relationship and becoming your supervisee's therapist, you shouldn't use your therapy skills in supervision.

(Campbell, 2006 p. 269)

SUPERVISION MYTHS

WHAT ARE SOME OTHER MYTHS YOU'VE ENCOUNTERED RELATED TO SUPERVISION?

HOW MIGHT THESE BELIEFS AND ATTITUDES AFFECT HOW SUPERVISORS AND TRAINEES ENGAGE IN SUPERVISION?

WHAT KINDS OF FEELINGS COME TO MIND WHEN YOU THINK ABOUT SUPERVISION?

Excitement
Curiosity
Anxiety
Hopefulness
Dread
Annoyance
Fear
Discouraged
Ashamed
Happy
Pessimistic
Cheerful
Eager
Peaceful
Calm
Resentful
Insecure
Nervous

Other Feelings:

ARE THESE FEELINGS BASED ON EXPERIENCE, MYTHS, OR?

Supervision Anxiety: It's Not Just for Trainees

We want to zoom in for a moment on a specific attitude-related factor that can have different impacts on supervision: **anxiety**. When we think about anxiety, we most often think of the performance-related anxiety that trainees so often report. But more recently researchers have explored the presence and potential impacts of *supervisor* anxiety as well. As you read through this information, consider how these aspects of anxiety may or may not relate to your experiences or anticipation of supervision, and how you might utilize your individual strengths and the supervision process itself to mitigate the unwanted effects of anxiety.

Types of anxiety associated with supervision are generally focused in three categories: anticipatory (inability to control a future outcome), approval (desire for recognition and acceptance), and dominance (centered on a response to power differentials). Below, we've summarized the different sources of **supervision anxiety** that have been documented among trainees and supervisors. You'll notice that they all may overlap with two or more of the three anxiety types (Kuo et al., 2016). We can't stress enough the importance of recognizing that anxiety, for trainees and supervisors, is *normal*. Avoiding discussion of, or self-reflection on, anxiety can rob both trainees and supervisors of valuable opportunities to learn and grow. You might notice that several of the solutions offered below are also grounded in clinical interventions such as cognitive restructuring, behavioral exposure, and values-based work. To that end, we encourage you to explore how you can utilize your strengths as a clinician to help you overcome challenges associated with anxiety.

SOURCES OF SUPERVISOR ANXIETY

SOURCE	POTENTIAL IMPACTS	SOLUTIONS
Role of Evaluator Supervisors are often clinicians first, meaning that they are most comfortable in a non-judgmental supportive role. As such they can experience role conflict when faced with the responsibility to evaluate trainee's performance and readiness for the field.	• Avoidance of feedback in general or corrective feedback specifically • Over-reliance on trainee's self-report of clinical work • Inadequate assessment of trainee's competence and readiness for the field	• Practice pairing corrective and positive feedback (e.g., the sandwich approach). • Increase accountability by setting a clear expectation that both positive and corrective feedback will be given routinely (every session).
Personal Characteristics Individual differences between the supervisor and trainee such as gender, ethnicity, or religious/spiritual beliefs just to name a few. While the specific characteristics may or may not be a primary source of anxiety, it is generally a supervisor's anxiety about discussing these characteristics that is most prevalent.	• Avoidance of discussions related to individual differences within the supervision or trainee-client relationships • Difficulty or avoidance of modeling multicultural skills or competence within supervision	• Practice routinely incorporating discussions related to individual differences in supervision and all other clinical conversations. • Utilize evidence-based approaches such as the Hays ADDRESSING model to facilitate awareness and discussion of individual differences. • Consultation is another fantastic strategy for building confidence and competence in this area.
Lack of Training Having limited training in supervision can amplify supervisors' experiences of imposter syndrome regardless of whether or not their actual competence as a supervisor is in question.	• Discomfort or avoidance related to making decisions relative to supervisors' top priorities (protecting clients and the public) • Challenges in self-assessing competence to supervise generally or for specific populations or diagnostic presentations	• Take stock of your training, education, and supervision related experiences. Identify and prioritize gaps that need to be addressed to help you feel more prepared. • If formal training opportunities are not readily available, engage in regular consultation or consider supervision-of-supervision.
Organizational Culture These sources of anxiety are often reflected in supervisor caseloads, supervision loads, and the support or resources that are granted to the supervisor in order to feel that they have adequate time, energy, and resources to provide supervision.	• Overemphasis on administrative tasks during supervision sessions due to lack of time to complete tasks outside of session • Minimizing the importance and role of supervision	• Collaborate with your trainee(s) to identify what tasks to prioritize during sessions, keeping in mind that client care is primary. • Consider advocating for additional time to dedicate to supervision—this may include reducing your clinical or supervisory caseload.

Kuo, Connor, Landon & Chen, 2016

SOURCES OF TRAINEE ANXIETY

SOURCE	POTENTIAL IMPACTS	SOLUTIONS
Evaluation Inherent in the training and supervision process and also a high-stakes source of anxiety because trainee's entry into the profession is predicated on successful training outcomes.	• Avoidance of feedback in general or corrective feedback specifically • Minimizing mistakes, questions, or concerns • Positive skewing of self-report and self-assessment of clinical work	• Practice actively challenging beliefs or behavioral patterns that are interfering with your receptiveness to feedback. • Actively seek feedback, both positive and corrective, to help you and your supervisor understand the importance of all feedback in your training experiences. • Routinely engage in self-assessment and reflection. Pretend that these assessments will not be shared with anyone else: what areas do you feel most vulnerable about? Are you talking about those areas in supervision or avoiding them?
Unclear Expectations Tied to anticipatory anxiety, which can be alleviated by supervision contracts, clear and appropriate goals, and other means of transparent discussion of roles and expectations.	• Unstable supervision relationship, difficulty trusting in the supervisor or process that can reduce transparency and engagement. • Insecurity about what is needed to demonstrate increased competence and expected level of performance	• Advocate for a supervision contract that includes all of the elements outlined in the Supervision Contract worksheet in this chapter. Consider this an active document that can be used and referred to throughout the supervision process. • Empower yourself to be an active participant in the design and implementation of supervision. • ·Know your rights as a trainee, including the right to have clear goals and expectations. Know that you can seek additional support from training or program directors as needed to ensure that your training needs are met.
Conflicted Roles Centered on the difficulties in switching between the trainee's subordinate role as a student/learner and their role as a mental health provider.	• Confusion related to transitions between roles may skew characteristics depending on the context. Examples might include: taking a subordinate student/trainee role during clinical work, which can undermine clinical judgement; or taking a clinical/therapist role during supervision, which may present as arrogant or overly confident.	• Active and ongoing self-reflection and assessment of experiences in both roles to better identify when the role(s) are active or overlapping • Discussing role confusion during supervision and asking clarifying questions

Kuo, Connor, Landon & Chen, 2016

SUPERVISION ANXIETY WORKSHEET

Use this worksheet to summarize your reflections on any types or sources of anxiety that might impact supervision. We encourage you to utilize this document in supervision to talk about these factors and ways that supervision can help address them.

TYPES OF ANXIETY

Which of these types of anxiety apply to you?

___ Anticipatory Anxiety
Inability to control a future outcome

___ Approval Anxiety
Desire for recognition and acceptance

___ Dominance Anxiety
Response to power differentials

TRAINEE SOURCES OF ANXIETY

___ Unclear Expectations
___ Role Confusion
___ Evaluation
___ Others:

____
____
____

SUPERVISOR SOURCES OF ANXIETY

___ Evaluator Role
___ Lack of Training
___ Organizational Culture
___ Personal Characteristics
___ Others:

____
____
____

STRENGTHS AND SOLUTIONS

For each type or source of anxiety that might impact supervision, list the strengths and potential solutions that might help you address them.

Keep in mind that solutions and strengths can include your knowledge and skills as a clinician (e.g. exposure, CBT, or other clinical interventions).

Type or source of anxiety:

____

Applicable Strengths:

- ______________________________
- ______________________________

Potential Solutions:

- ______________________________
- ______________________________

Discuss in Supervision? Yes/No ___

Type or source of anxiety:

____

Applicable Strengths:

- ______________________________
- ______________________________

Potential Solutions:

- ______________________________
- ______________________________

Discuss in Supervision? Yes/No ___

Type or source of anxiety:

____

Applicable Strengths:

- ______________________________
- ______________________________

Potential Solutions:

- ______________________________
- ______________________________

Discuss in Supervision? Yes/No ___

Identifying and Amplifying Strengths

Attending to strengths is not a natural process for most of us. We are "wired" to attend and respond to potential threats in our environment (which in supervision can take the form of myriad problems or deficits). Overlooking the positive so that we can avoid the negative has helped our species to survive—but while survival is certainly useful, research shows that in some contexts attending to strengths is paramount. Strength-based approaches are often correlated to improved motivation, well-being, and overall growth or success in training and learning environments (Fialkov & Haddad, 2012; Seligman & Csikszentmihalyi, 2014).

> If you want to transform a situation or a relationship, focusing on strengths is often more effective than focusing on problems.
>
> (Fialkov and Haddad 2012, p.204)

Supervision is one of those environments where strength-based approaches are invaluable. In fact, the American Psychological Association (2014) has gone so far as to recommend the utilization of strength-based approaches as a component of **supervisory competence**. Shifting our attention to strengths takes practice, and there's arguably no better place to start than with identifying your own strengths. Identifying your strengths will help you integrate and amplify them within supervision and also help you better understand how to identify and amplify the strengths of your trainee (or your supervisor, or your clients). For example, if humor is a strength of yours, you might consider how humor can help establish rapport and facilitate openness and trust. You might use that to help normalize feedback or situations that are otherwise anxiety-provoking for your trainees.

We recommend considering the VIA Character Strengths Survey, which is a free and relatively brief online questionnaire. It describes six broad virtues that categorize 24 unique character strengths, summarized on the next page. Refer to Chapter 3 for a more detailed discussion of character strengths and other components of Positive Psychology.

SUMMARY OF CHARACTER STRENGTHS

VIRTUES	CHARACTER STRENGTHS
Wisdom	Creativity, Curiosity, Judgement, Love of Learning, Perspective
Courage	Bravery, Persistence, Honesty, Zest
Humility	Love, Kindness, Social Intelligence
Justice	Leadership, Teamwork, Fairness
Temperance	Forgiveness, Humility, Prudence, Self-Regulation
Transcendence	Appreciation of Beauty, Gratitude, Hope, Humor, Spirituality

You can likely imagine how many of these strengths are related to the work of supervisors and trainees. Trainees are likely to innately possess a high level of perseverance and courage based on their decision to engage in graduate-level education and clinical training. The supervisor roles necessitate aspects of wisdom, honesty, and hope that provide the oversight, training, feedback, and encouragement that trainees need to flourish. It is useful to consider what your individual strengths are across these categories and how you might amplify them to meet your goals in supervision.

In addition to the broader categories of strengths identified by the VIA, we also suggest using an **Appreciative Inquiry (AI)** approach for identifying and refining strengths relative to identifying goals and internal resources for meeting those goals. AI is most applicable to setting, monitoring, and adapting goals during supervision. We will discuss Appreciative Inquiry in much greater detail when we talk about setting strength-based goals later in this chapter.

Learning: Bringing Learning Theory and Learning Styles into the Practice of Supervision

Research on supervision competency and best practices suggests that **learning styles** and application of **learning theories** are important components of both the supervision process and the overall development of clinical and supervisory skills (Borders, 2014; Borders & Brown, 2006; Tangen et al., 2019; Watkins & Scaturo, 2013). This may seem self-evident because we know that supervision and training innately (ideally) involve *learning*. Here we'll encourage you to amplify the learning process through intentional integration of learning styles and associated processes. This is important for both roles:

- For supervisors, understanding the applications of learning theory and styles will help you identify and facilitate effective learning approaches based on your trainee's learning style, developmental level, and the particular training goal.
- For trainees, reflecting on learning theory and your styles of learning can help you play a more collaborative role in your learning process, in addition to providing self-reflection and feedback opportunities (e.g., reflecting on self-as-therapist/trainee and shaping your supervisor's teaching approaches).

For both roles, discussing learning theory, your individual learning styles, and the ways in which you might utilize them in supervision also fosters a collaborative and holistic supervision process. It's also worth noting that developmental level(s) in the context of specific competencies also plays a role in understanding the application of learning styles and techniques. For example, a trainee who is at beginning competency in cognitive-behavioral therapy and who has an auditory learning style may benefit from being introduced to specific CBT techniques by first listening to information and examples before shifting into application.

Learning Theory

For learning theory and its relationship to supervision we'll briefly review the work of Tangen et al. (2019) and their work on the application of learning theory in supervision:

APPLYING LEARNING THEORY IN SUPERVISION

THEORY	APPLICATION AND EXAMPLES
Behavioral	• Observation of behavior/performance • Stimuli and reinforcers • The learner is conceptualized as a passive participant in the learning process about those areas in supervision or avoiding them?
Cognitive	• Acquiring, integrating, and retrieving information • The learner is seen as a more active participant in the learning process
Person-Centered	• Integrates the learner's values, beliefs, and other individual and contextual factors • The goal is to facilitate the learner to be self-directed
Constructivist	• Learning is constructed through interactive processes between the learner and the environment (e.g., experimentation, collaboration, etc.)
Critical Pedagogy	• Emphasizes empowerment, viewing the learner and teacher as constructing knowledge and learning together (i.e., the teacher is also learning)
Experiential Learning	• Learning is an iterative process that integrates old and new information in the context of experiences through active engagement by the learner and facilitator/teacher.

Tangen et al. (2019)

You might be wondering, *all of these seem important to supervision, so how do I choose which one is best?* Tangen et al. (2019) propose that *each* learning theory plays a role in an optimal supervision process, depending on the context and developmental needs of the trainee. Behaviorism guides the direct and observable behaviors of students; cognitivism takes thinking processes into account; person-centered theory focuses more on the learner as a whole person; constructivism addresses the ways learners create their own knowledge; critical pedagogy examines the social context and power structures of education; and experiential learning offers perspective on the ways experiences affect learning.

Learning Styles

Learning styles help us think more specifically about what formats or techniques facilitate optimal learning at an individual level. Just as we did with strengths, we'll start by having you identify and reflect on your individual learning style before you bring it into the supervision dyad in that first session. There are many theories of learning styles and ways to identify learning styles, but the VARK is one that we believe corresponds best to the practice of supervision. You can access this short assessment at: https://vark-learn.com/the-vark-questionnaire/.

The VARK will help you identify your optimal learning style(s) across four categories: Visual, Aural, Read/Write, and Kinesthetic preferences. Often, individuals prefer two or more learning styles, which is considered a *multimodal* learning style. Keep in mind that learning styles can be contextual: what works in one setting or for a particular topic may not work the same for another setting or topic. For example, how we best learn complex mathematical formulas may not be how we best learn specific intervention skills.

Putting It All Together: Integrating Your Best Hopes, Strengths, and Learning Preferences to Set the Tone for Your First Session

The following worksheet is designed to help you conceptualize the big picture of how your individual attitudes, strengths, and learning preferences can set the stage for the first supervision session. We encourage you to consider this worksheet an important part of your preparation process, for it will help you keep your eye on your primary goals for this first session, despite all the other details that will be competing for your attention (such as administrative tasks). You might also consider referring back to this worksheet throughout the process of supervision, either on your own or with your supervisor or trainee(s), to measure alignment and progress, or to spur any necessary adjustments in your work together.

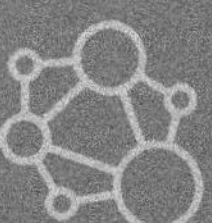

PUTTING IT ALL TOGETHER: WHAT I BRING TO THE SUPERVISION PROCESS

This worksheet is designed to help you synthesize your attitudes, strengths, and learning preferences in preparation for the first supervision session. Awareness of these elements will help you keep your eye on your primary goals for this first session, despite all the other details that will be competing for your attention.

MY BEST HOPES FOR THE FIRST SUPERVISION SESSION

Ultimate Outcome: What themes or feelings will encapsulate the first session? What will you each walk away from the session with?

Example: Our first session will feel collaborative and motivating. I will walk away feeling more confident in my role and that we're both on the same page.

____

____

____

____

____

____

____

MY ATTITUDE OR FEELINGS TOWARD SUPERVISION

What attitudes or feelings related to supervision do I want to amplify? Which attitudes or feelings might interfere with my best hopes for supervision?

____

____

____

____

____

____

____

____

____

MY STRENGTHS

1.______________________________
2. ______________________________
3. ______________________________
4. ______________________________
5. ______________________________

How will these strengths serve my goals and best hopes for supervision?

____

____

____

____

____

____

____

____

MY LEARNING PREFERENCES

1.______________________________
2. ______________________________
3. ______________________________

How will these learning preferences serve my goals and best hopes for supervision?

____

____

____

____

____

____

____

____

____

____

Self-Care in Supervision: Setting a Foundation for Effective Self-Care

Self-care has a mixed reputation among mental health providers, particularly within training programs and settings. On one hand we know that self-care is an ethical (Abramson, 2021), if not functional, imperative to ensuring clinical competence and effectiveness. On the other, self-care is often difficult to enact, difficult to discuss because it is personal in nature, and often best conceptualized as, *Do as I say, not as I do.* Still, as our attention shifts increasingly toward how to *do* self-care and not just *talk* about self-care, we're learning more and more about the role of supervision in reinforcing self-care and developing sustainable self-care practices.

> Supervisors have a deliberate role in shaping their students' competencies as novice clinicians; thus, supervision may provide time to actively teach and help graduate students foster self-care practices.
>
> (Moore et al. 2019, p.30)

For both supervisors and trainees, taking this time to reflect on and assess your self-care attitudes and practices serves two important purposes. First, it allows you to take stock of how you're functioning right now and to remedy any unmet self-care needs that may negatively impact your engagement in supervision. Second, it prepares you to discuss self-care in supervision so that you can harness the power of supervision to improve upon or amplify effective self-care practices. To that end, we invite you to consider the following self-care assessment and companion worksheet. Supervisors might consider sending this worksheet to trainees with a plan to discuss self-care as a developing competency in the initial and ongoing sessions.

SELF-CARE ASSESSMENT

The following self-care assessment includes a list of suggested self-care practices; you can add others that you feel are important to you. Higher scores indicate more robust self-care practices, low scores may indicate that it's a good time to take stock and determine what changes you want to make in your self-care practices. The companion worksheet can help you identify self-care goals and can also be used to facilitate discussion related to self-care in supervision.

0 = I never do this 1 = I rarely do this 2 = I do this some of the time 3 = I do this regularly

Physical Self-Care

___ Eat regularly (breakfast, lunch, and dinner) and healthily
___ Exercise, play sports or engage in physical activity
___ Get regular preventive and/or needed medical care
___ Take time off when sick
___ Get enough sleep
___ Take time to be physically intimate
___ Other:

Psychological Self-Care

___ Take day trips, mini-vacations, and/or vacations
___ Make time away from cell phones, email, social. media, and the Internet
___ Make time for self-reflection: notice inner experience (thoughts, beliefs, attitudes, feelings)
___ Have my own personal psychotherapy
___ Do something at which I am not expert or in charge
___ Engage my intelligence in a new area, e.g., go to an art show, sports event, theatre, read
___ Say no to extra responsibilities when needed
___ Other:

Emotional Self-Care

___ Accept and love myself
___ Spend time with others whose company I enjoy
___ Identify comforting activities, objects, people, places and seek them out
___ Allow myself to experience full range of emotions (happy, sad, angry, frustrated, hopeful, etc.)
___ Laugh and smile often
___ Express my outrage in social action, letters, donations, marches, protests
___ Give myself affirmations, praise myself
___ Other:

Relationship Self-Care

___ Schedule regular quality time with my partner or spouse, family members, friends etc.
___ Stay in contact with faraway friends and family
___ Make time to reply to personal emails and letters
___ Allow others to do things for me
___ Enlarge my social circle
___ Ask for help when I need it
___ Share a fear, hope, or secret with someone I trust
___ Other:

Workplace or Academic Self-Care

___ Take a break daily (e.g. lunch)
___ Make quiet time to complete tasks
___ Engage in projects or tasks that are exciting and rewarding
___ Set limits and boundaries with residents and peers
___ Balance my workload so that no one day or part of a day is "too much"
___ Arrange work space so it is comfortable and comforting
___ Have a peer support group
___ Other:

Spiritual Self-Care

___ Make time for reflection about values, meaning, and purpose in my life; practice gratitude
___ Spend time in nature
___ Connect with supportive spiritual community and engage in spiritual practice/ritual
___ Be open to inspiration; develop and cherish optimism and hope
___ Be open to not knowing
___ Meditate/pray/sing
___ Contribute to causes in which I believe
___ Other:

Adapted from Saakvitne, Pearlman, & Staff of TSI/CAAP (1996). Transforming the pain: A workbook on vicarious traumatization. Norton

SELF-CARE ASSESSMENT WORKSHEET

Incorporating your scores from the Self-Care Assessment, use this worksheet to explore your strengths and areas for growth in self-care practices. Consider which areas to prioritize based on how much of a positive impact you experience or might anticipate from specific categories of self-care. We encourage you to use this worksheet to facilitate discussions in supervision related to self-care and optimal wellbeing.

SELF-ASSESSMENT SCORES

Physical Self-Care Total: ______
Strength ____ or Area for Growth _____
How much of a positive impact does this aspect of self-care have on your wellbeing and functioning (circle one)?
(least impactful) 1 2 3 4 5 (most impactful)

Psychological Self-Care Total: ______
Strength ____ or Area for Growth _____
How much of a positive impact does this aspect of self-care have on your wellbeing and functioning (circle one)?
(least impactful) 1 2 3 4 5 (most impactful)

Emotional Self-Care Total: ______
Strength ____ or Area for Growth _____
How much of a positive impact does this aspect of self-care have on your wellbeing and functioning (circle one)?
(least impactful) 1 2 3 4 5 (most impactful)

Spiritual Self-Care Total: ______
Strength ____ or Area for Growth _____
How much of a positive impact does this aspect of self-care have on your wellbeing and functioning (circle one)?
(least impactful) 1 2 3 4 5 (most impactful)

Relationship Self-Care Total: ______
Strength ____ or Area for Growth _____
How much of a positive impact does this aspect of self-care have on your wellbeing and functioning (circle one)?
(least impactful) 1 2 3 4 5 (most impactful)

Workplace or Academic Self-Care Total: ______
Strength ____ or Area for Growth _____
How much of a positive impact does this aspect of self-care have on your wellbeing and functioning (circle one)?
(least impactful) 1 2 3 4 5 (most impactful)

GOALS AND NEXT STEPS

Of the six self-care categories and activities, which three do you want to focus on improving most during this year/term?

1. ______________________________
2. ______________________________
3. ______________________________

What specific behaviors will help you improve in each of these areas? For example, if your goal is to improve psychological self-care, you might measure improvement by taking more vacation time.

Goal 1: ______________________________
____
____

Goal 2: ______________________________
____
____

Goal 3: ______________________________
____
____

BENEFITS

When these areas improve, what benefits or positive differences might you notice?

Goal 1: ______________________________
____
____

Goal 2: ______________________________
____
____

Goal 3: ______________________________
____
____

Practical Next Steps for First Session Preparation

Now that we've explored what internal resources (attitudes, strengths, and learning style) that you bring to the supervision relationship, let's address the practical next steps in the preparation process. These include scheduling, setting mutual expectations for what will take place in the first session, and preparing to introduce yourself. These steps are often undervalued for the opportunity they provide to establish a positive relationship: they provide transparency, collaboration, and a demonstration of commitment to the supervision process. We've summarized these preparation elements in the Supervision Contract Checklist at the end of this chapter.

While some of these elements may seem simple and self-explanatory, it's important not to undervalue any one of them, and so we've expanded on them in the following preparation task summaries for supervisors and trainees.

- Setting the place and time.
  - Consider a place and time that meet your respective scheduling needs and also provides a protected space for supervision (privacy, minimal disruption, etc.).
- **Preparation expectations**, including what you each need to bring to the meeting. At minimum these should include:
  - Supervision contract plus any site/setting or program documents that need to be reviewed and completed to formally recognize and record the supervision relationship.
  - Self-assessments and previous supervisor evaluations—these can help inform goals and better understand what training goals have already been accomplished or are in process.

You might also consider bringing in additional measures or tools, such as the **Best Hopes** worksheet, or the outcomes of learning style or strengths assessments like the VARK or VIA.

- **First session expectations**: Setting the expectations for what you need to cover in the first session.
  - For supervisors, we recommend sending your trainee the First Supervision Session Checklist we've included at the end of this chapter. This is a way of providing them with an outline of the first session's goals and tasks, and it's an opportunity to consider what they may want to add to the process.
- Prepare your introduction.

For Supervisors: Your **introduction to supervision** should cover informed consent and an introduction to your model/approach of supervision. For example:

> It's great to meet you, Rashid! I'm really looking forward to working with you this year. I saw that you were at Great Clinic in your last training experience, and I want to hear more about how that experience was for you! Before we jump into that and some of the other things on our agenda today, I thought we would introduce ourselves and just say a little about our experiences and what we're hoping to get out of our work together, generally. I'll start ... I graduated in 2012 from University of Clinical Social Work program and many of my training experiences also included hospitals and outpatient clinics like this one.

> I've been working here for the past three years as a clinician and clinical supervisor. In terms of my training in supervision, my graduate program had a semester-long course in supervision, and my internship also included supervision training. Since graduation I've been trying to attend CE on supervision at least once a year; I also read the *Journal of Wonderful Supervision* to keep up with the latest research. My approach to supervision mirrors my theoretical orientation which is an integration of CBT, ACT, and Positive Psychology. We can talk more about what this means in practical terms as it relates to our work together, but in general I tend to focus a lot on behaviorism as well as strengths versus deficits. I take my work as a supervisor very seriously, and I want to be sure that you get what you need out of this training experience so that you're ready to move on to the next steps.

For Trainees: Prepare your introduction and consider integrating your best hopes, strengths, and learning preferences, or other information that you feel like it's important for your supervisor to know in this first session. For example:

> I'm really excited to be here. I learned a lot during my first practicum at The Other Clinic and I think I'm ready to move my skills to the next level this year. I'm hoping to come away with more competency in risk assessment and to also have a better sense of my theoretical orientation. I've noticed that when it comes to things that make me more anxious, like risk assessments, I tend to learn best with concrete examples and instructions, but in other areas like treatment planning, I'm working on coming up with my own plan or ideas, first by using literature reviews and then discussing them for feedback. One of my strengths is curiosity; I think it's helped me try to remain open in my clinical work. I'm working on applying it more to my approach to training, particularly when I'm feeling anxious and wanting to do things perfectly.

- Consider what questions you want to ask.
  - What information is most important for you to gather in this first session?
  - What are you curious about in terms of your supervisor, the setting, etc.?

For trainees, we encourage you to think of this as a prioritized list depending on what your goals and experiences are. For example, if you're brand new to training and this is your first supervision experience you might consider some of the following ideas:

> This is my first time being supervised. I really want to learn what supervision is and how to effectively utilize supervision so that I'm successful not only in this training experience, but all the others yet to come.
>
> I'm feeling really anxious about my performance, I might need some reassurance as well as challenges to give me opportunities to build confidence and make mistakes that I can learn from.
>
> I think that my theoretical orientation is primarily psychodynamic, but I'm open to learning new theories and interventions.

And, if you're in a more advanced developmental stage such as internship or post-graduate work, you might be more focused on things like this:

> I've had a lot of opportunities to practice different approaches to clinical work, so I'd really like to spend this year refining my use of CBT and ACT.

I've noticed that my confidence has increased a lot in terms of differential diagnoses, but I also want to work on improving treatment planning based more on symptoms than a diagnosis for cases where the diagnosis may not be as clear or where there is significant comorbidity.

I'd like to be a supervisor one day and at this point I haven't had a lot of training in supervision, so I'm hoping that's something we can incorporate into our work.

We've developed a First Supervision Session Checklist to help supervisors and trainees organize these next steps in the preparation process. We've included an overview of the essential tasks and goals of the first session, as well as a checklist to help you remember and attend to each of those elements in addition to your individual goals and aspirations for the first session. We've also included a checklist for the supervision contract and what elements need to be included or considered in finalizing that important document. We encourage both supervisor and trainee to use these tools as a way to establish and reinforce expectations for your work together in that first session; we also suggest reviewing this checklist prior to supervision.

CHECKLIST FOR THE FIRST SUPERVISION SESSION

ESSENTIAL TASKS AND GOALS

Provide informed consent
Establish positive working relationship
Develop goals and next steps

INFORMED CONSENT

- ☐ Define supervision
- ☐ Define the roles and responsibilities of the supervisor
- ☐ Discuss limits of confidentiality
- ☐ Review and discuss the supervision contract
- ☐ Review and discuss evaluation forms and processes

RELATIONSHIP

- ☐ Set mutual expectations for supervision
- ☐ Ask about best hopes for supervision and the training term
- ☐ Ask about what worked well in previous supervision experiences
- ☐ Talk about self-care and provide relevant self-disclosure

GOAL SETTING & NEXT STEPS

- ☐ Identify developmental level and competencies
- ☐ Discuss self-assessment
- ☐ Identify strengths (characteristic and clinical)
- ☐ Collaborate on next steps and progress indicators using behavioral anchors
- ☐ Document goals and progress indicators

YOUR BEST HOPES SUMMARY

____
____
____

ADDITIONAL GOALS & QUESTIONS FOR THE FIRST SESSION

____

NEXT STEPS BETWEEN NOW AND THE NEXT SESSION

Supervisor

1: ____________________
2: ____________________
3: ____________________

Trainee

1: ____________________
2: ____________________
3: ____________________

SUPERVISION CONTRACT CHECKLIST

ESSENTIAL ELEMENTS OF THE SUPERVISION CONTRACT	OTHER ELEMENTS OR TASKS - SUCH AS THOSE REQUIRED BY THE PROGRAM OR IDENTIFIED IN THE FIRST SESSION

1. Overview of what supervision is/is not
2. Program's/setting's role and responsibilities related to supervision
3. Supervisor's roles and responsibilities
4. Limits of confidentiality in supervision
5. Trainee's roles and responsibilities
6. Method and logistics
  a. Time/Day
  b. Where (office, conference room)
  c. How it will take place (video conference, in-person)
7. Expectations for preparation (observation, progress note completion, and review, etc.)
8. Procedural expectations related to:
  a. Routine clinical work (documentation completion, administrative processes)
  b. Ethical problem-solving
  c. Risk situations (decision-making steps, emergency contact, etc.)
9. Expectations for trainee's developmental level and competence
10. Criteria and processes for evaluation of trainee's performance (evaluation forms, timelines)
11. Trainee's individual goals and the (behavioral) criteria for evaluation of their progress toward those goals
12. Remediation processes, including which performance criteria would indicate the need for remediation
	• ______
	• ______
	• ______
	• ______
	• ______
	• ______
	• ______
	• ______
	• ______
	• ______
	• ______
	• ______
	• ______
	• ______

INFORMED CONSENT WORKSHEET FOR SUPERVISORS

ESSENTIAL ELEMENTS OF INFORMED CONSENT

- Define supervision including the responsibilities of the supervisor
- Supervisor's approach/model of supervision
- Limits of confidentiality

DEFINING SUPERVISION

Supervision is distinct from consultation, therapy, or other clinical interventions. It is innately hierarchical in that a more senior/advanced clinician is overseeing the work and development of a more junior clinician

PRIMARY ROLES & RESPONSIBILITIES

- Protect the public
- Ensure quality of care for trainee's clients
- Gatekeeping and ensuring the competence of professionals entering the field

YOUR APPROACH TO SUPERVISION

Foundation (theoretical orientation):

____

____

____

Assumptions:

____

____

____

Examples of Tasks or Processes:

____

____

____

____

PUTTING IT ALL TOGETHER

Example:
Let's talk for a moment about supervision so that we make sure we're both on the same page about what it is/isn't and what some of my responsibilities are as your supervisor.
Supervision is....

____

____

____

____

My approach to supervision is____

____

____

____

and here are some examples of what that might look like in our work together____

____

____

____

____

____

____

____

____

____

____

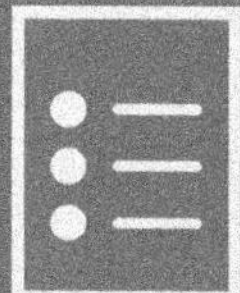

CHAPTER 4 TAKEAWAYS AND RESOURCES

TAKEAWAYS

- Preparing for the first session of supervision is just as important as preparing for an intake or first session with a client.
- The first session, and even what happens before the first session, set the stage for successful supervision.
- Supervision starts even before the first session. Reflecting on your individual attitudes, goals, best hopes, strengths, and learning preferences can help you understand and amplify what you bring to the process before it even starts!
- There are several essential tasks of the first supervision session including informed consent, establishing the supervision contract, building rapport, and goal setting.

RESOURCES

- Tangen, J. L., DiAnne Borders, L., & Fickling, M. J. (2019). The Supervision Guide: Informed by Theory, Ready for Practice. *International Journal for the Advancement of Counselling, 41*(2), 240–251.
- Falender, C. A., & Shafranske, E. P. (2012). *Getting the most out of clinical training and supervision: A guide for practicum students and interns.* American Psychological Association.
- Cooper, L. D., & Wieckowski, A. T. (2017). A structured approach to reflective practice training in a clinical practicum. *Training and Education in Professional Psychology, 11*(4), 252–259.

What are your top 3 takeaways from this chapter?

1. ________________
2. ________________
3. ________________

What do you wish you would have learned and how can you learn this?

- ________________
- ________________
- ________________

What is one thing that you want to do differently moving forward and how will you do this?

____

CHAPTER 5

THE ROLE OF CULTURAL COMPETENCE AND SOCIAL JUSTICE IN EFFECTIVE STRENGTH-BASED SUPERVISION

CHAPTER 5 GOALS

INFORM	ENGAGE
• Learn about the importance of multicultural competence and social justice in supervision • Understand how supervision can facilitate increased multicultural competence and promote advocacy for diverse client populations	• Discuss and reflect on your attitudes and experiences in regard to multicultural competence and social justice in clinical work and training • Engage in practices to facilitate multicultural awareness within the supervision relationship and between trainee and client(s) • Practice talking about multicultural and social justice factors within supervision as a way to enhance competence and model ethical, evidence-based practices

DOI: 10.4324/9781003006558-7

Multicultural and Social Justice Factors in Supervision: Moving beyond Multicultural Awareness toward Allyship, Advocacy, and Action

Reflection Question

How do you define multicultural competence and what are your beliefs and assumptions about the role of multicultural factors in supervision?

Mental health professionals are becoming increasingly attuned to how best to integrate **multicultural** factors into clinical work and supervision, including clients', supervisors', and/or trainees' individual differences and similarities. Tohidian and Quek (2017) define **multicultural supervision** as encompassing the following factors: attending to conversations in supervision that are specific to **culture/cultural difference**, suggesting interventions and assessments that are **culturally sensitive**, and assessing/evaluating the **multicultural competency** of trainees.

Reflection Question

How were you taught to explore your personal biases and areas for multicultural growth? How does this influence your work within supervision?

Practicing multicultural supervision includes, broadly, the following suggested techniques and processes (Tohidian & Quek, 2017; Tsui et al., 2014):

- Initiating conversations in supervision related to known/potential multicultural factors
- Exploring culturally based assumptions that occur from supervisor and/or trainee
- Awareness and exploration of cultural factors of both supervisor, trainee, and/or client, including: political context (individual ideology); cultural context (values, norms); organizational context (power differentials); professional context (interactions, clinical expertise); and personal context (background, age, gender, race, religion, etc.)
- Facilitating learning/growth related to multicultural factors via exploration or sharing of resources, examples, etc.
- Providing feedback on trainee's demonstrated facility with or areas for growth pertaining to multicultural awareness and competence
- Facilitating case conceptualizations from multicultural perspectives, including possibility of influence from cultural factors related to client presentation, symptomology, course of treatment, and other clinical contexts

One tool that we recommend using to facilitate discussions related to multicultural factors and competence in supervision is Hays's (2008) **ADDRESSING** model, included in the table on the next page. We encourage supervisors and trainees to use this table throughout supervision to increase awareness and dialogue concerning the individual similarities and differences between trainee and supervisor, trainee and client, and supervisor and client.

ADDRESSING MODEL IN SUPERVISION

ADDRESSING COMPONENT	SUPERVISOR	TRAINEE	CLIENT
Age / Generation			
Disability Status - Developmental			
Disability Status - Acquired			
Religion / Spiritual Orientation			
Ethnicity			
Socioeconomic Status			
Sexual Orientation			
Indigenous Heritage			
National Origin			
Gender			

Hays, 2008

Social Justice and Supervision

Social justice refers to fairness in how wealth, opportunities, and privileges are distributed within a society. When teaching or learning social justice, it is helpful to understand its components. The **Integrated Social Justice Model (ISJ)**, developed by Enns and Sinacore (2005), does a nice job of identifying these components. The model incorporates multicultural approaches, including feminist and narrative theory and practice, to create a simple structure that can be used to teach or learn social justice. The ISJ Model includes four dimensions:

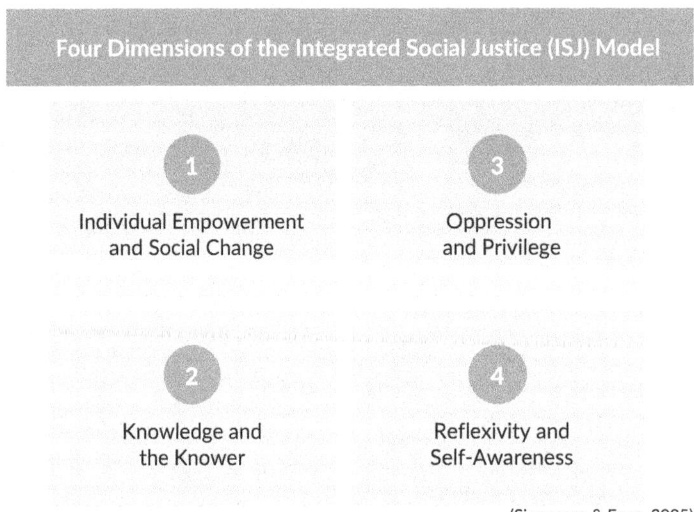

(Sinnacore & Enns, 2005)

The first dimension, **Individual Empowerment and Social Change**, refers to a continuum that charts positive changes within an individual to more broad systemic change across larger communities. From a strength-based perspective, it may include concepts such as resilience, well-being, character strengths, agency, self-efficacy, self-reliance, and psychological capital. As supervisors (and as therapists or counselors), we are typically focused on the individual side of the continuum, as our goals often include the development of both **agency** (competence: one's actual ability to bring about change) and **self-efficacy** (confidence: one's belief about their ability to bring about change) in our trainees and our clients.

The second dimension, **Knowledge and the Knower**, presents a continuum from giving voice to those whose voices have been marginalized or have gone unheard, to the expansion of our knowledge beyond the dominant sources. Strength-based concepts related to this dimension include valuing perspectives, diversity of ideas, and multiple forms of knowing. For supervisors, this means listening well and incorporating all voices into any decision-making process.

For example, Simpson-Southward et al. (2017) found that of the 52 supervision models published in the literature, very few include the voice of the client in trainee evaluations. In fact, only seven (14%) included client outcome measures in trainee evaluations, and only three (less than 5%) included actual client feedback. This means that most supervisors are evaluating their trainee's skills at working with clients without including the client's voice or perspective. Making sure to give voice to our clients is an important component of both therapy and supervision and is a social justice issue.

The third dimension, **Oppression and Privilege**, can be focused on single-identity oppression or multiple overlapping identities and issues. It addresses topics such as social position, social barriers, perspective, opportunities, and access. Use of the **ADDRESSING** Model (Hays, 2008) to understand similarities and differences between us and others is a popular method of applying this dimension. For clinical supervision, this may mean attending to similarities and differences between supervisor and trainee, trainee and client, or client and supervisor to better understand how the world impacts us. Doing so will bring context to individuals and our relationships within the supervision triad.

Finally, **Reflexivity and Self-Awareness** includes an understanding of the forces placed on us and the forces we place on others, as well as awareness of our social positions within our local community and the broader systems within which we live. It is consistently included as a key component of developing social justice competency (Caldwell & Vera, n.d.; Collins et al., 2013; Kassan et al., 2015). For many who teach social justice in courses and in clinical supervision, reflection papers are a common way to explore social justice and what it means to us as individuals within the broader system. We can also reflect on the other three dimensions and how we can apply social justice principles to help empower our trainees and our clients.

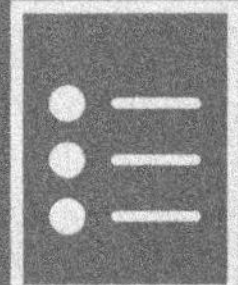

CHAPTER 5 TAKEAWAYS AND RESOURCES

TAKEAWAYS

- Supervision provides opportunities for developing and enhancing multicultural competence through discussion, modeling, and role-playing.
- Multicultural competence in supervision should attend to individual factors of the trainee, supervisor, and client(s) in addition to broader social, political, and cultural factors.
- Supervision can cultivate empowerment toward advocacy and other social justice oriented behaviors.

RESOURCES

- Falender, C. A., Shafranske, E. P., & Falicov, C. J. (2014). *Multiculturalism and diversity in clinical supervision: A competency-based approach* (pp. xv-296). American Psychological Association.
- Hall, J. C., & Theriot, M. T. (2016). Developing multicultural awareness, knowledge, and skills: Diversity training makes a difference?. *Multicultural Perspectives, 18*(1), 35-41.
- Hays, P. A. (2008). *Addressing cultural complexities in practice: Assessment, diagnosis, and therapy* Washington, DC: American Psychological Association.
- Hladik, J. (2016). Assessing multicultural competence of helping-profession students. *Multicultural Perspectives, 18*(1), 42-47.
- Presseau, C., Luu, L. P., Inman, A. G., & DeBlaere, C. (2019). Trainee social justice advocacy: Investigating the roles of training factors and multicultural competence. *Counselling Psychology Quarterly, 32*(2), 260-274.

What are your top 3 takeaways from this chapter?

1. ____________________
2. ____________________
3. ____________________

What do you wish you would have learned and how can you learn this?

- ____________________
- ____________________
- ____________________

What is one thing that you want to do differently moving forward and how will you do this?

____

____

____

____

CHAPTER 6

WE NEED TO TALK

The Relationship as a Foundation for Effective Strength-Based Supervision

INFORM	ENGAGE
• Understand why the supervision relationship is vital to the success of supervision • Learn about what factors contribute to positive supervision relationships • Learn the best practices and evidence-based techniques for building and monitoring a positive working relationship	• Reflect on individual relationship skills and experiences related to supervision • Practice effective relationship skills including active listening

Clinical supervision, like psychotherapy and counseling, is first and foremost a relationship. This is true regardless of the dyad's approach, location, setting, diagnosis or issue, and goals. Research suggests that the working alliance is critical in supervision (Bright & Evans, 2019; Sabella et al., 2020), so this chapter focuses entirely on cultivating and monitoring the supervision relationship. We will share the current best practices and evidence base for building effective relationships within the supervision dyad. We will also offer practical interventions that can be modeled by supervisors, practiced by trainees, and adapted to improve the trainee's work with clients.

Many have rightfully argued that relationship building interventions often come across as mechanical and overly structured, whereas the real supervision relationship is built through genuine curiosity, passion for growth, and a shared desire to move toward agreed-upon goals. We can't teach genuine curiosity from a workbook or text, but we can share with you effective interventions that you can adapt to your style as a clinical supervisor. We encourage the supervisor and trainee to work on these skills together.

DOI: 10.4324/9781003006558-8

The Supervision Relationship: Art, Science, and How Important Is It, Really?

When it comes to the supervision relationship (also referred to as the **working alliance**) we know one thing for certain: in supervision, there *is* a relationship. It is built into the process at the levels of dyad (supervisor and trainee) and triad (supervisor, trainee, and client); it plays a role in arguably *every* component of supervision, including self-disclosure, receptivity to feedback, motivation, satisfaction, self-efficacy, and goal achievement, among others (Cliffe et al., 2016; Enlow et al., 2019; Falender & Shafranske, 2017; Kangos et al., 2018; Kemer et al., 2019; Watkins & Scaturo, 2013).

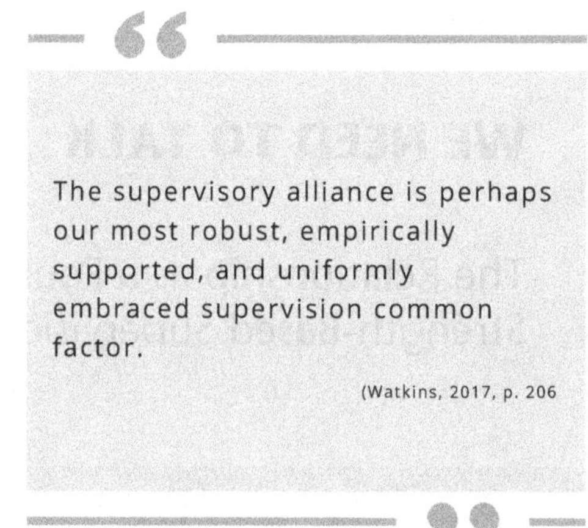

Similarly to Lambert's (1992) research on **common factors** in psychotherapy, researchers also believe that the quality of the supervisory relationship is even more impactful than the supervisor's theoretical model of supervision (Watkins & Scaturo, 2013). In essence, the specific techniques may vary wildly from supervisor to supervisor, trainee to trainee, setting to setting, but if the relationship is healthy and solid, supervision can be successful.

Research tells us several important things that contribute to a healthy supervision relationship, including:

1. A safe environment for exploration, growth, and learning.
2. Empathy, genuineness, and positive regard in all interactions.
3. Feedback that is delivered routinely and grounded in relevant, developmentally appropriate, and behaviorally (not personally/characteristically) anchored training goals.
4. Transparency, collaboration, and openness.
5. It's not all on the supervisor. Several studies have identified ways that trainees contribute to the health of the relationship (Stark et al., 2017).
6. A *good enough* relationship is good enough, particularly in contexts where individual factors are significantly misaligned, such as with significant personality or theoretical orientation differences (generally some combination thereof).

Carl Rogers argued that the therapeutic relationship is both necessary and sufficient to bring about positive change. He was referring to the therapist–client relationship, but we would argue that it applies equally to the supervisor–trainee relationship. The same could be argued for what is often referred to as the **common factors model** or the **common factors theory** of psychotherapeutic change. Lambert (1992) argued that as little as 15% of change that occurs in therapy is related to the therapeutic approach of the counselor. The remaining 85% represents hope (15%), extratherapeutic factors (40%), and the relationship (30%). According to Lambert, then, the relationship accounts for between a quarter and a third of therapeutic outcome. This mirrors the outcomes of supervision research, which tend to find that the relationship between the supervisor and trainee moderates the success of nearly every aspect of supervision.

Relationship-Building Skills

The relationship-building skills discussed in this chapter are focused on developing an effective working alliance in clinical supervision, but they are also used for other purposes. For example, many of the skills are also used to identify and develop strengths, to set goals and plan to achieve them, and to use as models in psychotherapy or counseling. We argue that having a solid relationship makes the work of a supervisor or trainee much more enjoyable as well. We will build on this relationship-building skillset in the next chapter focused on developing strength-based goals.

The key to making these skills work for you is threefold: Practice, Get Feedback, and Make Them Your Own. Initially this may feel robotic or sterile, but the more you bring in your own style and your own way of communicating, the more natural the skills will become. And we realize that many of these skills may be familiar to you and that you may even consider yourself quite capable in some of them. This is great! Build on your strengths and practice applying your skills in different contexts.

Keys to Effective Relationship Skills:

1. Practice
2. Get Feedback
3. Make Them Your Own

All of these skills build on the evidence-based practices of clinical supervision discussed in Section I, including a genuine curiosity about the members of the supervision dyad and the processes involved, respect and positive regard, collaboration, and a true desire to help each other grow.

These relationship-building skills are common across all professions and approaches. Recall that Carl Rogers stressed the importance of being genuinely curious, congruent, and non-judgmental. Other specific relationship skills are detailed in the Basic Listening Sequence by Ivey, Ivey, and Zalaquett (2018). These skills include questioning, encouraging, paraphrasing, reflecting, and summarizing. They are also an integral part of Motivational Interviewing skills that form the acronym OARS: open questioning, affirming, reflective listening, and summarizing. We've categorized these skills into two groups: **Questions** and **Reflective Listening**.

Questions facilitate the continuation of a conversation. They can be used broadly (Can you tell me more about that?) or can be very focused (What courses do you still have to take?). Questions steer the conversation but at the same time narrow it. Like any skill, questioning should be used to move supervision and the relationship forward. We've included five broad types of questions that can be used to get to know your interviewee (trainee in our case) and begin building a positive relationship. The first two are likely the most familiar. They include open questions that give limited direction and inspire a lengthy response or discussion, and closed questions that give a lot of direction and inspire only a short response. Both types have their benefits, but when used inappropriately or too frequently, both can fracture a relationship rather than help build it.

The last three questions come from Norcross (2011), who assert that certain questions can increase treatment effectiveness by 26% if used in some form on a regular basis. These three questions ask about the relationship, progress toward goals, and the process itself. Relationship questions seek to understand the relationship and how it can be improved. Progress questions seek to understand progress toward supervision goals and how it can be improved. Process questions seek to understand the supervision process and how it can be improved.

Reflective listening pays attention to verbal and nonverbal behaviors then reflects these back to the speaker, often with interpretation or some other addition. Reflections can range from simply repeating a single word, to focusing on its deeper meaning, to reflectively summarizing an entire conversation. Along with empathic reflections, we've included three additional broad reflective skills: **encouragers**, **paraphrases**, and **summarizations**.

Encouragers are a variety of verbal and nonverbal behaviors used to encourage others to continue talking. They include head nods, affirmative-to-neutral vocalizations like "Uh-huh," and the repetition of a keyword or phrase (sometimes referred to as a restatement). Whereas a restatement typically uses the same words as the original speaker, paraphrases reword what was said to check in and make sure the individual understands correctly (Ivey et al., 2018).

Paraphrases catch the essence of what is being said and reflect it back. They can take the form of a statement or a question if you are seeking confirmation on the accuracy of your reflection. Paraphrase reflections can be categorized as subtractive, basic, and additive (Truax & Carkhuff, 1967). Subtractive reflections are those that take away from the relationship or the discussion. They often miss the mark, minimize or exaggerate something, or otherwise fail to capture the essence of the topic. Basic reflections capture the essence but do not go beyond. Additive reflections capture the essence and add something to the reflection that, although it was not directly said, is accurate or inspires deeper thought. Additive reflections are sometimes called empathic reflections and can focus on feelings, content, process, or meaning.

Finally, **summarizations** draw together the interviewee's perspective and reflect it back to them. They can be used to begin a supervision session, to transition to a new topic, to provide clarity in lengthy and complex topics, or to end a supervision session or series of sessions. It is often helpful to ask the trainee to summarize a topic or session, as this allows the supervisor to understand how the trainee sees the session and what aspects were important.

Like any skill, practice your questioning and reflective listening skills in different contexts, get feedback on how to improve them, and adjust them to fit your style.

RELATIONSHIP BUILDING SKILLS: ASKING QUESTIONS

Questions facilitate the continuation of a conversation. Questions steer the conversation but at the same time narrow it. Like any skill, questions should be used to move supervision and the relationship forward.

OPEN QUESTIONS

Open questions elicit more information and give the client more room to respond. They tend to start with words such as *what* (leads to facts), *why* (leads to answers), *how* (leads to exploration), or *could/can/would* (very open-ended).

- *What else can you tell me about that?*
- *What other things are happening during your training or coursework this year?*
- *How do you assess the relationship when working with a client?*
- *What happened during your first week at the new clinic?*
- *What could happen if you tried this intervention?*
- *Why might that intervention not work with this client?*
- *Tell me about your past experiences in supervision?*

CLOSED QUESTIONS

Closed questions elicit shorter responses and provide specific information. They tend to start with words such as *is, are, do, how many, when,* etc.

- *How many clients have you seen so far?*
- *Do you feel like you understand the client's presenting issues?*
- *Is this your first time using this CBT intervention?*

PROGRESS QUESTIONS

Progress questions seek to understand the forward movement of supervision toward the trainee's goals. Similar to how we would ask these questions in therapy, supervisors can ask their trainees about the relationship, goals, and activities.

- *How is our relationship?*
- *How did today's supervision session feel?*
- *What did you like most about today? What did you like least?*
- *Are we making progress toward achieving goals?*
- *What would you like us to do more of? What should we do less of? What else could we be doing?*
- *What was it like for you when you heard my feedback about that intervention?*

RELATIONSHIP BUILDING SKILLS: REFLECTIVE LISTENING

Reflective listening skills pay attention to verbal and nonverbal behaviors, then reflect these back often with interpretation or some other addition. Reflections can range from simply repeating a single word, to focusing on its deeper meaning, to reflectively summarizing an entire conversation.

BASIC AND ADDITIVE (EMPATHIC) REFLECTIONS

- Reflections refer to reflecting or giving back to the trainee what you heard, saw, or otherwise considered. Basic reflections show understanding and accurately reflect the trainee's story.
- Additive or empathic reflections add to basic reflections by reading between the lines to get at aspects of training that may be unspoken or unseen.

- ***Basic Reflection:*** *It sounds like you enjoyed the session but wished you had been more active.*
- ***Additive Reflection:*** *It sounds like you enjoyed the session but wished you had been more active. I wonder if going over some specific skills to use with this client might help for next week's session?*

ENCOURAGERS

- Repeating a word or phrase to focus the trainee's attention.

- *If a trainee says: I really enjoyed the session but wished I had been more active.*
- *Supervisor: You enjoyed the session? (encouraging the trainee to focus on their level of enjoyment)*
- *Supervisor: More active? (encouraging the trainee to focus on their level of activity during the session)*

PARAPHRASES

- Paraphrasing is not repetition; it is using some of your own words plus the important main words of the trainee. It allows you to shorten or clarify the essence of what has been said. Paraphrases are often offered back to the trainee in a questioning tone of voice or offers a question at the end to deepen the discussion.

- *After trainee discusses their experience with a new client, Supervisor responds with this paraphrase:*
- *Thanks for sharing your experience with this client. I hear you saying it was a challenge. You said he talked a lot and you struggled to say much. I wonder if we could talk about some specific techniques that might help you feel more confident going into next week's session?*

SUMMARIZATIONS

- Similar to paraphrasing, summarizing involved offering back to the trainee your experiences during a discussion or interaction. Summarizations typically cover a longer period of time and are often used to begin or end the session.

- *Thanks for sharing your experience with this client. I hear you saying it was a challenge. You said he talked a lot and you struggled to say much. I'm glad you spent some time researching techniques that might help you feel more prepared for your next session. I think you've come up with some solid ideas and I'm looking forward to hearing how they worked. Let's make sure to talk about this next week.*

BUILDING RAPPORT BY ASKING QUESTIONS

This worksheet provides some examples of questions to consider asking your supervisor or trainee during the initial supervision sessions to get to know each other better.

EXAMPLE QUESTIONS

- What led you to this field?
- What do you do outside of work that's rewarding or just for fun?
- Do you have a specialty that you're interested in?
- What do you find easiest about your work with clients so far? What's hardest?
- How do you think you'll look back on this experience in five years?
- What advice do you wish you had been given at this stage of the training/education process?
- What have you enjoyed most about your training/education work so far? How about the least?
- What do you like most about working/training at this site? What's the most challenging?
- What do you think has helped you succeed in your career/training so far?
- If you could design a perfect day, what would it look like?
- What have been your favorite classes or subjects in your education so far?
- How do you identify new learning opportunities outside of what's provided in your setting/program?
- How do you feel you learn best?
- Tell me about your experiences in supervision so far, what's worked well and what hasn't worked so well?

YOUR QUESTIONS

- ______________________
- ______________________
- ______________________
- ______________________
- ______________________
- ______________________
- ______________________
- ______________________
- ______________________

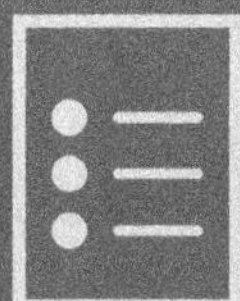

CHAPTER 6 TAKEAWAYS AND RESOURCES

TAKEAWAYS

- Similar to common factors in psychotherapy, the relationship is key to the success of supervision.
- Evidence suggests several factors contribute to a positive supervision relationship, including genuineness, commitment, collaboration, and transparency.
- Reflecting on and honing your relationship skills (active listening, reflection...) and applying those intentionally throughout supervision is an excellent way to establish and maintain a good supervisory relationship.

RESOURCES

- Bright, S., & Evans, A. M. (2019). Supervision development and working alliance: A survey of counseling supervisors. *The Journal of Counselor Preparation and Supervision, 12*(1), 1.
- Johnson, J., Corker, C., & O'Connor, D. B. (2020). Burnout in psychological therapists: A cross-sectional study investigating the role of supervisory relationship quality. *The Clinical Psychologist, 24*(3), 223–235.
- Ivey, A. E., Ivey, M. B., & Zalaquett, C. P. (2013; 9th ed. 2018). *Intentional interviewing and counseling: Facilitating client development in a multicultural society.* Cengage Learning.
- Kim, L., Wilson, E. E., ChenFeng, J., & Knudson-Martin, C. (2017). Towards Safe and Equitable Relationships: Sociocultural Attunementin Supervision. In R. Allan & S. Singh Poulsen (Eds.), *Creating Cultural Safety in Couple and Family Therapy: Supervision and Training* (pp. 57–70). Springer International Publishing.
- Sabella, S. A., Schultz, J. C., & Landon, T. J. (2020). Validation of a brief form of the supervisory working alliance inventory. *Rehabilitation Counseling Bulletin, 63*(2), 115–124.
- Watkins, C. E. (2012). Psychotherapy Supervision in the New Millennium: Competency-Based, Evidence-Based, Particularized, and Energized. *Journal of Contemporary Psychotherapy, 42*(3), 193–203.

What are your top 3 takeaways from this chapter?

1. __________
2. __________
3. __________

What do you wish you would have learned and how can you learn this?

- __________
- __________
- __________

What is one thing that you want to do differently moving forward and how will you do this?

____

CHAPTER 7

START WITH THE END IN MIND

Developing Strength-Based Supervision Goals

CHAPTER 7 GOALS

INFORM

- Understand the importance of collaborative goal-setting
- Understand the mechanics of goal-setting, including the evidence-based best practices and the four intervention questions.
- Learn Appreciative Inquiry (AI) as a strength-based approach to goal-setting within supervision as well as within counseling or psychotherapy.

ENGAGE

- Reflect on your own strengths and goals while developing a plan to identify and amplify your strengths and other resources as a means of moving forward toward your preferred future.
- Practice asking and formulating questions that elicit best hopes, showcase strengths, and help clarify training goals
- Learn specific relationship-building and solution-focused skills that bring life to strength-based clinical supervision.

Starting with the end in mind is the mantra of **solution-focused** interventions. It refers to the idea that we should point ourselves forward and look to the future, or our ***preferred future*** as it is often referred to, rather than dwelling in the past. Just like in therapy, supervision requires goals toward which the supervisor and trainee can work together. Without goals, we are just wandering around aimlessly.

Establishing goals in supervision is a vital component that, evidence suggests, can often be overlooked or can be overly ambiguous. In this chapter, supervisors and trainees will learn why establishing clear, developmentally appropriate, and behaviorally anchored goals is crucial to the success of supervision. We will also address how to implement different strategies for

DOI: 10.4324/9781003006558-9

establishing goals using strength-based approaches such as **Appreciative Inquiry (AI)** (Cooperrider, 1986; Cooperrider & Whitney, 2001).

Goal-setting has a lot to do with what the trainee plans to achieve over the course of the training experience, but it also has to do with goals for the relationship, goals for the process of supervision, and plans for achieving these goals. Goal-setting is more than just determining where you are going; it is about how you will get there and how the process will enhance your work as a supervisor, a trainee, and a clinician. Some goals are common across trainees at specific developmental levels, and some are specific to the trainee, the training program, or the training site.

Goal-setting is more than just determing where you are going; it is about how you will get there and how the process will enhance your work as a supervisor, a trainee, and as a clinician.

Collective (Shared) and Individual Goals

Both shared and individual goals should be strength-based. When designing any goals, we need both a starting point and an ending point. Oftentimes, the starting point is developed through the deficit model—tell me about your weaknesses, tell me what you wish you could do better, tell me what you struggle with. Endpoints are then written as either deficit-based (How will you fix or minimize your weakness?) or strength-based (How will you use your strengths and other resources to overcome this obstacle?).

Unfortunately, because the traditional model of goal development is based in the deficit model, we often spend supervision working to overcome what is wrong. If we focus solely on the developmental approach, meaning that our goal is to develop a minimum level of competency only, we miss opportunities for individualized growth and development—and therefore miss the opportunity to develop the trainee's strengths. Our goal should be broader: to help the trainee achieve the minimum level of competency for their training level *and* to identify and expand on strengths to help the trainee build their own identity as a clinician.

The Four Intervention Questions in Action in Supervision

As mental health professionals, we often wear different hats and perform different tasks, but we tend to ask the same **intervention questions** whether we are doing therapy with a client, offering consultation to a colleague, or performing clinical supervision with a trainee. Most often, these four **intervention questions** are asked about the client by the therapist or counselor with the goal of understanding where the client is, how they got to that point, where they are headed, and how we can help them get there. In other words, these four questions allow you to collaboratively develop a treatment plan with your clients. The four questions look something like this:

- **Where is the client now?** What deficits is the client experiencing that they want to reduce or eliminate?
- **How did they get here?** What is causing the problems in the client's life? What deficits exist in their sense of self, their relationships with others, and their view of the past and future? What is preventing forward movement?

- **Where should the client be?** What would it look like to eliminate or minimize the client's deficits (reduce depression, anxiety, etc.)?
- **How do we help the client get there?** How do we as therapists or counselors help the client eliminate these deficits? What is our treatment plan?

Notice how these questions are worded to focus on the client's deficits. Using the medical model of disease treatment, we often spend our time focused on what is wrong. As Martin Seligman (2004) argues, our traditional approach to treatment was aimed at getting the client to neutral, to zero. While these **intervention questions** work well to understand the client's current deficits, and we would argue that they are necessary, they fall short when it comes to identifying what is going well in the client's life. When seen through a strength-based lens, these four **intervention questions** look a little different:

- **Where is the client now?** What is going well for the client? In what ways is the client being successful?
- **How did they get here?** What strengths exist in their sense of self, their relationships with others, and their view of the past and future? What has helped amplify forward movement?
- **Where should the client be?** What would it look like to enhance the client's strengths and other resources?
- **How do we help the client get there?** How do we as therapists or counselors help the client identify and amplify their strengths and resources? What is our treatment plan?

Goal-Setting and Appreciative Inquiry

Appreciative Inquiry (AI) was developed through the organizational psychology arm of professional psychology to help supervisors work with employees from a strength-based perspective rather than a deficit-based one (Cooperrider & Whitney, 2001). Appreciative Inquiry asks what is good about us; it is an exploration of our strengths and ourselves at our best. AI pulls from various theories and has been successfully integrated in the fields of organizational development, education, medicine, psychology, social work, and counseling. It is a strength-based, integrative, and atheoretical approach to identifying and amplifying what is already going well in pursuit of a preferred future.

AI usually includes between four and six stages, all beginning with the letter D (it was at one time referred to as the 4D Model). These stages aim to build the relationship, identify strengths, and amplify strengths as a means to achieve goals. It is unstructured but often includes prompts and questions at each stage, similar to the four intervention questions. In the graphic on p. 102, we've focused the four questions on the trainee and share some ways each question can be put into action in strength-based clinical supervision.

THE FOUR INTERVENTION QUESTIONS IN ACTION IN SUPERVISION

QUESTION 1: WHERE IS THE TRAINEE NOW?

The first question asks about the current status of the trainee. It looks at where the trainee is now, relative to their developmental level within their training program, across the various domains that will be included in the supervision experience. We also want to ask about the trainee's strengths relative to the current competencies, as well as where the trainee excels and what the trainee enjoys. We also want to address areas where the trainee struggles in terms of competencies, but we do so relative to their strengths.

QUESTION 2: HOW DID THE TRAINEE GET HERE?

Consider the previous experience of the trainee as well as the approaches to learning and training that have worked for them in the past. In the more traditional deficit-based approach, this question would look at the struggles and negative issues impacting the trainee's ability to meet competency. From a strengths-based perspective, it focuses more on what in the past has been effective in helping the trainee move forward. In other words, rather than asking what went wrong, we ask what went well.

QUESTION 3: WHERE SHOULD THE TRAINEE BE?

The third question focuses on the goals for supervision. It is traditionally focused only on the trainee, but we believe goals should include the entire supervision triad—trainee, clients, and supervisor. This set of questions focuses on where the trainee should be at the end of the training experience as well as the processes involved in getting there. It can also focus on the relationship between the trainee and the supervisor, and their goals for their work together. The supervisor should also consider what they can learn and how they can grow as a result of this supervision experience. Finally, and most importantly, goals should be set for the trainee's work with clients. We need to consider minimum competencies based on the trainee's developmental level as well as areas where the trainee can shine by amplifying strengths and other resources in the pursuit of professional growth.

QUESTION 4: HOW WILL THE TRAINEE GET THERE?

The final question, or set of questions, is about planning and working collaboratively to determine how to achieve the outcome and process goals identified in the previous questions. How will the trainee advance from their current knowledge and skill level to a higher level after the training experience? What has worked in the past? How does the trainee learn best? What approaches have been most effective? Consider again that small steps lead to big steps. And remember to be operational and concrete at times so it is clear where supervision is headed.

There are many skills, even within a strength-based perspective, that can help get you where you want to be. We've identified a few of our favorite skills that build on the relationship-building skills discussed in the previous chapter and include **solution-focused** skills like asking trainee-focused questions and identifying positive differences.

SOLUTION-FOCUSED SKILLS: TRAINEE FOCUS

Solution-focused **questions change the emphasis of the conversation from past problems to current and future solutions.**

BEST HOPES, PREFERRED FUTURE

Asking about **best hopes** or preferred future helps the trainee imagine where they are going so we can better determine how to get there.

- **"Miracle Question"**: Imagine you go to sleep tonight just like any other night. Tonight, however, while you are sleeping a miracle occurs and you become a master therapist. You wake up, but because you were sleeping at the time, you don't know a miracle happened. During your next therapy session, you start to notice differences. What might be the first thing you notice? What might you notice next? What else?
- What are your **best hopes** for our supervision session today? What else?
- What could occur today for you to say, Wow, that was a really good supervision session?
- Imagine where you would like to be as a counselor at the end of our year together. This is your preferred future. What does it look like?

ASKING PERMISSION

Helps everyone feel a part of the process and minimizes any unnecessary power differentials.

- What would you like to focus on today?
- Do you mind if we spend sometime today on relationship building? You did some great work with your client and I bet we can find some ways to polish your skills even more.
- I struggled with my client this week. I hope we can make some time to talk about that today?

HIDDEN COMPLIMENTS

Hidden compliments are questions about the successes that provide an opportunity for the interviewee to compliment themselves.

- You formed a really nice working relationship with your client. How did you do that?
- Wow, you know a lot about this treatment protocol. How do you know so much?
- How did you get so comfortable with solution-focused interventions?

SOLUTION-FOCUSED SKILLS: POSITIVE DIFFERENCES

Positive Differences refer to times when a problem did not occur or when the problem was reduced or has less of an impact. Identifying these times then exploring what the trainee was doing allows for the further exploration of strengths and skills that could be used to minimize or eliminate obstacles.

EXCEPTIONS

Exceptions are times when a problem does not occur.

- I noticed this week you were more active with your client and actually redirected him a few times. What was different this week?
- Nice job getting all your notes completed this week. What helped you stay caught up?
- You seemed more confident today compared to the last couple of weeks. Tell me about that?

POSITIVE PRESUPPOSITIONS

A presupposition is an assumption that something is present without asking. For example, "Did anything go well this week?" could be asked "What went well this week?" In our experience, presuppositions result in more quality responses that more effectively emphasize strengths.

- What went well in your session with your client?
- What went well today in our supervision session?
- What did you enjoy about that training?
- Tell me three things you want to do this week to help strengthen your relationship-building skills?
- And our favorite: What else? This is especially useful when asking your trainee about their strengths or what went well. What else? How else? etc.

BROADEN AND BUILD

Broaden and Build (Fredrickson, 2001, 2013) initially referred to positive emotions but in supervision it can help identify anything that is going well. After a productive counseling session, for example, a supervisor might ask the trainee how they could build on what they learned and apply it to other areas.

- You did a nice job asking solution-focused questions with that client. How could you do that with your other client?
- You worked hard with this client. What did you learn about yourself? How could you build on this?
- You have a lot of confidence with assessment. What might help this confidence spread to therapy?

FLAGGING THE MINEFIELD

"Flagging the minefield" is a solution-focused process of identifying potential obstacles and then developing a plan to eliminate or reduce their impact.

- What could get in the way of you achieving your goals? What else?
- What could we do now to minimize its negative impact? What else?
- What could we do now to avoid this obstacle? What else?

Organizations concerned with the training and competence of mental health professionals, including the APA and the ACA, explicitly endorse and encourage the use of strength-based approaches in training and supervision. The APA's (2014) most recent Supervision Guidelines assumes clinical supervision is strength-based, leaving no wiggle room for whether supervisors should incorporate a strength-based approach in their supervision model. When **Appreciative Inquiry** is applied to supervision, it is a flexible approach to identifying the best in your trainee and sets the stage for strength-based supervision.

We want to encourage you to take advantage of the powerful tool of modeling and use the ROPES Model, Appreciative Inquiry, and Scaling to identify and develop your strengths as a supervisor so that you can build on those strengths and teach the process to your trainees. Those trainees can then build on their own strengths and will be better equipped to help their clients identify their own strengths and how to build on them. We can then set objective goals and measure change through the process of scaling. Let's dive into these a little deeper so you can learn how to apply them.

Appreciative Goal-Setting

Appreciative Inquiry (AI) and **ROPES** are both strength-based and **solution-focused**, so they overlap in how they focus on an individual's resources and build on these in pursuit of a **preferred future**. AI is a developmental model that provides a structure for strength-based goal development; ROPES provides a strength-based model of movement. It can be used throughout supervision and fits nicely within the Appreciative Inquiry developmental approach. As we stated before, **solution-focused** interventions give action to positive psychology to help bring about forward movement.

APPRECIATIVE GOAL-SETTING

THE R.O.P.E.S MODEL FOR SOLUTION-FOCUSED STRENGTH DEVELOPMENT

ROPES is an acronym for Resources, Options, Possibilities, Exceptions, and Solutions. It was developed by Greybeal (2001) as a strengths-based model to identify solutions that facilitate forward movement toward the preferred future. Use these questions as a starting point, but work to make them your own.

RESOURCES

Resources include internal (strengths, etc.) and external (VIPs, trainings, books, articles, roleplaying, etc.) assets that can be activated or amplified to move the trainee closer to their goals

- What resources are available that will help you reach your goals?
- What have you done in the past that has been helpful?
- What helps you be successful? What else?

OPTIONS

Options refer to how the trainee's resources can be put into play in the pursuit of goal achievement.

- What options are currently available to help you move forward?
- What are the different ways you could work on achieving your goals?
- What are the pros and cons of various options? What else?

POSSIBILITIES

Possibilities refers to resources and options that may have been missed or that could be activated or amplified in pursuit of goal achievement.

- What other possible options might exist?
- How can we think outside the box?
- What could we do better?
- What could we be missing? What else?

EXCEPTIONS

Exceptions are those times when things went well. The idea is to identify the reasons for success and work to put them into play again.

- When have you overcome similar obstacles? How did you do this?
- When are you at your best? What do you excel at?
- What has made you successful in the past? What else?

SOLUTIONS

Solutions refers to what is currently going well, what has gone well in the past, or on what is likely to go well. Again, the idea is to understand the reasons for success.

- What is going well? What are you doing that is working well?
- What have others complimented you on? What have others thanked you for?
- What are you proud of? What was the most enjoyable?

Our Appreciative Inquiry model has six stages. We see AI, especially when applied to supervision, as having three related and sequential tasks, each with two stages: Define and Discover, Dream and Design, and Deliver but Don't Settle. As you move through these stages, you will notice similarities across AI, the ROPES Model, and the four Intervention Questions discussed in the previous section.

SIX STAGES OF APPRECIATIVE INQUIRY

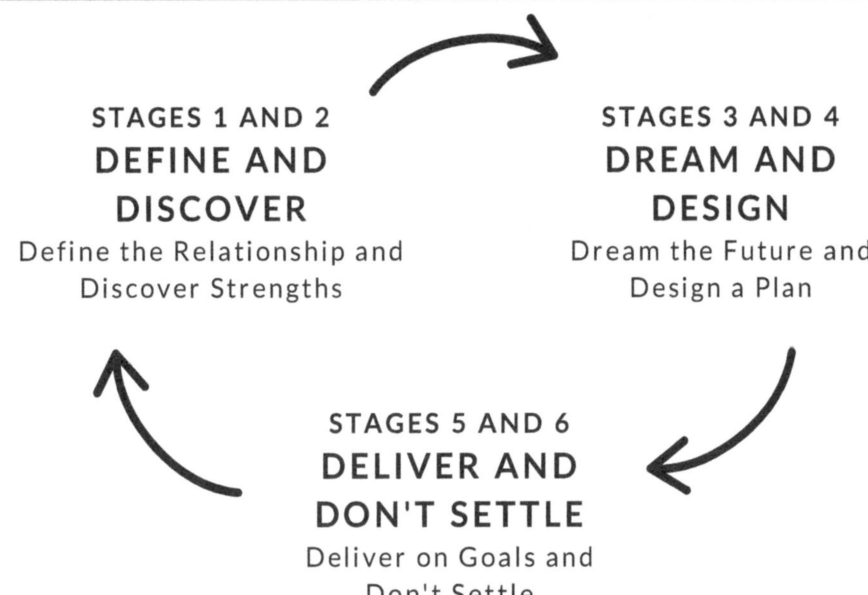

In Stage 1, the goal is to define the expectations of the relationship and the work that will be done together in order to maximize success. Relationship building begins immediately and continues throughout the supervision (or therapy) process. As the interviewer asks questions aimed at getting to know the interviewee, strengths may become more obvious and interviewers should pay attention to (1) anything identified as a strength, (2) anything others praised or highlighted as strengths or skills, and (3) anything the interviewee expresses enjoyment in, finds fulfilling, or gets meaning from.

APPRECIATIVE INQUIRY GOAL-SETTING

1: DEFINE THE RELATIONSHIP

Begin defining a collaborative relationship. Create a safe and welcoming environment and get to know the interviewee from a strengths-based perspective. Pay attention to (and make notes regarding) strengths, exceptions, internal and external resources, diversity issues, past experiences, and what brings joy and inspiration to the interviewee.

SKILLS	PROMPTS
Consider Intervention Question 1: Where is the trainee now? Apply relationship building skills by asking open questions. Use limited closed questions. Engage in reflective listening by using reflections and encouragers to deepen and broaden the interview. Ask permission and use hidden compliments to help empower your trainee. Begin the process of identifying strengths and resources.	• What are you most proud of? Tell me more about that? • What do you enjoy doing? Tell me more about that? • What motivates or inspires you? What else? • Who has been most helpful to you? How have they been helpful? • What inspired you to choose this field? • Tell me about a time when you've overcome something really challenging? • Tell me about a day that's gone really well recently?

NOTES

Stage 2, which occurs simultaneously with Stage 1, looks for the interviewee's strengths by asking questions designed specifically for this exploration. The goal is to identify your interviewee's resources, including internal resources like strengths and external resources like VIPs (very important people), textbooks, video trainings, etc. As you reach the end of the first two stages you should have a strong working alliance with your trainee and should have a good sense of what the trainee's strengths and resources are.

While this stage of AI is not the only time you should investigate strengths of both the trainee and supervisor, it often represents the first opportunity to bring strengths into the supervision process. It may be a great time to take the Values in Action Strengths Survey at viacharacter.org/character-strengths. Or as a supervisor, you could introduce the concept of strengths using Peterson and Seligman's (2004) model or another model of individual strengths. This would allow you to discuss your similarities and differences, much like you would use the ADDRESSING Model (Hays, 2008), and set the stage for how you could amplify these strengths during this goal-setting exercise and throughout the supervision process.

APPRECIATIVE INQUIRY GOAL-SETTING

2. DISCOVER & REFLECT ON STRENGTHS

Discover and reflect on your interviewee's strengths and other resources, both internal and external. Identify what is going well for the interviewee and where they find joy and inspiration.

SKILLS

Consider Intervention Question 2: How did the trainee get here?
Apply relationship building skills by asking open questions. Use limited closed questions. Engage in reflective listening by using reflections and encouragers to deepen the discussion. Use presuppositions ("what else?") to broaden the discussion. Ask permission and use hidden compliments to help empower your trainee. Identify and call out trainee strengths and resources. Use Solution-Focused skills of exceptions and positive presuppositions. Paraphrase and summarize, or ask the trainee to, in order to ensure agreement and collaboration. Begin applying the ROPES model, especially as you explore resources and begin looking at trainee options, possibilities, and exceptions.

PROMPTS

- What are your strengths? Say more about that?
- What have others said you are good at? What else?
- What do you enjoy doing? Tell me why you enjoy it?
- What motivates or inspires you?
- Who has been most helpful to you? How have they been helpful?
- What resources have been useful?
- What are you good at? Share more about that?
- What do you wish you could do more of? What else?

NOTES

Stage 3 begins moving the relationship forward. It is called "Dream" because it affords the dyad the opportunity to consider their **best hopes** for their work together. The goals are not merely for the trainee to demonstrate the minimum level of competency; the goals are to work together to achieve competency, then amplify strengths and build on what is already working well.

APPRECIATIVE INQUIRY GOAL-SETTING

3. DREAM THE FUTURE

Identify and describe the interviewee's preferred future as a clinical supervisor. Focus on process goals as well as outcome goals. Build on the interviewee's strengths. Allow the trainee to dream of their preferred future with a focus on ownership.

SKILLS	PROMPTS
Consider Interventions Question 3: Where should the trainee be? Continue using relationship-building skills. Apply solution-focused skills and reflect on trainee strengths and resources. Continue applying ROPES Model, with a focus on finding solutions. Focus on the trainee by using Solution-Focused skills like the Miracle Question and providing direct and hidden (indirect) compliments. Use paraphrases and summarizations to ensure agreement and collaboration	• Use the Miracle Question (or frame it as a magic wand, fairy godmother, etc.). • What are your best hopes for the training year? Tell me more about that? • What inspires you about your work? • What do you admire most about your past supervisors? • How can we continue your progress or successes? How else?

NOTES

As you begin to set formal goals for supervision, including those that are common across all trainees, you will start identifying and defining the process that will be used to maximize success in achieving these goals. Stage 4 is called "Design" because it builds the process of getting from where we are now to where we want to be. By the end of Stage 4, the trainee and supervisor will have identified goals for the trainee and for their relationship and work together. You will have collaboratively developed a plan to achieve these goals and will have done so from a strength-based perspective.

APPRECIATIVE INQUIRY GOAL-SETTING

4. DESIGN A PLAN

Begin discussing how the preferred future could be attained. Focus on what is achievable (best hopes) and how strengths can be amplified to help ensure success. Consider small steps and process goals as a means to achieving larger outcome goals.

SKILLS	PROMPTS
Consider Interventions Question 4: How will the trainee get there? Continue using relationship-building skills and solution-focused skills, especially broaden and build, as this helps to develop a plan based on strengths that builds on what is already going well. Use scaling to help identify small steps toward goals. Continue applying ROPES Model and look for resources, options, possibilities and exceptions and how these can be used to design a strength-based training plan. Look for potential obstacles and make contingency plans.	• How do you best learn? How else? • What has worked well in the past to develop new skills? What else? • What activities help you improve your knowledge and/or skills? Say more about that? • Small steps (mini goals)—What can you do in the next week? Next month? • What might prevent forward movement ("Flag the Minefield")? • How might you activate your resources to overcome obstacles? • What strengths and resources are available and how might you use these?

NOTES

Returning to the concept of grit is important here. Duckworth (2016) reminds us that that grit is about holding the same top-level goals for a long time. If we have too many top-level goals or they are not mapped to our daily activities, we will struggle to achieve any of them. Therefore, identifying but limiting our top-level goals, those focused on the more distant future, allows us to better tailor our daily activities in pursuit of those goals.

For supervision, this helps us turn goals into action. Imagine a trainee plans to work in the field of trauma after graduation. This could be considered a top-level goal or long-term goal, one that will take some time to achieve. What could the trainee be doing during this training year to move closer to that long-term goal? Consider that a mid-term goal, one that can be achieved in the training year that will move the trainee closer to their top-level goal. Now consider the shorter term, perhaps this month. What could the trainee be doing this month to move them closer to their mid-term goals? And finally, consider the trainee's daily or weekly activities. What could the trainee do today or this week to move them close to their short-term goals? Using this approach allows us to move from stage 3 to stage 4 where we translate goals into action.

MAPPING DAILY ACTIVITIES TO GOALS

Daily Activities → Short-Term Goal
Daily Activities → Short-Term Goal
Daily Activities → Short-Term Goal
Daily Activities → Short-Term Goal

Short-Term Goal + Short-Term Goal → Mid-Term Goal
Short-Term Goal + Short-Term Goal → Mid-Term Goal

Mid-Term Goal + Mid-Term Goal → Long-Term Goal

A final **solution-focused** technique we want to share regarding goal-setting is the tool of scaling. Strength-based, **solution-focused** scaling flips the traditional approach to scaling problems, which is often referred to as SUDS—subjective units of distress scale. When using SUDS, you would ask a client to rate their anxiety, for example, on a scale from one to ten with ten being the most anxious they have felt. SUDS works well to track the growth or reduction in a problem.

The solution approach scales the solution, not the problem. For example, rather than asking the client how bad their anxiety is today, a counselor may ask the client to describe the absence of anxiety or what it would look like to not have anxiety. The miracle question is often used to explore what it will look like when the problem is gone and then this preferred future is assigned a value of 10. This flips it to the positive so scaling can be used to track how successful they are in moving toward their goals.

In this scenario, the prompt might sound something like this: "On a scale of one to ten, with ten being the best you have done in controlling your anxiety and one being the opposite, where are you today?" Follow-up questions help the client understand what they are doing well and what they should continue doing. For example, "What did you do that worked to move you closer to your goal of being anxiety free?" or when comparing scaling across sessions, "What strengths did you use to increase this number [or to maintain the number, or prevent it from going even lower]?

Let's move **solution-focused** scaling to the supervision process and imagine a trainee and supervisor discussing strengths and goals. They decide to work on relationship building as a goal. Applying scaling in supervision might look something like this:

Supervisor: On a scale of one to ten, with ten representing your goal of forming solid therapeutic relationships with clients, one representing the opposite, where are you now?

Trainee: I do okay in this area but it has not been consistent. Last year I had a few clients that I struggled with, so I would like to do better.

Supervisor: So on the ten-point sale, with ten being your goal, where are you now?

Trainee: Maybe a seven.

Supervisor: That's great! That says you have some strengths and skills in this area. Tell me why you are at a seven instead of a six or a five. What are you doing that works?

Trainee: I have good listening skills. I think I come across as non-judgmental. I try to connect with my clients and see the world through their eyes.

Supervisor: These are obviously important, so I am glad you feel comfortable with these skills. Let's make sure to discuss these more. What else are you doing that is working in forming the therapeutic alliance with your clients?

Trainee: Well, I'm respectful, I think I ask good questions, but I am working on getting better with reflections and expressing empathy. I struggle with that and sometimes catch myself wondering how to respond to my client, especially if I don't know them well.

Supervisor: It sounds like you have some good insight into your skillset including your strengths and areas for growth. If you are at a seven now, what would help you move to an eight?

Trainee: I think I could continue what I am doing and work on reflections and how to demonstrate empathy with my clients.

Supervisor: Great, let's write that down and discuss how that will look. What else?

Trainee: Maybe work on my anxiety in counseling. Sometimes when I don't know how to respond to a client, I find myself getting lost in my thoughts and maybe the client sees this. Now that I think about it, maybe I should work more on being less anxious in counseling.

Supervisor: You are not the first trainee to tell me this. Let's make sure to focus on anxiety and how you can reduce that during sessions as we move forward. What else would help you be more present in a counseling session?

Trainee: Sleep, better preparation before each session, maybe more skills or tools would help as well.

Supervisor: So far we've identified a few specific ways to improve your work with clients this year. You want to improve your skills at reflection and empathic reflections, specifically; you want to reduce anxiety during counseling and be more present focused when with clients; and you also mentioned better prep, including getting enough sleep.

Trainee: Yes, I would love to improve those areas this year.
Supervisor: Great, let's talk about what this will look like and what you and I will do to help you achieve your goals for this year.

Along with scaling goals, **solution-focused** scaling can also look at motivation and confidence. For example: "On a scale of one to ten, how confident are you that you can achieve these goals, with ten being very confident and one being the opposite?" The supervisor can then go through the process as indicated above to determine what the trainee could do to improve their confidence (or move the scale upward). The same works for motivation by asking the trainee to scale how motivated they are to achieve a particular goal.

Appreciative Goal-Setting Sample Transcript

The following is an excerpt taken from an initial clinical supervision session. The interviewer is a **solution-focused**, strength-based supervisor. The interviewee is a second-year doctoral student in psychology about to begin their first clinical training experience. The setting is a university-based community clinic. There was discussion of the process and administrative requirements prior to this.

APPRECIATIVE GOAL-SETTING
SAMPLE TRANSCRIPT

Supervisor: I would like to spend some time today getting to know you a little better. You completed your first year of the program, so congratulations on your progress.

Trainee: Thanks. There were some hiccups, but so far so good. I'm excited about doing therapy but really nervous too.

Supervisor: I'm excited to work with you this year. The first year of a graduate program isn't easy; how did you make it successful?

Trainee: I think just a lot of hard work.

Supervisor: I'm sure it was a lot of hard work. What helped you be successful?

Trainee: I'm lucky that I really like what I am studying. I like to learn, that helps a lot. Sometimes, though, I catch myself going off on learning tangents, so I have to make sure to focus myself. So I guess focusing is really the hardest part.

Supervisor: Well you've obviously focused enough to get you this far. What have you found helpful so far?

Trainee: I think self-care is important, and I think having friends in the program is important. I don't think I would be here if I didn't have people to help me.

Supervisor: I was the same way in grad school. It helps a lot, huh?

Trainee: No doubt.

Supervisor: So one of the toughest challenges in your first year has been focusing, but you've been able to do it successfully because of things like self-care and help from your fellow students. It sounds like relationships are important to you and I'm glad you've found them positive. What else helped you be successful in your first year?

After paraphrasing the strengths of the trainee (success in first year, ability to focus, recognizing importance of relationships, self-care, enjoyment of learning) and resources (fellow students) mentioned by the trainee, the supervisor asked, "What else?" to identify additional strengths and resources. This process can continue as the relationship develops and the trainee's resources are explored. The supervisor can reflect back to the trainee frequently through paraphrases and summarizations and can ask the trainee to summarize as well.

Refining and Documenting Training Goals

Once you have established some initial goals or best hopes for the training term, you can then refine those goals (if needed) and document them collaboratively (e.g., confirming and clarifying to make sure you're both on the same page). We suggest using the following framework for refining and documenting goals. This structure includes (1) defining the goal, (2) identifying what will be different when the goal is met, and (3) discussing how progress will be monitored and evaluated:

> Goal 1 is to ______________. Here's what will be happening or be different when this goal is met: ______________. Here is how we'll monitor and evaluate progress toward this goal: ______________.

Using this framework helps ensure that the goals have been developed using evidence-based best practices including that they are developmentally appropriate, behaviorally anchored, and can feasibly be achieved in the training term.

You may need to refine the goals until they are easily articulated and behaviorally anchored. For example, a trainee who is new to DBT interventions may initially identify a goal of *"Being more confident introducing DBT skills to clients."* If we apply our framework to refine the goal, that might look like:

> My first goal is to feel more confident when I introduce clients to DBT mindfulness skills. I'll know that I've met this goal when I am consistently (in more than half of my sessions) introducing 3–5 mindfulness skills without reading verbatim from the corresponding handouts. We'll monitor this goal by (1) reviewing segments of video each week where I am introducing mindfulness skills and (2) practicing and demonstrating introducing those skills in supervision.

It is also important to ensure that goals are developmentally appropriate. For example, early in training we often want to jump to more exciting and advanced intervention skills and overlook the importance of foundational skills like establishing rapport and building the positive working alliance. Supervisors can help shift attention to developmentally appropriate goals by reframing advanced goals within the trainee's developmental context. Using resources like the IDM can help provide a common language for discussing developmental stages.

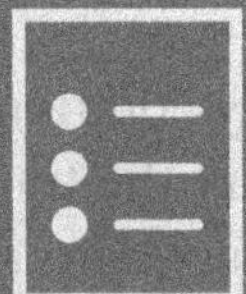

CHAPTER 7 TAKEAWAYS AND RESOURCES

TAKEAWAYS

- The four intervention questions are key to understanding the trainee's successes and setting goals to continue momentum.
- Solution-focused skills work well to move us forward toward our goals. The Miracle Question helps to identify an aspirational preferred future. Looking for and building on successes uses our own momentum to achieve our goals. And flagging the minefield allows us to imagine obstacles and make plans to minimize or overcome them.
- Appreciative Inquiry offers a way to use relational and solution-focused skills to help build a solid working relationship, identify strengths and resources, develop aspirational goals, and design a plan, based on strengths and resources, to achieve these goals.

RESOURCES

- Lutz, A. B. (2013). *Learning solution-focused therapy: An illustrated guide.* American Psychiatric Pub.
- Wade, J., & Jones, J. (2015). *Strength-based clinical supervision: A positive psychology approach to clinical training.* Springer.

What are your top 3 takeaways from this chapter?

1. ______
2. ______
3. ______

What do you wish you would have learned and how can you learn this?

- ______
- ______
- ______

What is one thing that you want to do differently moving forward and how will you do this?

______
______
______
______

SECTION III

MOVING FORWARD

Building on Strengths in Ongoing and Final Supervision Sessions

Introduction to Section III

In the previous section we focused on the individual and collaborative work that's needed in order to prepare for and engage in the first supervision session, including:

- Learning that preparing for supervision is just as important as preparing to see a new client: it sets the relationship up for success by ensuring that the relationship starts with self-awareness, intentionality, and organization.
- Reflecting on the attitudes, strengths, learning preferences, experiences, and expectations that you bring to supervision so that you can focus on your strengths, advocate for your learning needs, and bring awareness to any potential internal barriers—like anxiety—that may impact your experience.
- Understanding what tasks are essential in the first session and how to engage in them using evidence-based practices related to informed consent, the supervision contract, building rapport, and establishing goals.
- Learning best practices for goal-setting by emphasizing strengths and collaboration toward goals that are attainable, developmentally appropriate, and behaviorally anchored.
- Putting positive psychology into action by applying relationship-building skills and solution-focused skills, both aimed at identifying and moving forward toward a preferred future. You also learned about a structured strength-based approach to goal-setting called the Appreciative Inquiry (AI) model that starts with a positive relationship and the identification of strengths.

From here we take all of the work that you have put into starting this relationship and set it into action throughout the ongoing sessions of supervision. Essentially, we address everything that happens until your final session. There will be many things that capture your attention throughout the course of supervision; our goal in this section is to keep you focused on the essential components of ongoing sessions, including:

1. Monitoring Clinical Work
2. Providing Effective Strength-Based Feedback
3. Monitoring Caseloads and Talking about Clients in Supervision
4. Addressing Obstacles, Including Repairing the Relationship and Remediation.

DOI: 10.4324/9781003006558-10

CHAPTER 8

IT'S A JOURNEY AND A DESTINATION

Essential Tasks and Goals of Ongoing Supervision Sessions

CHAPTER 8 GOALS

INFORM

- Understand the supervision learning cycle and its role in ongoing supervision sessions
- Understand the evidence-based best practices for ongoing supervision sessions, including monitoring and observing clinical work and providing routine, strength-based feedback
- Learn about processes for remediating or resolving issues that may arise in supervision
- Learn how to prioritize your preparation and in-supervision time to meet the goals and needs of trainees, supervisors, and clients
- Understand the importance of self-care in supervision for supervisors and trainees.

ENGAGE

- Discussion points to spark conversations about how to structure supervision time and collaborate on "if-this-then-that" processes for when things don't go as planned
- Worksheets for monitoring and observing clinical work, formulating feedback, monitoring and adapting goals, and addressing potential issues (including remediation)
- Resources for added depth and context for key topics that arise in ongoing supervision sessions.

Now that you've prepared for your first supervision session and have laid the foundation for an effective (and hopefully fun) supervision process, it's time to shift your attention to the focus of ongoing supervision sessions. In this introduction we'll provide an overview of supervisor

DOI: 10.4324/9781003006558-11

and trainee essential tasks and goals for ongoing supervision sessions that build upon elements from the first session.

Laying the foundation for a positive working relationship really sets the stage for successful supervision. Chapters in this section will go into more depth on several of the ongoing session tasks, such as monitoring and observation, conducting evaluation and feedback, handling anxieties, and remediating or addressing other issues that may arise. Collectively, these tasks all reflect the fundamental responsibilities of supervisors and trainees across the course of supervision. We've reviewed them in the diagram below.

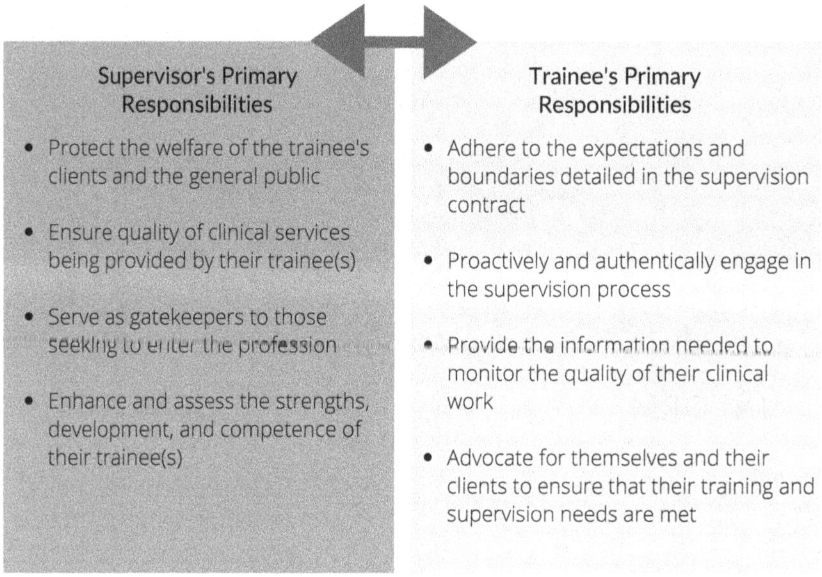

The Supervision Learning Cycle

Before we jump into specific tasks, we wanted to give you an overview of ongoing supervision sessions. This is best captured by supervision gurus Shafranske and Falender (2016) in their **learning cycle**, which we've adapted below. This cycle starts with the trainee's performance; it continues through observation, reflection, evaluation and feedback, goal setting and planning; then it repeats throughout the supervision process. If you're wondering how this cycle is connected to the work you did in Section I to lay the foundation for supervision, remember that each of these elements are grounded in expectations, transparency, a positive relationship, previously established goals, and assessments of the trainee's needs and developmental level. The foundations of the first session, paired with this cycle, set the stage for the ongoing session tasks.

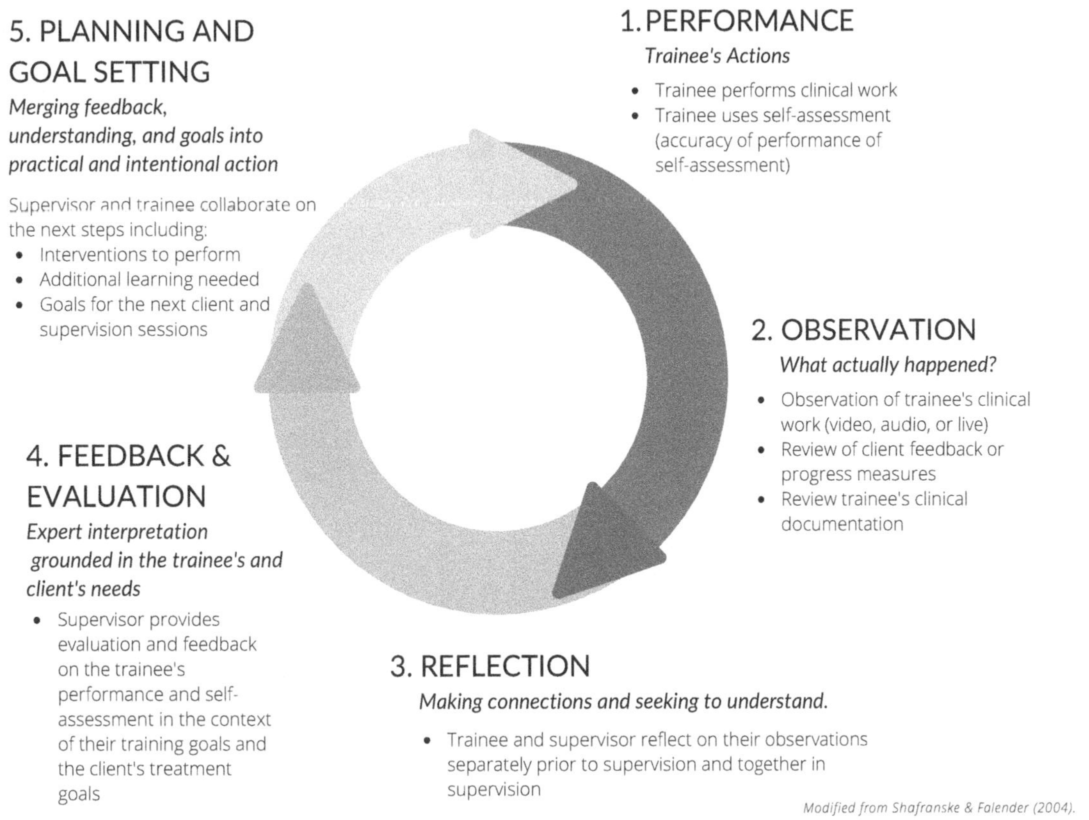

1. PERFORMANCE

Trainee's Actions

- Trainee performs clinical work
- Trainee uses self-assessment (accuracy of performance of self-assessment)

2. OBSERVATION

What actually happened?

- Observation of trainee's clinical work (video, audio, or live)
- Review of client feedback or progress measures
- Review trainee's clinical documentation

3. REFLECTION

Making connections and seeking to understand.

- Trainee and supervisor reflect on their observations separately prior to supervision and together in supervision

4. FEEDBACK & EVALUATION

Expert interpretation grounded in the trainee's and client's needs

- Supervisor provides evaluation and feedback on the trainee's performance and self-assessment in the context of their training goals and the client's treatment goals

5. PLANNING AND GOAL SETTING

Merging feedback, understanding, and goals into practical and intentional action

Supervisor and trainee collaborate on the next steps including:

- Interventions to perform
- Additional learning needed
- Goals for the next client and supervision sessions

Modified from Shafranske & Falender (2004).

Overview of Tasks and Priorities in Ongoing Supervision Sessions

Ongoing supervision sessions generally encompass several different themes in terms of goals, priorities, and tasks for supervisors and trainees. Each session will likely vary depending on the context of the week, the trainee's caseload, setting considerations, the trainee's developmental level, training goals, and progress or barriers toward goals or implementing feedback from previous sessions. That's a lot for both trainees and supervisors to consider as they collaborate on setting the agendas for their sessions and adapting when new content arises or things don't go as planned. In general, both trainees and supervisors should attend to the following essential tasks of ongoing sessions.

OVERVIEW OF TASKS AND PRIORITIES IN ONGOING SUPERVISION SESSIONS

ESSENTIAL TASKS FOR TRAINEES AND SUPERVISORS
Monitoring the quality of the trainee's clinical work.
Monitoring the trainee's caseload, including progress or barriers to progress and treatment goals.
Providing evaluation and feedback on the trainee's clinical work, training goals, and competencies.
Keeping an eye on the goals that the supervisor and their trainee set for the term and adapting them as necessary.
Monitoring the relationship/working alliance and repairing ruptures if they occur.
Continuously assessing the trainee's developmental level and progress, keeping in mind that most development will occur non-linearly.
Monitoring and adjusting supervisor and trainee self-care practices.

We've incorporated these into the checklist at the end of this chapter, which can serve as a big-picture reminder of priorities for ongoing supervision sessions. In the following chapters we'll start to break down monitoring and observation, feedback, and what to do when things go awry. We've also included the following example of a supervision timeline to consider as you plan the course of supervision from start to finish. Keeping the timeline of supervision in mind—whether it's a 12-week term, a semester, or a year—helps to keep things like evaluations from sneaking up on you.

12-WEEK SUPERVISION TIMELINE

Week One	Provide informed consent, review and revise the supervision contract, get to know each other, and set—or starting to set—goals.
Week Two	Refine goals, continue to establish rapport, and begin to observe and provide feedback on the trainee's clinical work.
Weeks Three and Four	Keep an eye on the relationship, observe clinical work and provide informal feedback, and monitor progress toward goals.
Week Five	Same as above, plus prepare for the mid-term formal evaluation. Some aspects of this session should include discussing the form and inviting the trainee to complete it from their perspective (focusing on their development and progress for discussion in the next session).
Week Six	Set aside time to review trainee's self-assessment of their mid-term evaluation, compare and contrast to the supervisor's evaluation, and determine what to include on the final document. The goal is to have the document finalized and agreed upon by the end of session.
Week Seven	Check in on the relationship relative to your first formal evaluation process. Continue monitoring clinical work and providing formative feedback.
Weeks Eight to Nine	Continue to monitor the relationship, observe clinical work, provide formative feedback, and assess progress toward goals.
Week Nine	Start to talk about the forthcoming end of supervision. This might include asking trainees to prepare a list of recommendations for their caseload (in terms of what clients are ready to terminate treatment or need to transfer to a different clinician). Continue to observe clinical work and provide feedback.
Week Ten	By this session, supervisor and trainee should have agreed upon a plan for each client and should be able to take steps to terminate or transfer services as needed before the end of supervision in Week Twelve. Time should be set aside in this session to preview the summative evaluation form, with the goal that trainee and supervisor complete it separately before the next session.
Week Eleven	Continue to monitor any remaining clients and clinical work. Set aside time to discuss the preliminary summative evaluation forms with a goal of finalizing the evaluation before the next and final session. Supervisor and trainee should discuss what they want to focus on in their last session, including reflecting on any lingering questions or feedback that they may have.
Week Twelve	Finalize the summative evaluation, process the experience of supervision, reinforce strengths and successes, and discuss ongoing goals and areas for growth, which may include next steps in training or professional development.

SAMPLE 12-WEEK SUPERVISION TIMELINE

SESSION #	MONITORING THE SUPERVISORY RELATIONSHIP	CONTRACT AND INFORMED CONSENT	GOAL SETTING	PROVIDING FORMATIVE FEEDBACK	MONITORING PROGRESS TOWARD GOALS	DIRECTLY OBSERVING CLINICAL WORK	FORMAL EVALUATION AND FEEDBACK	MONITORING CASELOAD	CASELOAD TERMINATION OR TRANSFER
Week 1	✓	✓	✓			✓		✓	
Week 2	✓	*Reinforce as needed	✓	✓		✓		✓	
Weeks 3-6	✓			✓	✓	✓	*Draft Mid-Term Evaluation	✓	
Week 6	✓			✓	✓	✓	✓	✓	
Weeks 7-9	✓			✓	✓	✓		✓	
Week 9	✓			✓	✓	✓		✓	✓ Planning
Week 10	✓			✓	✓	✓		✓	✓ Planning
Week 11	✓			✓	✓	✓	*Draft Summative Evaluation	✓	✓ Finalizing
Week 12	✓			✓	✓	✓	✓	✓	✓

Self-Care in Supervision: Monitoring, Modeling, and Enhancing Resilience

Self-care or personal well-being among licensed clinicians and clinicians-in-training has been a somewhat controversial topic in recent years. Though recognized as essential to preventing burnout and adhering to the ethical guidelines pertaining to clinical competence, self-care and individual well-being can often be misconceptualized as: *Do as I say, not as I do.* Trainees and licensed professionals alike indicate that even when self-care is discussed or implicitly or explicitly encouraged, it is difficult to prioritize self-care in the face of real-world demands and expectations.

> As many as 70% of trainees report significant levels of distress and even burnout before their professional careers have even started.

This is particularly true in training programs, where trainees are often asked, if not required, to commit to many weekly hours of clinical work, supervision, coursework, and other tasks of training like applying and interviewing for their next clinical placement, working on research teams, preparing for oral or written examinations, and more. They're expected to do all this while receiving little, if any, financial compensation, and more likely incurring debt. It is no wonder that up to 70% of mental health trainees report significant levels of distress and even burnout before their professional careers have even started (El-Ghoroury et al., 2012; Kaeding et al., 2017; Richardson et al., 2020).

Supervisors are no less susceptible. While the research on burnout and stress specific to the role of being a supervisor is limited, supervisors rarely serve as *just* supervisors—they are likely to maintain their own clinical practice, in addition to teaching, research, consultation, and other activities. Evidence suggests that 20–40% of mental health professionals endorse significant symptoms of burnout, with the most prevalent being emotional exhaustion (O'Connor et al., 2018). We also know that the majority of mental health professionals will supervise to varying degrees throughout their careers. Given the demands of supervision, one might wonder how supervision contributes to or can perhaps mitigate the impacts of burnout. Sadly, research has not yet answered this question. However, we would posit that supervision can protect trainees and supervisors from burnout. We know that trainee well-being and self-care are highly influenced by supervision; we also know that supervisors can experience benefits from supervision. These benefits include feeling more up-to-date on emerging trends and research, and there are even altruistic benefits to paying forward the knowledge gained by their experiences, successes, and mistakes.

Supervision can play an invaluable role in shaping the success of trainees as not only competent but *well* clinicians who both understand and enact important self-care practices. But how can supervisors accomplish this during supervision? We've adapted the best practices suggested by Moore et al. (2019) to foster self-care within supervision:

> Supervision can play an invaluable role in shaping the success of trainees as not only competent but *well* clinicians who understand and enact self-care practices.

- Regularly discuss trainee's self-care
- Set clear expectations for supervision
- Demonstrate empathy for and interest in the supervisee
- Model self-care.

We also believe that supervisors have a clinical and ethical responsibility to monitor their trainee's self-care, resilience, and general well-being throughout training.

There are several ways that supervisors and trainees can effectively implement self-care monitoring and growth in their work together. First, they can indicate their willingness to talk about and target this important task. This conversation often starts with supervisors because of their inherent power in the relationship: they set the tone for what is expected and normal within supervision, and they can quickly normalize self-care by bringing it up in the first and subsequent sessions. This is one area of supervision where self-disclosure can be immensely useful and appropriate: supervisors can talk about their own experiences during training, their own path to cultivating professional and personal resilience, and their desire to help their trainees meet their goals without sacrificing their well-being.

Monitoring and discussing self-care can be as simple as asking, "How are you doing?" each week. It can also be more formal, involving self-care self-assessment measures like the Self-Care Behavior Inventory (SCBI), the Professional Self-Care Scale (PSCS), or the Mindful Self-Care Scale (MSCS). It can also be useful for supervisors to contextualize challenges in supervision that may be the result of increased stress or burnout. For example, imagine a trainee who is normally on time for supervision each week suddenly starts coming late and is no longer as prepared as they normally are. Changes like these are more often an indication of challenges to the trainee's resilience, not problems of competency. When challenges involving self-care arrive, we encourage supervisors to take a compassionate and supportive approach that leans into the challenge and seeks to activate the trainee's strengths. Practically, this might include advocating for the resources and time a trainee needs to regain their footing without shaming or diminishing their needs. As busy professionals, it can be hard to advocate for changes to workloads that we have long accommodated, but we can help promote change in our fields—change that can enhance the longevity of the next generations of clinicians.

Self-Care Assessment Tools

- Self-Care Behavior Inventory (SCBI)
- Professional Self-Care Scale (PSCS)
- Mindful Self-Care Scale (MSCS)

BEST PRACTICES FOR MONITORING AND PROMOTING SELF-CARE IN SUPERVISION

1

Start in the First Session & Set Expectations

Identify self-care as a vital component of the training process in the *first* session to set the stage for how you will both monitor and promote self-care in your work together. This can also be didactic in nature if a trainee is just getting started, or have yet to be introduced to the role of self-care.

- *Tell me what you know about self-care and its role in training and the work that we do as therapists?*
- *How do you see self-care fitting into our work together?*
- *Can we come up with 2-3 strategies that we can use in our work together to ensure that we're keeping an eye on how you're doing and how supervision can help promote and protect your self-care practices?*
- *Consider reviewing and determining what measures you might use such as the:*
  - *Self-Care Behavior Inventory (SCBI)*
  - *Professional Self-Care Scale (PSCS)*
  - *Mindful Self-Care Scale (MSCS)*

2

Bring it up Regularly

Talking about self-care routinely helps to both promote the use of effective self-care strategies, lookout for signs of burnout, and normalize talking about self-care as one of many aspects of developing clinical competence. Self-care is personal, so collaborate for how to best initiate these conversations and respect boundaries.

- *It can be as simple as "How are you doing?"*
- *Clinical skills are often helpful in noticing discrepancies such as changes in body language or incongruent affect: "I may be off-base here, but you seem less enthusiastic talking about these clients today. Is that true? Do you want to talk about it?"*

3

Demonstrate Empathy and Interest

Supervisors' use of self-disclosure can be highly effective here and can validate and normalize the challenges that trainees experience as well as demonstrate that the supervisor has an understanding - or a desire to understand - what the trainee is experiencing.

- *It makes sense that you're feeling overwhelmed. You have all of these assignments on top of your work here at the clinic, not to mention trying to have a life at the same time! When I was in grad school there were so many days when I felt too tired to do anything at the end of the day. Have you been feeling that way?*
- *Be flexible. If an opportunity to discuss self-care is competing with other agenda items, consider which can be put off until the next session. Demonstrate that the trainee's well-being is a priority. After all, it impacts not only their well-being but their ability to learn and work effectively with clients.*

4

Demonstrate Willingness to Support Growth in Self-Care Practices

Go beyond simply asking how a trainee is doing, and acknowledge that their role(s) are stressful and demanding. This can help reinforce that self-care is an important part of training, in addition to showing that their supervisor is truly ready and willing to tackle challenges with them.

- *What do you think about spending some additional time today or this week talking about these challenges and seeing if we can come up with some solutions together? I know how important this work is to you; you're becoming an excellent clinician. And I know that trainees experience really high rates of burnout before they're ever licensed. I want to do everything I can to help ensure that you have a long and healthy career.*

Keeping an Eye on the Supervision Relationship

The supervision working alliance is one of the core components of effective supervision and successful supervision outcomes. Setting the relationship up for success plays an important role—providing informed consent, setting up clear and behaviorally anchored expectations, and so forth—and it's important to monitor the relationship throughout the course of supervision. We suggest checking in on the relationship in some way during each session. There are several different formal and informal ways to do this.

First, different formal measures and tools have been established to help supervisors monitor and assess the working alliance, such as the Supervision Working Alliance Inventory (SWAI) (Efstation et al., 1990), or the FAP Supervision Bridging Questions (Tsai et al., 2009). Informal methods can include routinely asking questions like: *What has been helpful or unhelpful in our work together so far? What would you like more or less of? How are we doing as a team? Have there been any topics or concerns that you've been reluctant to speak up about?* Such questions can be valuable and perhaps more efficient than formal methods, depending on the context of supervision and demands of the site. There are risks and benefits to formal and informal methods, and ideally we suggest using both to provide opportunities for self-reporting and reflection outside of the supervision session (formal measures) and within the session (informal questions).

MONITORING THE RELATIONSHIP

Use this worksheet to facilitate discussion about how to keep an eye on the supervision relationship and what measures and approaches you both want to use.

QUESTION TO CONSIDER TO MONITOR THE RELATIONSHIP	RELATIONSHIP CUES
• *What was helpful or unhelpful about today's supervision?* • *What would you like more of or less of in our work together?* • *What else can I do, or what could I be doing to help you meet your goals?* • *What has been on your mind lately that you have been hesitant to talk about?* Other relationship monitoring questions: ____________________ ____________________ ____________________ ____________________ ____________________ ____________________ ____________________ ____________________ ____________________ ____________________ ____________________ ____________________ What other methods will we use to monitor the relationship? 1.____________________ 2.____________________ 3.____________________ 4.____________________	What are some signs that things are going well in our relationship? *Example: Trainee feels comfortable being open and honest.* 1. ____________________ ____________________ ____________________ 2. ____________________ ____________________ 3. ____________________ ____________________ ____________________ 4. ____________________ ____________________ ____________________ How about signs that things aren't going well? *Example: Supervisor notices defensiveness when they provide feedback.* 1. ____________________ ____________________ ____________________ 2. ____________________ ____________________ 3. ____________________ ____________________ ____________________ 4. ____________________ ____________________ __________

ONGOING SUPERVISION SESSIONS CHECKLIST

Use this checklist to keep an eye on essential tasks, session priorities, larger goals, and mutual expectations

ESSENTIAL TASKS AND GOALS

1. Monitor the quality of clinical work
2. Review goals and provide feedback
3. Keep an eye on the supervision relationship

Top Three Priorities or Goals for this Supervision Session

1.________________________

2.________________________

3.________________________

Observation and monitoring of clinical work

- ❑ *Best practice* - Video/audio recording review or live observation
- ❑ Review of client progress measures

Self-report and discussion of clinical work and caseload

- ❑ Caseload concerns/priorities
- ❑ Case presentation(s)

Feedback on goals and competencies

- ❑ Review goals and identify progress or barriers
- ❑ Provide formative and strength-based feedback on goals and relevant competencies

Check on the relationship

- ❑ How was today and what would you like more or less of?
- ❑ How are we doing? Is there any other feedback you want to give me?

Experience and Self-Care Check-In

- ❑ How is the training experience going in general?
- ❑ How are you doing? How has your self-care been?

GOALS AND BEST HOPES FOR THIS TRAINING TERM

Consider your best hopes for this session or the term as a whole + your top three training goals. This helps you keep an eye on the bigger picture while attending to all the other tasks of supervision.

Best Hopes:

____

____

____

Training Goals:

1. ________________________
2. ________________________
3. ________________________

NOTES AND NEXT STEPS

Notes from Today:

____

____

____

Supervisor Next Steps:

1. ________________________
2. ________________________
3. ________________________

Trainee Next Steps:

1. ________________________
2. ________________________
3. ________________________

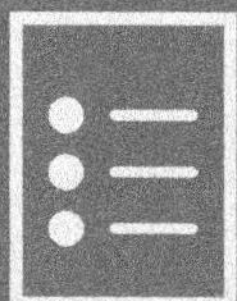

CHAPTER 8 TAKEAWAYS AND RESOURCES

TAKEAWAYS

- The learning process in supervision includes a cycle of elements starting with the trainee's performance and continuing through feedback implementation.
- Ongoing supervision sessions include the essential elements of monitoring the trainee's clinical work, reviewing goals and providing feedback, and keeping an eye on the supervision relationship.
- Ongoing supervision sessions also provide valuable opportunities for learning and assessing self-care practices which can help set trainees up for longer, healthier careers.

RESOURCES

- Falender, C. A., & Shafranske, E. P. (2004). *Clinical supervision: A competency-based approach*. American Psychological Association.
- Falender, C. A., & Shafranske, E. P. (2012). *Getting the most out of clinical training and supervision: A guide for practicum students and interns.* American Psychological Association.
- Kaeding, A., Sougleris, C., Reid, C., van Vreeswijk, M. F., Hayes, C., Dorrian, J., & Simpson, S. (2017). Professional burnout, early maladaptive schemas, and physical health in clinical and counselling psychology trainees. *Journal of Clinical Psychology, 73*(12), 1782–1796.
- Richardson, C. M., Trusty, W. T., & George, K. A. (2020). Trainee wellness: self-critical perfectionism, self-compassion, depression, and burnout among doctoral trainees in psychology. *Counselling Psychology Quarterly, 33*(2), 187–198.

What are your top 3 takeaways from this chapter?

1. __________
2. __________
3. __________

What do you wish you would have learned and how can you learn this?

- __________
- __________
- __________

What is one thing that you want to do differently moving forward and how will you do this?

CHAPTER 9

WHAT YOU SEE IS WHAT YOU GET

Monitoring and Observing Clinical Work

CHAPTER 9 GOALS

INFORM	ENGAGE
• Understand why monitoring and observing trainees' clinical work is ethically, legally, and developmentally vital • Compare and contrast the advantages and disadvantages of live, video, and audio observation • Learn specific skills for reflecting on and discussing clinical observations, including Give-me-five and I-spy techniques • Understand how to integrate a variety of complementary observation and monitoring methods	• Discussion points to open a collaborative dialogue with your supervisor or trainee about observation and monitoring and their role in your work together • Worksheets for trainees and supervisors to help prioritize your video review time by focusing on specific training goals, strengths, and treatment considerations • Opportunities to practice different approaches to reviewing and discussing clinical work during video or live observation

As we mentioned earlier, ongoing supervision includes *many* different tasks. While they're all important, some, such as observing trainees' actual clinic work, are *vital*. After all, how can we ensure the quality of services that clients receive (supervisors' #1 priority) and accurately assess a trainee's development if we don't *see* their work?

Unfortunately, research on observation of trainees' work has demonstrated that, in most cases, observation isn't happening, or is happening on a very limited basis. One study showed that out of 150 supervisees in a one-month period, only 3–11% reported that their supervisor

DOI: 10.4324/9781003006558-12

had observed their clinical work in either video, audio, or live formats (Amerikaner & Rose, 2012); 49% of those same supervisees reported that their supervisors "never" observed their clinical work; and only 24% reported that their work was observed "regularly." We can't stress enough the importance of this task. You have the opportunity to create change in your training environment by expecting and engaging in observation.

IN A ONE-MONTH SNAPSHOT OF SUPERVISION OF 150 TRAINEES

49%

Of trainees reported that their supervisor "never" observed their clinical work.

24%

Of trainees reported that their supervisor observed their clinical work "regularly"

Of the supervisors who reported observing their trainees' clinical work...

11%

Used video observation

4%

Used audio observation

3%

Used live observation

Amerikaner, M., & Rose, T. (2012). Direct observation of psychology supervisees' clinical work: A snapshot of current practice. *The Clinical Supervisor, 31*(1), 61-80.

Monitoring of clinical work falls within three categories:

1. **Direct observation** of clinical work.
2. **Secondary monitoring** using trainees' **self-report** or **documentation** of clinical work.
3. **Client outcome** or progress measures.

Each of these data points is useful in monitoring a trainee's clinical work and ensuring the quality of care being provided to clients. Each plays a role in enhancing the growth and competence of trainees. On their own they have limited utility—you can imagine how only reviewing a trainee's progress notes would provide a narrow and potentially inaccurate view. However, when used in combination, these data points help supervisors gather a robust and accurate picture of what's happening with the client and the trainee. Of these monitoring methods, the importance of **direct observation** cannot be overstated ... although we will certainly try as we move through this and the following chapters.

A special note to trainees: if your supervisor isn't observing your clinical work, remember that you have the right to advocate for this! Later in this chapter we share some ideas about how you can advocate for more observation with your supervisor directly or with your training director(s) if needed.

> The absence of observation alone is considered enough to define supervision as *inadequate*.
>
> Ellis et al., 2015

First, a Note about Informed Consent as It Relates to Supervision and Observation

Ethically and legally, trainees and their supervisors (as always, we encourage that you confirm the specific requirements in your profession and jurisdiction) are **generally required to provide the following information to clients related to the training status of the trainee:**

1. Information about the trainee's training status (e.g., unlicensed) and assurance that they are under the supervision of a licensed professional, who is ultimately responsible for the trainee's work.
2. The name and contact information for their supervisor.
3. Any information about requirements to record or otherwise document their clinical work, plus the assurance that the recordings and documentation are viewable by the supervisor and utilized in supervision, case consultation, or other training formats as indicated by their setting or training program. In the case of recordings, trainees should also inform clients how recordings are secured and for how long they are retained (e.g., stored electronically on a secure server, used only for supervision purposes, deleted within two weeks).

The following is an example script of how a trainee may provide informed consent related to their training and supervision status. We encourage supervisors and trainees to develop and practice an informed consent script that encompasses these elements and others required by their setting.

Trainee to Client during First Session:

As you may have guessed by the size of my office, I am currently in training as an intern at Best Counseling Services as a part of my work to complete a doctorate degree in clinical psychology.

Because I'm in training, I am under the supervision of one of our licensed psychologists, Dr. Amazing Supervisor, who oversees my work. Dr. Supervisor will have access to the documentation that I create from our appointment today and to the recording of today's session. Dr. Supervisor's contact information is on this business card; you can reach out to them if you ever have any questions or concerns about my work.

Part of my training includes recording sessions using the webcam that you can see above my desk. These recordings are only used for training and supervision purposes. They are stored on a secure server and deleted every two weeks. The webcam is not currently recording and will only be used if you agree to have your sessions recorded by signing this "consent to recording and notice of supervision" form.

Do you have any questions or concerns about any of the information that I've mentioned so far?

Trainees (and supervisors) should also be prepared to answer a client's questions about the trainee, supervisor, or the training program or setting if they arise. For example, clients may wonder how many years of experience or training a trainee and/or their supervisor has, or if they have any specialty training or experience in the client's presenting concerns.

Is It a One-Way or Two-Way Mirror? The Evidence for Direct Observation in Clinical Supervision

Evidence suggests that supervisors, trainees, training programs, accrediting bodies, and other stakeholders understand and agree that **direct monitoring** and **observation** of clinical work is crucial. In fact, the absence of observation alone is considered enough to determine if supervision is **inadequate** (Ellis et al., 2015).

Yet trainees and supervisors report relatively infrequent use of **direct observation** in their work together (Amerikaner & Rose, 2012; Cook & Sackett, 2018). We know that monitoring and observation serve several purposes. Among them are:

- **Ensuring the quality of clinical work** (also known as the #1 priority for supervisors regarding their responsibility to protect the trainee's clients).
- Providing a **behavioral basis** for assessing and providing feedback on a trainee's developing competencies (which are also behavioral or behaviorally linked, such as the integration of self-awareness in clinical work).
- **Improving the supervisory relationship** through several mechanisms, including enhancing trainees' perception of their supervisors' commitment to training and their work as a supervisor.

We would also argue that the use of observation allows supervisors to **model evidence-based practices** by utilizing the best available evidence (i.e., actual clinical work) in their evaluation of trainees' work. After all, it's difficult to provide effective feedback, monitor goals and progress, or remediate problems if we're unaware of what's actually happening in the clinical environment. We also know that **self-reporting** clinical work provides a subjective, limited, and often inaccurate or incomplete picture—particularly among clinicians-in-training who are at varying stages of not knowing what they don't know.

Watch, Listen, and Learn: Advantages, Disadvantages, and Setting Considerations for Different Types of Observation and Monitoring Methods

We know that observation and monitoring are important. It also matters *how* we observe and monitor trainees' work. Many factors can impact our choice of methods, such as our setting, the trainee's developmental level, observation anxiety, the supervisor's schedule, clients' needs, and access to technology, just to name a few.

Many aspects of observation are dependent on the context and resources of the training setting. For example, video or audio recording capabilities are generally limited in primary care settings, where clinical work often takes place in rotating or as-available exam rooms. Other settings may have built-in observational capabilities, such as university counseling centers that are often attached to training programs. Regardless, we encourage supervisors and trainees to take advantage of the tools available for observation or to get creative (ethically, of course) to ensure that they can observe and review actual clinical work.

OBSERVATION METHODS

OBSERVATION METHOD	BENEFITS AND CHALLENGES
Live Observation *Research suggests that this is the most effective observation method (Beddoe et al., 2011; Cook & Sackett, 2018; Johnson, 2019; Vezer, 2020).*	Live observation provides several opportunities, including allowing the supervisor to view all aspects of verbal/non-verbal communication and even to provide immediate feedback. There are several ways to conduct live observation, including sitting in on the session, observing through a one-way mirror, watching a live video feed, or using reflecting teams. Live observation can provide an added challenge to trainees who are anxious about feedback, so you should consider your trainee's developmental level. Supervisors and trainees will want to collaborate before and after using this method to monitor its effectiveness relative to the anxiety of the trainee and their ability to perform clinical skills in the presence of their supervisor. Use of technology in live observation formats can also provide opportunities to provide immediate feedback (also known as live supervision) and direction for trainees. However, evidence suggests that such feedback can be distracting. Newer technologies (including the unfortunately-named Bug in the Eye, or BITE, which projects text messages to a monitor visible only to the trainee) are being adapted to help reduce feedback interference.
Audio Observation	Audio and video observation techniques can be paused and restarted throughout their use in supervision, allowing the supervisor or trainee to ask questions and provide feedback without disrupting the flow of the session. One drawback of audio-only recordings is that it leaves out much of the non-verbal communication between the trainee and their client(s). Although audio-only is certainly better than no observation at all, it is generally considered the least effective observation method.
Video Observation	Like audio observation, video recording trainees' clinical work has several advantages, including: • Being available after the session for review in supervision, case presentation, etc. • Pausing and restarting to reflect on or clarify different aspects of the session • Providing information on non-verbal communication between a trainee and client, allowing for feedback that might not otherwise happen with audio-only recordings.

Applications and Limitations of Self-Report and Clinical Documentation Review as Methods of Monitoring Clinical Work

Self-report and documentation review are widely utilized methods for monitoring trainees' clinical work. Not only are they less time-consuming, but in many cases they are required, such as when supervisors must review and sign progress notes. As an informal means of self-assessment, self-report (in the form of case presentation or updates) and documentation review can give supervisors an accurate idea of what the trainee *thinks* is happening with their clients and their training progress.

However, when self-report and documentation review are used in isolation (e.g., absent a supervisor's viewing actual clinical work via live or audio/video observation), the stage is set for inadequate supervision. Supervisors and trainees in higher-volume settings should work together to determine the best method for monitoring the work with all their clients. This may include prioritizing discussions based on predetermined factors, such as estimated level of risk or number of sessions remaining. We've included additional ideas and worksheets in the chapter on case presentation.

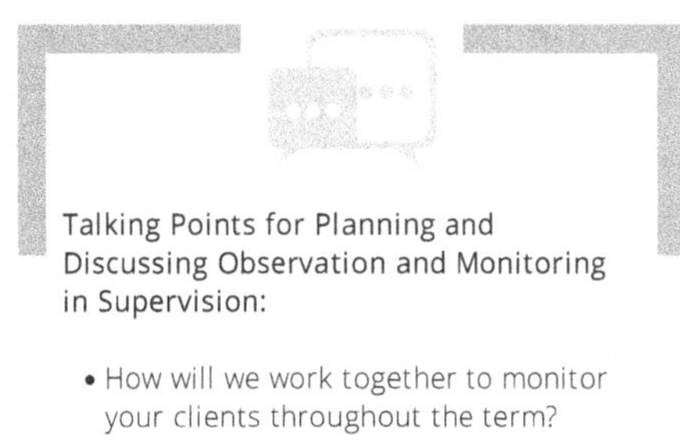

Talking Points for Planning and Discussing Observation and Monitoring in Supervision:

- How will we work together to monitor your clients throughout the term?
- What information should we plan to discuss every session? What information can we be flexible on, depending on our supervision time and priorities?

Documentation review, including progress notes, is another form of self-report. It is a way to supplement observations and monitor a trainee's clinical work in between supervision sessions or outside of audio/video review. Documentation review provides additional opportunities to develop competency across many areas including (though certainly not limited to) client conceptualization and the ethical and regulatory requirements pertaining to documentation. Documentation also allows trainees and supervisors to collaboratively enhance a trainee's clinical voice and clinical writing skills in preparation for independent practice. For example: in the developmental stages of training, a trainee may be encouraged to model the documentation style of their supervisor, whereas in later stages we encourage a more autonomous approach to documentation that incorporates the trainee's theoretical orientation and empowers their own voice and preferences for format and content.

Talking about Clinical Work: Case Presentation

Case presentation is an important component of monitoring client care and facilitating trainee growth. It can be either formal or informal, and ideally it should allow for discussion of the case *and* how it relates to the training and development of the trainee. For example, discussing a client's presenting symptoms can facilitate dialogue on differential diagnosis for that client in addition to providing the supervisor and trainee with an assessment of the trainee's strengths and areas for improvement in considering diagnostic options. Presenting cases also provides trainees with an opportunity to assess and communicate their client's and their own strengths and challenges. We encourage trainees and supervisors to be strength-focused, but not problem-phobic, in conceptualizing and presenting their clients.

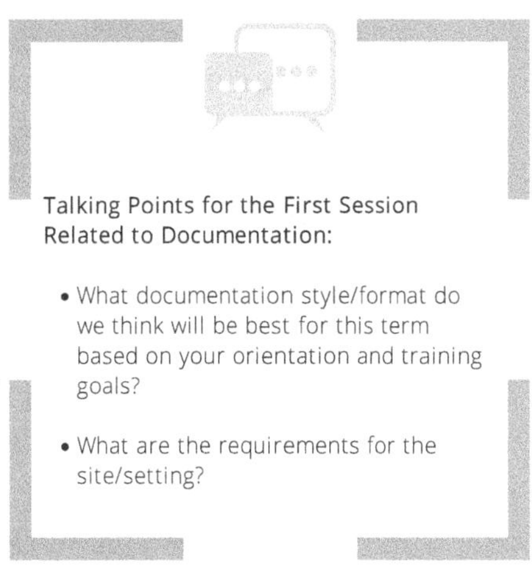

Talking Points for the First Session Related to Documentation:

- What documentation style/format do we think will be best for this term based on your orientation and training goals?
- What are the requirements for the site/setting?

Trainee Guidelines for Preparing a Case Presentation

A major component of clinical supervision is presenting cases to your supervisor. Doing so both demonstrates and improves your skills and ensures and improves the treatment the client receives. Case presentations are useful beyond the clinical training period—consider grand rounds in medical settings. Honing these skills will set trainees up for success in communicating clinical information to other professionals throughout their career. Case presentations, like grand rounds in a medical setting, are especially helpful in the real world where they are presented to and discussed with a diverse team of professionals from a variety of fields. In this text, we will assume that you are presenting to your supervisor. Keep in mind that although we address case presentations from a generic strength-based perspective, your supervisor, or the setting at which you are presenting, may have specific requirements and you may have specific goals for the presentation. Try to start with the end in mind so you know where you are heading as you develop your presentation. You also need to consider the focus of the presentation—are you introducing a client to a treatment team or are you demonstrating your clinical skills to your professors? The first scenario looks at where the client is and how they got here. The second focuses more on the client's goals and the work done in pursuit of these goals. Revisiting the four intervention questions may provide some structure for your case presentation.

The Four Intervention Questions as a Structure for Case Presentations

We hope you are seeing the benefits and flexibility of the **four intervention questions** to structure strength-based growth for supervisors, trainees, and clients alike. Below we address each of these questions as they may be used for case presentations.

1. **Where is the client now?**
   - Traditionally, this is where the trainee presents information regarding an intake interview, diagnostic assessment, mental status, and other considerations to paint a psychological picture of how the client is functioning at the present time. Often this focuses exclusively on the client's problems; however, best-practices indicate that case presentations should *also* include a discussion of the client's strengths.
   - Looking at both obstacles that encumber forward movement as well as strengths and resources that facilitate forward movement provides a full picture of the client.
2. **How did the client get here?**
   - Case conceptualization allows the trainee and supervisor to understand what the client experienced that contributed to the development of the client's present status. Traditionally, we use this section to discuss negative events and other biopsychosocial issues known to cause or amplify mental illness. Don't skip this part just because it is problem-focused. Remember, be **strength-based** and **solution-focused** but not problem-phobic. The strength-based perspective adds the client's strengths and what has gone well in their development. It works to identify positive aspects of the client's psychological capital, such as resilience, hope, optimism, and self-efficacy. It can also help you better understand how effectively—and in what contexts—the client is using their strengths and resources.
   - The result of this question should be an understanding of the client's deficits and strengths in enough detail to lead to a discussion of the client's goals and to the development and implementation of a treatment plan.
3. **Where does the client want to be?**
   - Here the trainee and supervisor discuss goals for the client, including how the goals have changed over time depending on where they are at in treatment. Goals should be attainable and should be agreed upon by both the client and the therapist. Strength-based goals are often worded in the addition or amplification of the

positive, rather than merely the elimination of the negative. For example, rather than stating that the client will report less sadness, we may add that the client will also identify and amplify more positive emotions like joy, gratitude, pride, or awe.
   - Consider the answer to this question to be the client's preferred future. We should begin our treatment planning with this end in mind.

4. **How can they get there?**
   - This fourth question focuses on your treatment plan.
     - What theories, approaches, techniques, and interventions will you employ to help your client reach their goals?
     - How does the research support this plan from an evidence-based perspective? What are the client's preferences?
     - Have they been in counseling before?
     - What worked and what did not work at that time?
     - What did the client enjoy most about or get the most out of previous treatment? Look for positive differences—times when therapy in the past worked and build on this.
   - Combined, information gathered through this question will help you and your client create a roadmap to their preferred future using evidence-based practices that match their treatment goals, individual factors, and your competencies as a clinician.

For case presentations focused on clients that are in or have completed treatment, it is important to readdress these four questions with updated information on treatment progress. You will want to consider what is and is not working, what has been learned, and how treatment goals and the treatment plan changed as a result? To help answer these questions you might include qualitative progress indicators, such as a quote from the client discussing improvements in their functioning or psychological well-being. You could also include quantitative progress or outcome measures. We will discuss these in more detail next.

Integrating Client Progress, Outcome, and Feedback Measures

Combined with observation methods, the use of client progress, outcome, and/or feedback measures in supervision is an excellent way to monitor and evaluate clinical work—not to mention another great way to integrate evidence-based practices into the training process (Lambert et al., 2018). If your setting is not already routinely using progress measures, we encourage you to work together in supervision to determine what measures are most appropriate for your client(s) and the setting. Progress measures might include those that have been formally developed to assess treatment outcomes and progress, and/or those that are specific to a client's symptoms or the therapeutic relationship. We've included a non-exhaustive list of potential progress, symptom, or relationship/working alliance measures below.

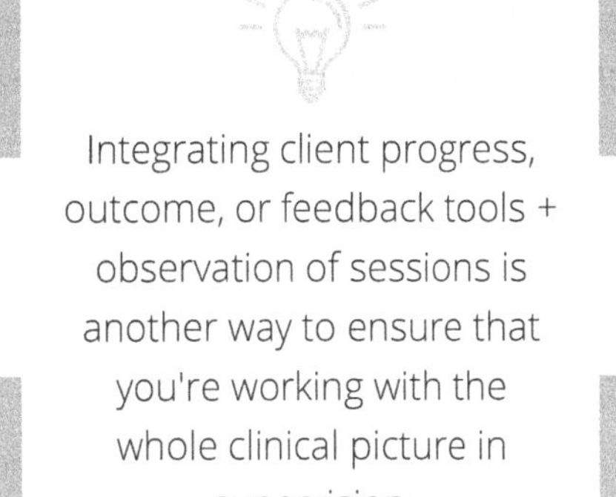

- Partners for Change Outcome Management System (PCOMS)
- Outcome Questionnaire System (OQS)

- Patient Health Questionnaire 9 (PHQ-9)
- Generalized Anxiety Questionnaire 7 (GAD-7)
- Counseling Center Assessment of Psychological Symptoms (CCAPS)
- Cross-Cutting Symptom Measures
- Session Rating Scale (SRS)
- Outcome Rating Scale (ORS)

Manring et al. (2019, p. 351) provide an excellent overview and rationale for the applications and integrations of progress and outcome measures in supervision. They recommend several questions to prompt discussion of the use of progress measures in supervision, some of which we've adapted below.

Questions for facilitating discussion of progress and outcome measure results:

- What is your experience in using progress measures in your training or work so far?
- Do you have concerns about using them (in general or specifically) in our supervision work together?
- Which measures do you think would be most useful for the most common concerns or needs of the clients seen in our setting?

Questions for facilitating discussion of progress and outcome measure results:

- How soon might you expect to see change on this measure based on the interventions you've selected/implemented?
- Are you surprised by the client's responses to this measure? If so, or if not, why?
- What do you think may have contributed to their responses, other than the interventions?
- Do you plan to use or share the results of this measure in your work with the client? How will you do this?

Reducing Trainee Anxiety Regarding Observation: Normalize, Normalize, Normalize

As the evidence suggests, observation is underutilized. Some trainees may find their work goes unobserved for long periods of time, if not the entirety of their training. In establishing rapport and setting expectations for supervision it will be important to understand what the role of observation has been in the trainee's experience thus far. The same is true for trainees: we encourage you to talk to your supervisor about their perceptions and uses of observation, then collaborate on how to increase observation if you feel that it may be underutilized. For new trainees or trainees whose work has gone largely unobserved, anxiety about being observed may impact this crucial supervision task.

> The first strategy supervisors can use to reduce trainee anxiety is to build a positive, collaborative, and trusting relationship.
>
> (Topor et al., 2017)

Topor et al. (2017) discuss several reasons that trainees may be anxious about having their work observed by their supervisors. These reasons fall across several dimensions, including **individual characteristics** (general anxiety, high need for achievement, etc.) and **experiences** (e.g., negative experiences in supervision or with feedback in general). Several methods have been proposed to reduce trainees' anxiety related to observation. These should facilitate the use of observation in supervision (a must) and increase the confidence and self-efficacy of the trainee as they learn about their strengths and receive reinforcing feedback based on their observed work.

Topor et al. (2017) suggest a step-wise approach that addresses the following:

- **Supervisory relationship:** Establish a positive working relationship that facilitates trust through transparency, collaboration, and clear communication of expectations.
- **Supervision/Learning contract:** Reinforce the use of observational methods and their uses and applications within the supervision contract. We would add that it is also beneficial to frame observation as something that protects both the client *and* the trainee, in the sense that a supervisor's evaluations and feedback will be based on observation of actual clinic work and the trainee's demonstrated skills and competencies.
- **Exposure:** Frequent and routine use of audio/visual recording or other observation methods is important in increasing comfort with being observed and use of related technology/equipment.
- **Informed consent:** Collaborate with the trainee to develop an approach for introducing observation to clients, including providing information on the uses and benefits of recording.
- **Developmental level:** Supervisors are encouraged to tailor their observational feedback to their trainee's developmental level. Topor et al. (2017) encourage using the IDM's specific interventions, which are correlated to various developmental stages. It's also important to consider that the trainee's developmental level will shift depending on the client's presenting concerns and individual factors. A trainee who is proficient working with Black American clients presenting with anxiety may experience a shift in developmental level across several domains when they are assigned an Asian American client experiencing their first depressive episode. Trainees may also experience shifts in developmental level based on experiences outside of training, including personal stressors or those related to education/training milestones. It's important to normalize these experiences and adapt the scaffold of supervision accordingly.

These factors are also congruent with Ellis et al.'s (2015) role induction intervention for mitigating trainee anxiety. Role induction in supervision promotes all the above factors, with an emphasis on routinely reinforcing and clarifying the roles of supervisor and trainee, as well as the expectations for each role in supervision. Key elements of role induction and examples are summarized in the following handout.

ROLE INDUCTION SUMMARY FOR ADDRESSING TRAINEE ANXIETY

NORMALIZING ANXIETY

Example: *When I was in training I felt really anxious about having my supervisor observe me when I was working with clients. Even now, when colleagues observe my work it still makes me a little nervous. How about you?*

NORMALIZING THE NON-LINEAR DEVELOPMENTAL TRAJECTORY OF TRAINING

Example: *You're right, your use of silence in therapy has improved a lot with several of your clients. And, based off what you just said about "I should have known better" with this client, I wonder if you're expecting your skills to be the same with every client, every time, no exceptions?*

EMPHASIZING THE SUPERVISOR AS SOMEONE WHO IS INVESTED IN HELPING THE TRAINEE LEARN, GROW, AND SUCCEED

Example: *I'm excited to watch your work with Client X today. I've learned that actually seeing my trainees in action is the best way for me to help them understand what they're doing well and to help reach their internship goals.*

PROVIDING METHODS FOR TRAINEES TO EXPRESS THEIR ANXIETY AND MOVE TOWARD OR AWAY FROM IT IF APPROPRIATE

(e.g., spending a few moments on an anxiety-provoking topic, then shifting to a topic they're more comfortable with)

Example: *Last week we talked about what aspects of observation make you most and least anxious. I was thinking we could use that to help us structure how we spend our video review time today. For example, we could start or end with the clips that you're most or least anxious about. What do you think?*

We would also add that having trainees observe their supervisor(s), their peers, and other clinical staff can go a long way towards normalizing and reinforcing the importance of observation at every stage of development.

Reflection, Inquiry, and Feedback: Specific Methods to Consider During Observation

Interpersonal Process Recall (IPR) is a popular method for facilitating learning and growth during observation. It amplifies a trainee's attention on self and others while they receive non-judgmental feedback and guidance from a supervisor (Falender & Shafranske 2012). The approach centers on reviewing video footage of sessions while pausing the tape and posing questions that elicit the trainee's recall of the thoughts, feelings, or specific moments they experienced during the session (Ivers et al., 2017). IPR has broad applications in supervision and training, including increasing awareness of self-as-therapist, increasing comfort with expressing thoughts and feelings with supervisors or peers, and increasing a trainee's ability to engage in here-and-now interventions (Falender & Shafranske, 2012; Ivers et al., 2017). It is particularly useful for improving multicultural competence (Ivers et al., 2017).

Examples of IPR questions include:

- What were you thinking and feeling in this moment?
- What would it have been like to tell the client what you were thinking and feeling? How do you think they would have responded?
- Does this client remind you of anyone else in your life?
- What do you think the client thought about you? How did you want them to think about you?
- You mentioned X feeling; how do you feel about having that feeling?

Other techniques ask the observer to focus on specific aspects of a session. They are useful in zeroing in on specific patterns, skills, and behaviors. The ***Give-me-five*** and ***I-spy*** approaches are two examples.

Give-me-five **technique:**

- Trainee and supervisor observe a 15–20 minute video clip with the goal of identifying five key points and noting any related inferences or conclusions.
- Starting with the trainee, they then compare and discuss their five key points and incorporate them into role-plays, learning experiences, and goal-setting.
- The five points can be general or thematic, such as looking for five demonstrations of a specific skill, or identifying five important topics, strengths, or patterns/themes.

I-spy **technique:**

- This technique is most useful for enhancing the development of specific skills and techniques. Gonsalvez et al. (2016) describe it as a find-and-replace strategy that allows trainees to identify where specific skills could have been applied or improved.
- The trainee and supervisor again review a 15–20 minute video clip. In contrast to *Give-me-five*, they look for only one specific skill, or a time when the skill could have been used.
- Trainee and supervisor then review and discuss the flagged moments.

Opportunities to enhance observation are also provided in treatment fidelity measures, which often include specific rating systems and criteria for observing different therapeutic approaches.

The Yale University Psychotherapy Development Center's Adherence and Competence Scale (YACS; Carroll et al., 2000) provides clinicians and supervisors with different fidelity measures for common evidence-based treatments, including motivational interviewing.

QUESTIONS TO CONSIDER WHEN OBSERVING CLINICAL WORK

SUPERVISOR QUESTIONS TO CONSIDER DURING OBSERVATION OF CLINICAL WORK

- Tell me more about what's happening here?
- How was this moment for you?
- Tell me more about how you chose this/X intervention?
- What alternative interventions were you considering then, or now?
- What did you notice about your client's response when you said/did X?
- What did you notice about your client's body language during the session?
- Does this remind you of anything that's happened in previous sessions with this client?

TRAINEE QUESTIONS TO CONSIDER DURING OBSERVATION OF CLINICAL WORK

These reflection questions can be helpful as you review your own work or observe others. They can also facilitate discussion during supervision. For example, you might share your reflections with your supervisor and then ask for their input.

- What's going well in this session?
- What strengths am I demonstrating?
- What strengths is my client demonstrating?
- If I were giving feedback to a peer, what would I tell them about this moment?
- What approach or intervention was I aiming for here?
- What alternative approaches might I have considered?
- What moments am I excited to show my supervisor?
- Based on this session/moment, what do I want to do differently or the same in the next session with this client?

Putting It All Together: Integrating Monitoring Methods

Ideally, monitoring of clinical work will encompass discussion (self-report), documentation (self-report), observation of actual clinical work, and progress or outcome measures. We realize that not all settings may allow for this, so we encourage supervisors and trainees to use as many of those methods as possible. Additionally, consider how to prioritize methods based on the developmental level of the trainee, the acuity of the client, and resources of the setting.

We've provided worksheets that you can use in preparation for or during supervision regarding the observation of clinical work via video review. As you consider the elements in the worksheets, also take into account:

- The trainee's documentation of the session(s) and its congruence or incongruence with what is observed in the session(s). This can promote valuable discussion and improve self-assessment. For example, if there are many positive moments or strengths observed in the session(s) but the trainee's documentation is problem-focused, you might consider discussing how this impacts the trainee's view of their work and the client.
- The trainee's level of development and anxiety related to observing their work and having their work observed. It can be useful to use general or scaling questions to assess and monitor this, such as: *How was it observing the video of this session—did any feelings come up for you? What aspects of our watching this video together are most worrisome for you? Which are the least worrisome?*
- The trainee's goals in the context of focusing in on certain aspects of the session based on their training goals or treatment goals. This can be accomplished by limiting the focus of observation (and feedback) to no more than five aspects of the session, a technique utilized in CBT supervision called *Give-me-five* (Gonsalvez et al., 2016). Or the *I-Spy* technique, which asks for the observer to only look at specific microskills (reflective listening, question types, etc.).
- While the *Give-me-five* technique is designed to provide a broad perspective on the session, trainees and supervisors who are focusing on specific skills might consider utilizing the *I-Spy technique.*

TRAINEE VIDEO REVIEW WORKSHEET

Use this worksheet as a part of your video review process in preparation for supervision to help prioritize questions and areas where you'd like additional feedback.

Client Identifier: ____________

Session Type/# ____________

Related Treatment Goals

____

____

SESSION GOALS

(CLIENT AND/OR THERAPIST GOALS)

1.____________________

____

2.____________________

____

3____________________

____

PRIORITIES FOR VIDEO REVIEW

(E.G., LOOKING FOR SPECIFIC SKILL DEMONSTRATION, MOMENTS YOU'D LIKE FEEDBACK ON, ETC.)

1.____________________

____

2.____________________

____

3____________________

____

TIMESTAMPS & NOTES/QUESTIONS

(ASPECTS OF THE VIDEO THAT YOU WOULD LIKE TO REVIEW)

___:___

____

____

____

____

____

___:___

____

____

____

____

____

___:___

____

____

____

____

IN TERMS OF TRAINING GOALS, WHAT STRENGTHS ARE DEMONSTRATED?

1.____________________

____

2.____________________

____

3____________________

____

IN TERMS OF TREATMENT GOALS, WHAT STRENGTHS ARE DEMONSTRATED?

1.____________________

____

2.____________________

____

3____________________

____

SUPERVISOR VIDEO REVIEW WORKSHEET

Use this worksheet in preparation for or during supervision as a way to structure priorities for video review and feedback, based on variables such as trainee's developmental level and goals, client presentation, therapeutic approach (CBT, etc.), and setting factors (e.g., session limits).

Client Identifier: ____________

Session Type/# ____________

Related Treatment Goals

____

____

What are your top priorities in terms of what you're watching for in this video?
Consider your trainee's short- and long-term goals and any immediate needs concerning the client's presentation.

1. ______________________________

____

2. ______________________________

____

3 ______________________________

____

TIMESTAMPS & NOTES/QUESTIONS
WHAT MOMENTS DO YOU WANT TO DISCUSS AND PROVIDE FEEDBACK ON DURING SUPERVISION?

___:___

____

____

____

____

____

___:___

____

____

____

____

____

___:___

____

____

____

____

What strengths does your trainee demonstrate during this session?
Be specific and anchor these strengths to moments in the video.

1. ______________________________

____

2. ______________________________

____

3 ______________________________

____

For next steps, what would you like your trainee to focus on in the next session regarding their **development**?

1. ______________________________

____

2. ______________________________

____

3 ______________________________

____

For next steps, what would you like your trainee to focus on in the next session regarding the **client**?

1. ______________________________

____

2. ______________________________

____

3 ______________________________

____

CLIENT MONITORING WORKSHEET

This worksheet was designed to help supervisors and trainees collaboratively monitor the trainee's entire caseload. Consider which of these elements should be prioritized on a weekly or monthly basis. For example, you might review all elements on a monthly basis and only certain elements on a weekly basis.

CLIENT ID: _______	PROGRESS AND NEXT STEPS
Treatment Goal Summary: ____________________ ____________________ Risk Factors: ▯ Suicidality ▯ Homicidality/Violence Toward Others ▯ Self-Injurious Behaviors ▯ Substance Abuse ▯ Other Risk Behaviors ____________________ ____________________ ____________________	Session #: ___ Progress Scale: ▯ 1 (limited) ▯ 2▯ 3 ▯ 4 ▯ 5 (significant) Strengths and What's Going Well: ____________________ ____________________ ____________________ ____________________ Barriers/Challenges: ____________________ ____________________ ____________________ Supervision Feedback and Next Steps: ____________________ ____________________ ____________________

CLIENT ID: _______	PROGRESS AND NEXT STEPS
Treatment Goal Summary: ____________________ ____________________ Risk Factors: ▯ Suicidality ▯ Homicidality/Violence Toward Others ▯ Self-Injurious Behaviors ▯ Substance Abuse ▯ Other Risk Behaviors ____________________ ____________________ ____________________	Session #: ___ Progress Scale: ▯ 1 (limited) ▯ 2▯ 3 ▯ 4 ▯ 5 (significant) Strengths and What's Going Well: ____________________ ____________________ ____________________ ____________________ Barriers/Challenges: ____________________ ____________________ ____________________ Supervision Feedback and Next Steps: ____________________ ____________________ ____________________

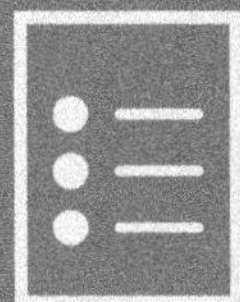

CHAPTER 9 TAKEAWAYS AND RESOURCES

TAKEAWAYS

- Observation of trainees' actual clinical work is crucial to fulfilling the ethical and legal responsibilities that supervisors have to trainees and their clients.
- There are many different ways to use monitoring and observation. It's best to combine several approaches, such as progress or symptom measures, clinical documentation, and video observation, to capture a full picture of the client and the trainee.
- Observation can produce anxiety for trainees (and supervisors!). There are several ways to mitigate anxiety, including Role Induction, which normalizes anxiety and clarifies and reinforces roles and expectations.

RESOURCES

- Yale Adherence and Competence Scale: https://medicine.yale.edu/psychiatry/research/programs/clinical_people/pdc/YACSII_176838_284_46619_v1.pdf
- McComb, J. L., Diamond, R. M., Breunlin, D. C., Chambers, A. L., & Murray, K. S. (2019). Introducing client feedback into marriage and family therapy supervision: a qualitative study examining the transition to empirically informed supervision. Journal of Family Therapy, 41(2), 214-231.
- Gonsalvez, C. J., Brockman, R. N., & Hill, H. R. (2016). Video feedback in CBT supervision: review and illustration of two specific techniques. The Cognitive Behaviour Therapist, 9 (e24), 1-15.
- Hagstrom, S. L., & Maranzan, K. A. (2019). Bridging the gap between technological advance and professional psychology training: A way forward. Canadian Psychology/Psychologie canadienne, 60(4), 281.

What are your top 3 takeaways from this chapter?

1. ____________________
2. ____________________
3. ____________________

What do you wish you would have learned and how can you learn this?

- ____________________
- ____________________
- ____________________

What is one thing that you want to do differently moving forward and how will you do this?

____
____
____
____

CHAPTER 10

EFFECTIVE FEEDBACK

Best Practices for Giving Trainees More of What They Want (Hint: Feedback)

CHAPTER 10 GOALS

INFORM	ENGAGE
• Understand the importance and role of feedback in clinical training • Learn the evidence-based best practices for delivering effective feedback on strengths and areas for growth • Understand how to improve implementation of feedback • Learn how to provide strength-based corrective and positive feedback	• Practice developing effective feedback statements • Discuss feedback expectations • Evaluate feedback statements • Discuss what feedback strategies will work best in your supervision relationship • Reflect on thoughts, feelings, or assumptions about feedback including feedback anxiety

Although supervisors are responsible for monitoring the quality of their trainees' work, their role goes beyond oversight to also include the responsibility for facilitating the *growth and development* of their trainees. Supervisors thus have a powerful opportunity to help their trainees evaluate and build on their clinical strengths, to address areas where additional growth is needed, and to demonstrate a developmentally appropriate level of competence. This is where **feedback** comes in. Feedback is so vital to the process that its absence alone can define harmful or negligent supervision.

DOI: 10.4324/9781003006558-13

Frequency and Context of Informal and Formal Feedback

Supervisors and trainees may ask, *how often should I be providing/receiving feedback?* The answer is in *every* supervision session and between sessions as needed. Providing feedback in every session (we also suggest frequently within each session) helps trainees and supervisors:

- Normalize giving and receiving feedback
- Stay on top of their goals and client's treatment needs
- Mitigate any surprises when it comes time for the trainee's summative evaluation. (Ideally, by the time you and your supervisor reach the summative evaluation there will be no surprises regarding progress toward training goals and remaining areas for growth.)

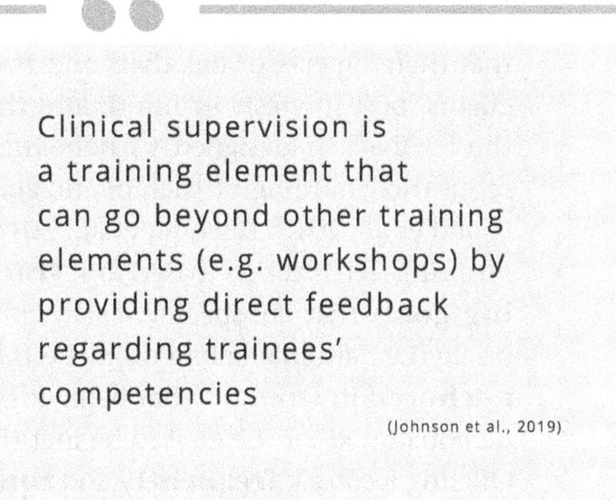

That being said, there are differences between informal and formal feedback. The latter generally comes as formative and summative evaluations that are kept as a part of the trainee's file or record. There should be congruence between informal feedback—e.g., the feedback that is perhaps more frequently and casually delivered throughout supervision—and formal, written feedback to help mitigate any surprises and promote a positive relationship. For example, a supervisor who has given their trainee only positive informal feedback throughout the first several months of supervision, only to provide critical feedback on the trainee's midterm evaluation, has perhaps lost some of their trainee's trust and has prevented them from addressing those areas prior to the midterm evaluation. Perhaps even more concerning, the trainee may have repeated something negative without any corrective action, making it even harder to remediate and possibly causing harm to clients.

Evidence for Effective Feedback

Feedback's importance to a trainee's development cannot be underestimated. Neither can its role in enhancing many aspects of supervision, which include:

- Improving the quality of clinical practice and clinical service to clients
- Promoting the trainee's development and competence
- Increasing the trainee's self-awareness and accuracy of their self-assessment of their clinical skills and developmental level
- Enhancing the therapeutic relationship by (a) reinforcing the supervisor's role in helping the trainee reach their full potential, and (b) demonstrating the supervisor's attentiveness and commitment to the process.

Providing any feedback is better than no feedback at all; however, the evidence suggests several key components of **effective feedback**, including:

> "When supervisees reflect on their supervision, what comes to mind most often is the *quality* and *quantity* of the feedback that they received"
>
> (Bernard & Goodyear, 2014, p. 233)

- Ensuring the conditions for a **strong working alliance** are in place: transparency, safety, understanding, and respect. This promotes the trainee's trust that their supervisor has their and their clients' best interests in mind, and that the feedback is designed to help them reach their training or therapeutic goals (Codd et al., 2016; Falender et al., 2016).
- Ensuring feedback is based on **training goals** that are specific, clear, collaboratively developed, developmentally appropriate (i.e., attainable based on the trainee's developmental level), and **behaviorally anchored** in terms of what behaviors are present now and what behaviors need to be demonstrated for the goal to be met (Falender & Shafranske, 2017).
- Offering feedback **frequently** and **routinely** to provide a trainee with continuous information regarding their performance and to normalize receiving feedback in order to minimize anxiety and reinforce the importance of feedback (Falender & Shafranske, 2017).
- Casting feedback as a **dynamic, collaborative, and iterative** process. According to Falender and Shafranske (2017) the evaluation and feedback process should encompass a cycle that includes assessment (supervisor) and self-assessment (trainee and supervisor). This becomes a dynamic conversation related to the outcomes of the assessment(s),

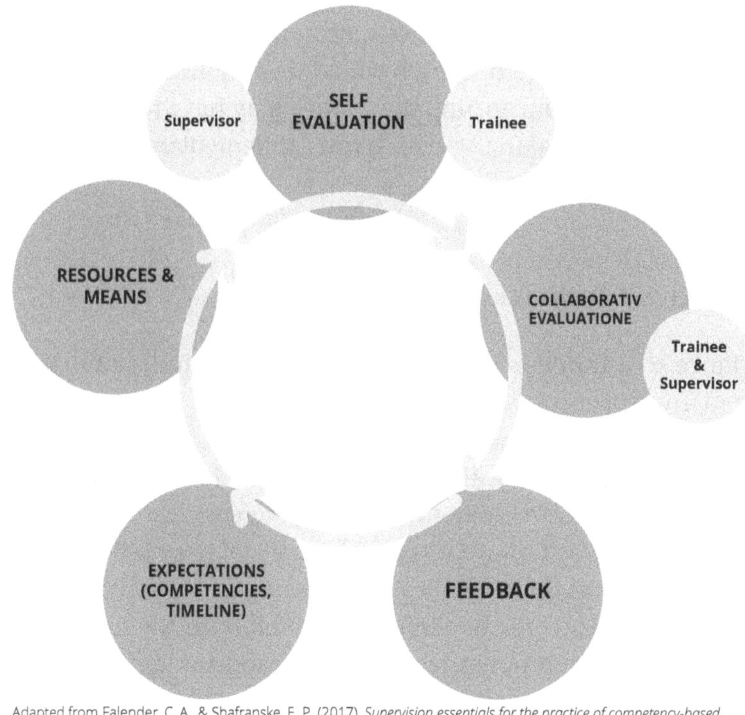

Adapted from Falender, C. A., & Shafranske, E. P. (2017). *Supervision essentials for the practice of competency-based supervision*. American Psychological Association

wherein feedback from both supervisor and trainee is translated into expectations and goals.

- Feedback (and evaluations) should be **clear and concise** and based on **observation of the trainee's actual clinical work,** including specific behaviors, tasks, and skills. This ensures that feedback is **focused on specific performance elements** versus broader personal/professional characteristics/attributes, which can increase the risk of internalization and reduce motivation (Falender & Shafranske, 2017; Weck et al., 2017). Outcome research also demonstrates that feedback based on observation is more effective than feedback based on self-report or other indirect methods for monitoring a trainee's work (Johnson, 2019).
- Effective feedback emphasizes a trainee's **strengths** and **opportunities for growth** by promoting the use of strengths to address deficiencies. This is also congruent with a developmental mindset, in which a trainee ideally can utilize their experiences in overcoming previous training challenges to promote their growth in new areas of development (Falender & Shafranske, 2017; Wade & Jones, 2015). It's important to understand that using a strength-based feedback approach doesn't just mean that you can only provide feedback on what's going well: using a strength-based approach can also provide critical feedback and address deficiencies. We'll provide some examples of that in the next part of this chapter.
- Frame feedback language, even critical language, in a way that lets the trainee know that their **supervisor is confident that they can reach the defined goal**. This reinforces the trainee's trust in the relationship and promotes motivation to try and implement the feedback—after all, why try when you're unsure about your ability to succeed (Holt et al., 2015)?
- Paired with observation of clinical work, feedback is best received and implemented when it is **focused on the task and the situation** instead of the individual. This helps trainees to conceptualize the task as temporary, limited in scope, common, and controllable, which represent an optimistic view (Seligman, 2006), compared to the more pessimistic way of seeing issues as permanent, pervasive, personal, and uncontrollable. According to Seligman, the optimistic view corresponds to increased success and improved well-being. This is particularly important if the trainee has experiences of unhelpful cognitive distortions, such as assuming that their supervisor is thinking negatively about them even in the absence of negative feedback, focusing only on negative information, and catastrophizing related to their potential to succeed (Rogers et al., 2019).

BEST PRACTICES FOR COMMUNICATION OF FORMATIVE FEEDBACK

1. Ensure that feedback is relevant to the trainee's training goals, expected competencies, and their stage of development.

2. Feedback statements should be clear, while avoiding being hurtful, threatening or humiliating. This is best done by using behavioral anchors to help externalize the target of feedback (e.g., mitigating internalizing feedback as a character flaw).

3. Feedback should be offered regularly throughout supervision, in every session.

4. Feedback should be based on direct observation of the trainee's actual clinical work. This helps to anchor it behaviorally.

5. Feedback should be balanced between supportive or reinforcing strengths ("what's going well") and providing challenge and correction.

6. When feedback is corrective it should be timely, specific, behavioral/actionable and nonjudgmental.

7. Trainees and supervisors should use reflection and questions to ensure that feedback is received and interpreted appropriately.

8. Frame feedback through the lens of individual perception (with the exception of feedback related to less subjective content, such as processes for managing safety, etc.).

9. Normalize that receiving feedback can be anxiety provoking. Explore what this means individually and within the relationship.

10. Remember that acceptance and integration of feedback is highly correlated to the state of the working alliance: if the relationship is positive, feedback is more likely to be well received and enacted.

11. Formative feedback is different from summative feedback: it is a way to progressively move toward a goal(s) before that progress is formally evaluated.

12. Whenever possible, feedback should be collaborative and bi-directional.

Thinking about Feedback as an Intervention

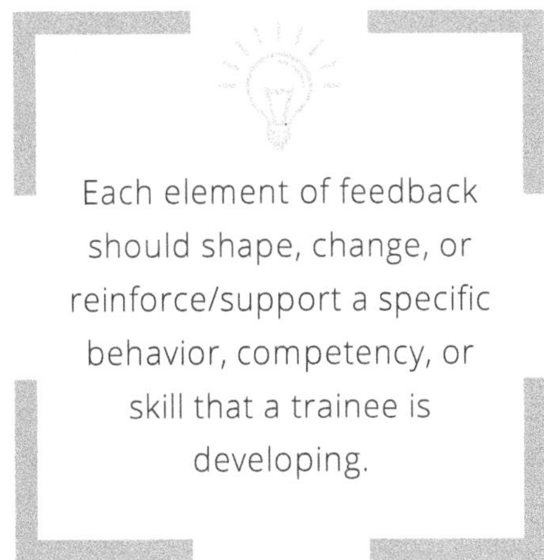

Just as we consider different types of interventions to utilize with clients, supervisors also have different options as they consider what their trainees need in a particular situation. There are generally three categories of supervision interventions:

1. Assessing the trainee (learning needs, developmental level, cognitions, behaviors, attitudes, and more)
2. Changing, shaping, or supporting a behavior or attitude
3. Evaluating the performance of the trainee (this often comes after the previous two interventions by evaluating whether or not the trainee's performance has improved as expected).

The second intervention—changing, shaping, or supporting behaviors and attitudes—is the *feedback* intervention. Each element of feedback should shape, change, or reinforce/support a specific behavior, competency, or skill that a trainee is developing. Corrective feedback is most often considered when we're trying to shape or alter a behavior, but it's also worth considering how positive feedback can accomplish this as well. For example, with clients who are discussing unwanted behavior, we often highlight times when this behavior has not been present or when exceptions to the behavior have occurred. This works well in supervision because it instills a sense of hope and self-efficacy, and also gives trainees a behavioral anchor for what they're aiming for: in essence, *do more of this, do more like this, etc.* If we think of feedback as an intervention, it adds an element of intentionality that leans on supervisors' clinical expertise and judgment to lend familiarity and confidence to a task that can sometimes feel uncomfortable.

Putting It into Action: How to Provide Effective Strength-Based Feedback to Amplify Strengths *and* Address Deficits

> Emphasizing strengths, or activating strengths to address deficiencies, helps to improve motivation and the implementation of feedback.

We've provided examples for both supervisor-to-trainee and trainee-to-supervisor. The necessity of supervisors providing feedback to trainees is well documented. A **trainee's feedback to their supervisor** is also a vital part of their development and contributes significantly to the success of the supervision process. Emphasizing strengths, or activating strengths to address deficiencies, helps to improve motivation and implement feedback. It also reinforces the supervisor's interest and commitment to a trainee's success, which has positive impacts on the working alliance.

Review the examples of effective strength-based feedback and see which of the elements of effective feedback—detailed earlier in this chapter—you notice (e.g., behaviorally anchored, strength-based, and so forth). Then complete some of the practice activities aimed at improving your skills with strength-based feedback.

EXAMPLES OF EFFECTIVE STRENGTH-BASED FEEDBACK FROM SUPERVISOR TO TRAINEE

1

"I noticed that you offered a re-frame of the client's experience. How can you continue to use this skill based on your client's goals for treatment?"

2

"I noticed that you seemed genuinely curious about your client and asked them several questions back-to-back during your session. What do you know about how clients respond when you ask them multiple questions in a row?"

3

"In your last session with this patient, you were able to put them at ease even though they told you they were reluctant to see you. Tell me more about how you were able to do that."

4

"In this session the client is presenting you with a lot of conflicting information. Tell me about a time when you pointed out something that was incongruent."

5

"You were more direct and structured in this session—I can tell that you've been working hard on developing those skills. What would it look like if you were to take that to the next level?"

6

"At the end of this session you used several skills, including redirection and affirmation, to help close the session and reinforce the goals that your patient established, even though it appears they have several other things they wanted to share with you. Tell me about how this experience was for you?"

7

"You mentioned that you are considering several different diagnoses based on the different symptoms that the client described in this intake session. What additional information, resources, or experiences can help you select the most appropriate diagnosis by the end of your next session?"

EXAMPLES OF EFFECTIVE STRENGTH-BASED FEEDBACK FROM TRAINEE TO SUPERVISOR

1

"In our last session, we watched a clip from my session with Client B and you pointed out a moment when I utilized reframing appropriately. I've noticed ever since then I've been able to use that skill more confidently and frequently."

2

"Watching this video has been really helpful, especially when you mentioned that I should try to focus on being more 'warm' with my client. Can we talk more about how I can demonstrate more warmth in my next session?"

3

"I appreciate how grounded you are in psychodynamic intervention. Could we explore conceptualizing and observing this next video clip from a cognitive-behavioral perspective to help me continue to refine my theoretical orientation?"

4

"Thank you for letting me borrow the book on DBT skills. I'm struggling to identify which mindfulness skill would be most appropriate for Client X. Can we take some time in our session today to review those skills in the context of Client X's treatment plan?"

5

"I'm excited about working with you to improve my brief therapy treatment planning skills. I know we have a goal for me to see clients for six sessions or fewer, and I'm wondering how I can talk to clients about that—could we role-play it in our supervision this week?"

6

"Thank you for the detailed feedback on my progress notes; it's really helping me understand how to present the most relevant information about clients in these intake sessions. Could we also watch a clip from the video of Client Z's intake session? I'd like to get your feedback on my documentation of their symptoms based on their presentation."

7

"I've noticed that you always have a lot of nice things to say to me in our supervision sessions, and it's really helped me feel more comfortable as I get used to working in this new clinic. Now that I'm more comfortable I feel like I'm ready to focus on areas where I need to improve; could we talk about those this week?"

PRACTICING EFFECTIVE STRENGTH-BASED FEEDBACK

This activity is designed to help you practice developing effective feedback statements. Consider engaging in this activity with your trainee or supervisor in order to learn more about their approaches to feedback and to collaborate on what will work best for your relationship.

SUMMARY OF THE ELEMENTS OF EFFECTIVE FEEDBACK

- Reflects a strong working alliance
- Clear and concise
- Anchored on a behavior, task, or skill relative to training goals and/or client's needs
- Focused on specific versus global elements
- Emphasizes strengths and ability to succeed
- Focused on the task and situation
- Dynamic and collaborative
- Based on observations of the trainee's clinical work

EXAMPLE FEEDBACK STATEMENTS

"You're clearly nervous in this session and it's very distracting. But don't worry, it will get better."

What do you like about this statement? What strengths are present?
Which elements of effective feedback (summarized above) are present, and which are missing?
What do you think the outcome of this statement might be for the trainee and the supervision relationship?

Your Reframe:

____

____

____

____

"I watched the video of your session with Client X last month. Great work. How are things going with your dissertation?"

What do you like about this statement? What strengths are present?
Which elements of effective feedback are present, and which are missing?
What do you think the outcome of this statement might be for the trainee and the supervision relationship?

Your Reframe:

____

____

____

____

PRACTICING EFFECTIVE STRENGTH-BASED FEEDBACK

"Your progress notes are too long."

What do you like about this statement? What strengths are present?

Which elements of effective feedback are present, and which are missing?

What do you think the outcome of this statement might be for the trainee and the supervision relationship?

Your Reframe:

"Ok, right there! The client handed you an important piece of information on a silver platter and you didn't use it!"

What do you like about this statement? What strengths are present?

Which elements of effective feedback are present, and which are missing?

What do you think the outcome of this statement might be for the trainee and the supervision relationship?

Your Reframe:

"You're making the client feel too comfortable. How can they grow when they're comfortable?"

What do you like about this statement? What strengths are present?

Which elements of effective feedback are present, and which are missing?

What do you think the outcome of this statement might be for the trainee and the supervision relationship?

Your Reframe:

"Your progress notes are always late and your sessions always go over time. We need to get this figured out because it's causing problems in the clinic."

What do you like about this statement? What strengths are present?

Which elements of effective feedback are present, and which are missing?

What do you think the outcome of this statement might be for the trainee and the supervision relationship?

Your Reframe:

REFLECTION ON THE ACTIVITY AND YOUR NEXT STEPS

What strengths of yours stood out to you as you worked through this activity?

What about your areas for improvement—either globally or with your current supervisor or trainee?

How will you incorporate what you've learned into supervision?

Monitoring the Impact of Feedback on the Supervision Relationship

Feedback generally strengthens the supervisory alliance by reinforcing the supervisor's role and motivation to help the trainee meet their training goals while ensuring appropriate care for clients. Feedback also increases transparency and accountability, which can foster trust and security in the relationship. In turn, these can increase a trainee's use of self-disclosure and appropriate risk-taking in exploring and expanding their skills and competence.

Sometimes, feedback can have a negative impact on the relationship. Generally, this can occur when a trainee isn't used to receiving feedback or when feedback is unexpected. This can happen for trainees who are new to supervision, or to those whose previous supervisors provided inadequate feedback or only positive affirmations. It can be important for supervisors and trainees to consider how comfortable they are with corrective and reinforcing feedback, then take steps to increase their comfort and utilization of both types of feedback.

Some considerations may include:

- Using the first supervision session to ask about your trainee's/supervisor's experience with providing and receiving feedback. What was helpful, what wasn't, was the feedback positive or negative, how did they feel about the feedback they received (motivated, anxious, excited, disappointed, etc.)?

- Providing reassurance related to the normalization of and motivation for providing feedback. For example, a supervisor meeting with a new trainee in their first practicum will want to normalize that the trainee should expect to receive a lot of feedback throughout their training experience: this is normal for all trainees and not just them individually. The supervisor might also provide reassurance that they are motivated to help support the trainee in meeting their goals, and that the primary goal for feedback is to help the supervisor and trainee get on the same page about where the trainee is now and where they will be at the end of the successful training term.
- Asking for feedback on feedback helps to monitor its effects, improve the relationship, and ensure that the feedback is understood and that the trainee knows how to implement it. For example, a supervisor who challenges a trainee to improve a particular skill might ask them how confident they feel in being able to demonstrate that skill, how it felt to receive that feedback, and whether or not they feel they need additional clarification in order to implement the feedback successfully.

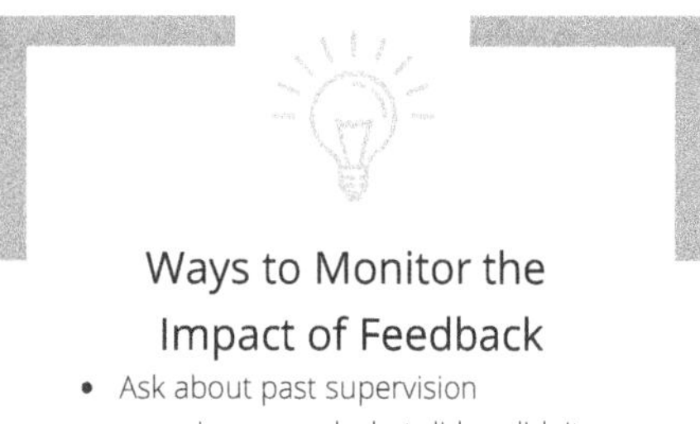

Ways to Monitor the Impact of Feedback

- Ask about past supervision experiences and what did or didn't work well in terms of feedback.
- Ask for feedback on your feedback.
- Normalize feedback—especially critical feedback—as a routine and expected part of development.

Considerations for Trainees in Implementing Feedback

Although receiving feedback is important, its utility is limited if trainees (and supervisors) don't fully understand how to implement it. Examples may include feedback that is too vague or unclear for the trainee to understand how to effectively apply it, or feedback that is based on trainee characteristics versus behaviors. Developmentally, feedback should challenge a trainee toward growth; it will thus be just beyond their current understanding or ability, which may necessitate questions to clarify their next steps on how they can successfully improve their performance. We invite trainees to consider the following questions as they receive and process feedback to ensure that they understand and feel confident in their endeavor to implement feedback.

Trainee Reflections on Feedback to Ensure Understanding

- Do I understand the feedback being given to me?
- Do I understand the value, rationale, and importance of this feedback?
- Is there any additional information/examples/resources I need to understand how to implement this feedback?
- Do I know what it will look like when I've successfully demonstrated that I understand and have applied this feedback?
- Do I know which of my behaviors will need to change for me to apply this feedback?

Managing Feedback Anxiety

Many trainees, and even experienced supervisors, report anxiety related to providing or receiving feedback (Borders et al., 2017). Anxiety is most often centered on fears related to negative or critical feedback and the vulnerability, uncertainty, or potential for confrontation that it can promote. Trainees are concerned with acquiring competence *and* progress or completion of their education and training, and overly critical feedback can make these goals feel less attainable. Supervisors are keen to help facilitate their trainees' growth, yet are sometimes uncomfortable providing critical feedback for fear of harming the relationship or making their trainees feel bad (Borders et al., 2017).

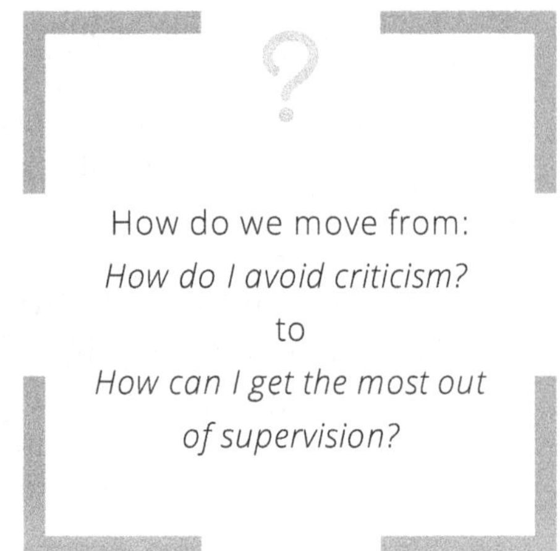

Research suggests that the following approaches can help mitigate the impacts of anxiety for supervisors and trainees related to critical feedback.

For Supervisors (adapted from Borders et al., 2017):

- Understand that it is normal for even the most experienced supervisors to experience anxiety related to delivering critical feedback.
- Keep in mind that trainees *want* constructive feedback; in fact, they generally report that they want *more* feedback in supervision and they want it to be more specific.
- Practice delivering critical feedback that is clear and direct versus tentative or indirect. This not only enhances the trainee's ability to understand and implement feedback, but also improves the supervisor's confidence in delivering and discussing feedback.
- Individualize feedback using the trainee's developmental level, learning style, personality, and so on. Consider breaking down a large piece of feedback into smaller and sequential elements; using humor or metaphor to frame the delivery; and tying the feedback into the trainee's goals, client needs, or other salient factors.
- Utilize the trainee's strengths in how you deliver feedback or establish a plan for next steps. Integrating strengths can help supervisors feel more comfortable in delivering critical feedback, as well as promote confidence in the trainee.
- Reflect on the fears related to delivering critical feedback and how those fears might be overcome by other factors, such as the desire for the trainee to grow/succeed, for the client's welfare to remain the highest priority, etc.
- Utilize consultation and supervision-of-supervision to practice, plan for, and reflect on delivering effective critical feedback.

For Trainees:

- Practice reflecting intentionally and positively on the relationship between feedback and your goals and success. Keep in mind that the feedback is for your benefit and that your supervisor is invested in your growth.
- Plan for critical feedback and expect it to occur routinely. If it's not, consider how you might ask your supervisor for more critical feedback to demonstrate your willingness to receive it.
- Consider what common cognitive distortions may be at play when you think about critical feedback. Thoughts associated with critical feedback might include things like,

"I should have known better than to do that" (shoulds); *"I'll never graduate"* (catastrophizing); *"my supervisor doesn't trust me anymore because of this mistake"* (mind reading); or *"I feel like a failure and I'll never make it through this internship"* (emotional reasoning).
- Reflect on how past experiences with critical feedback are at play in your perception of critical feedback now. Research suggests that attachment experiences, such as feeling criticized as a child, can play a role in the supervisory relationship.
- Discuss your thoughts and feelings associated with critical feedback in supervision. This can feel vulnerable, yet it offers you and your supervisor an opportunity to improve your relationship, discuss the feedback and next steps, and even collaborate on ways to improve the feedback process.

Evidence also suggests that the following factors can help improve trainees' receptiveness to feedback, which in turn can mitigate the potential impacts of anxiety and make feedback, whether corrective or positive, a more welcome experience:

- Acknowledge the power differential—it seems obvious, but it's important for trainees to know that their supervisor understands the impact that the power differential in supervision can have on their perception of feedback.
- Ensure that trainees clearly understand that feedback will be given and when/how it will be provided. This is best accomplished in the first session and in the supervision contract, but it doesn't hurt to have reminders from time to time. An example might sound like, *"We talked about feedback as being an important part of our work each week, and now we get to put that into action. I'm really excited to watch this video of your work, talk about it, and see if I can offer some help in areas that are important to you this term."*
- Keep an eye on the relationship and the potential impact of feedback on the relationship. Direct communication is generally best. For example: if a supervisor delivers corrective feedback, it's helpful to check in with the trainee to see how they're feeling about that experience.
- Engage the trainee's strengths and learning preferences as solutions and resources that they can utilize to *implement* feedback. This lets them know that you believe they can implement the feedback effectively, and it shows that you're willing to problem-solve any barriers with them.
- Maintain an attitude of optimism and find ways, explicit or implicit, to let trainees know that you believe they can achieve their goals. If you find your optimism slipping, this might be a good time to revisit their goals and determine if any adjustments or additional support/resources are needed.

Practicing Effective Feedback: Case Examples

We recommend engaging in this activity *with* your supervisor or trainee as a way to understand each other's approach to providing and receiving feedback. Collaborating on this activity will help enhance the use of feedback in your supervision relationship. For instance, a supervisor's typical approach to providing feedback may be incongruent with the feedback approach that a trainee has found most beneficial, so knowing this up front will help each to navigate and adapt feedback to ensure the success of their relationship and the trainee's growth.

PRACTICING EFFECTIVE STRENGTH-BASED FEEDBACK: CASE ONE

This activity is designed to help you practice developing effective-strength based feedback using case examples. It can also help you learn more about how your supervisor or trainee prefers to provide or receive feedback.

CASE EXAMPLE

Susan is a 2nd-year trainee whose goals include managing the pacing of sessions with her clients. She often finds herself feeling very curious and invested in what her clients are saying, or in questions that she has for them, which can make it hard for her to end the session on time.

Additional Context: Prior to this feedback session, Susan's supervisor watched the last ten minutes of three of Susan's most recent therapy sessions and noticed that one session ended on time and the other two went over time by more than ten minutes

GOALS TO KEEP IN MIND

1. How can I include at least one positive statement in my feedback?
2. How can I practice including detailed observations in my feedback?
3. How can I take their developmental level into account?
4. Your individual goal for feedback (optional). How can I...
   E.g., demonstrate why this feedback is important to their goals, relevant to their developmental level, etc.

YOUR FEEDBACK STATEMENT

____

____

____

____

____

____

____

____

____

____

PRACTICING EFFECTIVE STRENGTH-BASED FEEDBACK: CASE TWO

This activity is designed to help you practice developing effective-strength based feedback using case examples. It can also help you learn more about how your supervisor or trainee prefers to provide or receive feedback.

CASE EXAMPLE

Brian is a 4th-year trainee who is easily motivated and often takes on new projects at his internship site. Brian's internship setting expects him to see a higher volume of clients than his previous training settings, and it has been challenging for him to finish his progress notes on time (before supervision each week).

Additional Context: When they meet, Brian's supervisor notices that there are still several incomplete progress notes and Brian asks to talk about a new research project that's been started at the clinic.

GOALS TO KEEP IN MIND

1. How can I include at least one positive statement in my feedback?
2. How can I practice including detailed observations in my feedback?
3. How can I take their developmental level into account?
4. Your individual goal for feedback (optional). How can I...
   E.g., demonstrate why this feedback is important to their goals, relevant to their developmental level, etc.

YOUR FEEDBACK STATEMENT

____

____

____

____

____

____

____

____

____

____

PRACTICING EFFECTIVE STRENGTH-BASED FEEDBACK: CASE THREE

This activity is designed to help you practice developing effective-strength based feedback using case examples. It can also help you learn more about how your supervisor or trainee prefers to provide or receive feedback.

CASE EXAMPLE

Carol is a 1st-year trainee just starting her first practicum and her first experience of supervision. She meets her new supervisor for their first session; he seems to think that she's doing well and doesn't need much observation. She feels proud when he tells her that they don't need to watch her session tapes because he can tell how she's doing by her progress notes. Their session ends early, after he finishes signing her progress notes.

Later, Carol talks to a classmate who describes her first supervision session, which included reviewing and signing a supervision contract and planning to review video clips every week. Carol wants to give her supervisor feedback and request that they start to watch recordings together at their next session.

GOALS TO KEEP IN MIND

1. How can I include at least one positive statement in my feedback?
2. How can I practice including detailed observations in my feedback?
3. How can I take their developmental level into account?
4. Your individual goal for feedback (optional). How can I...
   E.g., demonstrate why this feedback is important to their goals, relevant to their developmental level, etc.

YOUR FEEDBACK STATEMENT

___

___

___

___

___

___

___

___

___

___

EFFECTIVE FEEDBACK SUPERVISOR WORKSHEET

Use this worksheet as a guide to help you plan and formulate an effective feedback approach that incorporates behavioral anchors, the trainee's goals/development, and their strengths.

WHAT SPECIFIC BEHAVIORS AND COMPETENCIES ARE THE TARGET OF THIS FEEDBACK?

Example: Observed trainee asking only closed-ended questions; intervention and assessment competencies

1. ____

2. ____

3. ____

WHAT IS YOUR BEST HOPE FOR HOW THIS FEEDBACK WILL BE RECEIVED?

Example: My trainee will understand how important this feedback is to the client's treatment, and they will feel confident in trying a new approach during the next session

WHAT ARE YOUR TRAINEE'S GOALS AND STRENGTHS THAT ARE ASSOCIATED WITH THIS FEEDBACK?

Example: This feedback is aligned with my trainee's goal for improving their rapport-building and clinical interview skills. Their curiosity and willingness to take risks are strengths to reinforce.

HOW WILL YOU PHRASE THIS FEEDBACK?

TRAINEE FEEDBACK IMPLEMENTATION WORKSHEET

Use this worksheet as a guide to monitoring feedback and planning for next steps. Also consider reflecting on how clear you feel about the feedback you've received, is additional clarification needed for you to best understand how to integrate this feedback in your clinical work?

FEEDBACK #1	IMPLEMENTATION
______________________	How and when will you implement this feedback?
______________________	______________________
______________________	______________________
______________________	______________________
______________________	What additional resources do you need to succeed?
______________________	______________________
______________________	______________________
______________________	______________________
	When will you and your supervisor follow up on this goal, and how will you know when it has been met?
	______________________
	______________________
	______________________

FEEDBACK #2	IMPLEMENTATION
______________________	How and when will you implement this feedback?
______________________	______________________
______________________	______________________
______________________	______________________
______________________	What additional resources do you need to succeed?
______________________	______________________
______________________	______________________
______________________	______________________
	When will you and your supervisor follow up on this goal, and how will you know when it has been met?
	______________________
	______________________
	______________________

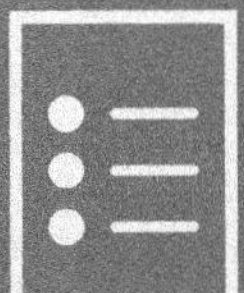

CHAPTER 10 TAKEAWAYS AND RESOURCES

TAKEAWAYS

- Trainees want more feedback.
- Effective feedback is clear, direct, behaviorally-anchored, and delivered in a way that lets the recipient know that they can succeed.
- Feedback isn't just for supervisor-to-trainee. Supervision relationships are best when feedback is dynamic (supervisor-to-trainee and trainee-to-supervisor) and collaborative.
- Using a strength-based approach doesn't mean you have to ignore deficits, but rather amplify strengths to address deficits or reinforce motivation.

RESOURCES

- McKibben, W. B., Borders, L. D., & Wahesh, E. (2019). Factors Influencing Supervisee Perceptions of Critical Feedback Validity. *Counselor Education and Supervision, 58*(4), 242–256.
- Rogers, J. L., Goodrich, K. M., Gilbride, D. D., & Luke, M. (2020). Preliminary Validation of the Feelings Experienced in Supervision Scale. *Counselor Education and Supervision, 59*(2), 129–144.
- Beddoe, L. (2017). Harmful supervision: A commentary. *The Clinical Supervisor, 36*(1), 88-101.
- Munson, C. (2012). *Handbook of clinical social work supervision*. Routledge.
- Rousmaniere, T., Goodyear, R. K., Miller, S. D., & Wampold, B. E. (Eds.). (2017). *The cycle of excellence: Using deliberate practice to improve supervision and training*. John Wiley & Sons.

What are your top 3 takeaways from this chapter?

1. ______________________________
2. ______________________________
3. ______________________________

What do you wish you would have learned and how can you learn this?

- ______________________________
- ______________________________
- ______________________________

What is one thing that you want to do differently moving forward and how will you do this?

____

____

____

____

CHAPTER 11

A FOCUS ON SOLUTIONS

Addressing Obstacles through Strength-Based Remediation and Rupture Repair

CHAPTER 11 GOALS

INFORM	ENGAGE
• Learn how to assess and remediate problems that may arise during the training process.	• Discuss how problems will be identified and addressed in supervision.
• Understand how to approach remediation from a strength-based perspective.	• Practice assessing for problems in case examples and considering next steps for remediation.
• Learn how to identify and repair ruptures in the supervision relationship.	• Discuss how to identify and handle ruptures in the relationship before they occur.
• Learn the ten elements of effective apologies and how to put them into action in supervision.	• Reflect on what behavior or attitude changes might indicate that a rupture has occurred.
	• Practice skills for effective apologies when mistakes are made.

Strength-Based Remediation and the Four Intervention Questions

Remediation refers to a formal process for addressing issues in performance. It can occur for many different reasons, most often when a trainee's competency is notably lower than expected for their stage of training *after* they have been given opportunities to improve that competency through formative feedback. For example, if a trainee receives feedback that they

DOI: 10.4324/9781003006558-14

need to complete their notes on time and yet fails to do this after a designated period (this is where collaborative goal-setting and having clear expectations becomes very important) then remediation is likely the next step. Remediation may also occur when a trainee engages in a behavior that warrants an immediate response, such as an ethical violation.

Remediation occurs when a trainee's competency is notably lower than expected for their stage of training *after* they have been given opportunities to improve.

Remediation works best when it is collaborative, well documented, and ideally focused on content that is not surprising to the trainee—e.g., after receiving formative feedback and having opportunities to resolve the performance issue outside of remediation. Thus, it should almost never be the first step in addressing performance problems, unless the behavior is egregious.

Strength-based remediation should be collaborative. Its goal is to develop competency through the identification and activation of strengths and other resources. Strength-based remediation should also consider the concept of **broaden and build** to expand positive development beyond competency and/or across areas. The Broaden and Build theory (Fredrickson, 2001) argues that a focus on positive emotions such as gratitude, pride, interest, hope, joy, or inspiration serves to broaden our awareness of other positive emotions and positive aspects in our work. It allows us to open our eyes to what else is going well and then to build on this awareness across other areas. Fredrickson (2013) concludes that focusing on the positive and working to build on this "quite literally widen people's outlook on the world around them" (p. 815). With this in mind, consider that, like goal-setting for both clients and trainees, remediation follows the **four intervention questions** and can take advantage of the ROPES Model and Appreciative Inquiry as appropriate. As a reminder, here are the **four intervention questions**:

- Where is the trainee now?
- How did they get here?
- Where should they be?
- How do they get there?

Additionally, we want to include a specific plan for measuring the success of the remediation. Strength-based remediation rests on the four intervention questions as well as updates specific to performance progress, just like case presentations would also include treatment progress.

Now we'll walk through a case example using the strength-based remediation approach outlined in the preceding handout. We'll take it one step at a time and invite you to consider what other factors or approaches you might include using your unique framework or perspective on supervision.

STRENGTHS-BASED REMEDIATION CASE EXAMPLE ONE

LIAM'S MINDFULNESS RETREAT EXPERIENCE

Liam is just past the halfway point of his first clinical training placement and he started a new rotation in your department last week, although he will continue with several of his previous clients. Feedback from his previous clinical supervisor was positive, noting Liam's enthusiasm, strong social skills, cultural humility, interest in diversity, and his willingness to take risks to be the most effective therapist he can be. In one of the formative evals, his supervisor described Liam as "one of the most culturally aware individuals I have worked with."

At the start of supervision today, Liam was noticeably excited. When asked, he revealed that he has a secret therapy weapon and that this is why he does such a "great job" with his clients. He reported that he read a lot about it and then spent the weekend at a mindfulness retreat that his client had recommended. His client also participated in this weekend activity and the two shared intimate details about themselves and their dreams for the future. Liam described it as a life-changing experience and said it helped him better understand himself and his client.

Before you could gather the words to respond to Liam's story, he stated enthusiastically that whenever he does something like this with a client, it always makes him a better clinician. He shared that he plans to join another client at her AA meeting later today, stating, "I need to know what it's like to be a recovering alcoholic. I think it is the only way to really understand what she is going through."

We'll use the four intervention questions discussed back in Section II:

1. Where is the trainee now?

____

____

2. How did they get here?

____

____

3. Where should they be?

____

____

4. How do they get there?

____

____

Let's start with the more traditional deficit-based approach to remediation, although we don't want to spend too much time here. Question 1 asks where the trainee is now. First, Liam's weekend at the mindfulness retreat with his client is a major concern. Second, Liam has planned to attend another client's AA meeting. And third, it appears that Liam has done this kind of activity before. Question 2 asks how Liam got to this point—that is, how he developed his poor boundaries with clients, which would require us to look at where his training had failed. The last two questions, from a deficit-based perspective, would have us focus on eliminating his behavior related to poor boundaries. Strengths would not become a focus unless they are purposely brought into the remediation.

This is where a strength-based perspective is different. We can tackle the same problem (or obstacle) with the same goal in mind, without focusing exclusively on clinical training failures. We may even help the trainee move forward in other related areas. Before we dive into the process, though, it is important to point out that Liam's behavior may cause harm to his clients. For this reason, we need to first address any immediate needs to ensure client safety and ethical compliance. We can then move on to remediation.

Now, back to the **four intervention questions**, but this time from a strength-based perspective. **Question 1** asks where Liam is now. Try to suspend your focus on the obvious problem with Liam's recent behavior and look at it from a strength perspective. Liam is demonstrating a passion for helping his clients. He is dedicated to putting in the time he feels is needed to serve them well. He is focused on learning about the activities (mindfulness retreat, AA meeting) before engaging in them. He is energetic and obviously takes pride in his work, based on his excitement as he shared his secret therapy weapon.

Doesn't even sound like the same trainee, does it? If we consider that Liam has good reasons for his actions, we can build on these to change his behavior to adhere to clinical standards and ethical principles. We've identified quite a few strengths. Although we don't know Liam's Signature Strengths (Peterson & Seligman, 2004), we might imagine Lifelong Learning is a strength of his, as well as Curiosity and Perspective. It is difficult to argue that he doesn't want to see the world through his clients' eyes. Finally, all of these strengths fall in the Virtue of Wisdom. Knowing the trainee's strengths and virtues, no matter how they are identified and labeled, allows us to use them to overcome the present obstacle and to help the trainee grow as a professional.

So let's move to **Question 2**: how did Liam get here? Obviously many successes have formed Liam's passion for learning and growth, as well as his desire to help others. Exploring what has worked in his past training allows us to build on those successes. Questions or prompts we might ask Liam include:

- You said you read something before the activity; tell me how reading is helpful to you.
- You talked about attending the mindfulness retreat and wanting to go to an AA meeting. Tell me more about why that is important.
- You work hard to understand your clients. Where does your passion for helping others come from?
- You take a lot of pride in serving your clients well. What brings you the greatest joy in your work with clients?

From these questions and similar ones, we can better understand the motivations for the trainee's behavior, which will help us design a remediation that build on them.

Question 3 asks where Liam should be. Obviously, his behaviors are concerning and his immediate and ongoing work with clients needs to be considered immediately. We can't ignore his behavior and will need it to stop. For this reason, some additional work regarding ethics and healthy boundaries with clients is warranted. However, stopping the behavior only brings us back to neutral; it does not advance Liam's learning or skills and it certainly does not build on his strengths. Not only do we want Liam to act in an ethical manner with his client's best interest in mind, we also want him to build on his existing strengths and broaden his knowledge, skills, and beliefs (or attitudes) regarding his work with clients. A few questions might include:

- What strengths and resources are available to you? What else?
- How could you learn about client's activities and interests while maintaining healthy boundaries?
- You seem to really enjoy learning. What are some ways you could do this while serving the best interests of your clients? What else?
- How will we know when you are successful? How else?

Moving to **Question 4**, "how does Liam get there," let's look again at his motivations and strengths. He seems to thrive when he feels he has a good understanding of his clients and he enjoys seeing the world from his clients' perspectives. From this knowledge alone, a few questions to ask Liam come to mind:

- What are your best hopes for this remediation? What would a positive solution look like? (Consider the **Miracle question** or your own derivative)
- What has worked in the past when you worked to learn new skills? What else?
- What strengths do you amplify when you work to get to know your clients? How could we use these?
- What resources are available? What else?
- What obstacles might get in the way of a successful remediation? How will you minimize or eliminate them? How else?

Responses to these and other questions, combined with behavioral anchors on the desired remediation outcome, will assist in developing a strength-based remediation plan that will not only eliminate the problem, but will help Liam develop new skills and a deeper understanding about how to best work with his clients.

Now It's Your Turn: Practicing Appreciative Remediation

We'll shift our attention now to Callie. Read the scenario below and consider how you might respond. This is another excellent activity for supervisors and trainees to engage in, either separately or together, to help learn more about the unique perspectives of both roles in the remediation process.

STRENGTHS-BASED REMEDIATION CASE EXAMPLE TWO

CALLIE'S LACK OF FOCUS

Callie is a new intern at your facility. She completed her dissertation early and already has three peer-reviewed publications. In her application, her academic references used terms such as bright, motivated, high-achiever, brilliant, and energetic to describe her. Her previous clinical supervisor was more cautious, referring to Callie as "a dedicated clinician who will benefit from additional practice to build confidence and competence as a therapist."

During your first supervision-of-supervision session with her she demonstrated good social skills, collaborated on appropriate goals, and seemed excited to see her first supervisee. Goals were set and Callie agreed to work on relationship-building skills and to set supervision goals in her first session with her supervisee. You and she also agreed to work on the development of a supervision model that fits with Callie's professional style. Callie had her first session as a supervisor later that day and you reviewed the video that evening. A few things stood out.

First, Callie did about 80% of the talking in the session, most of it related to the research on clinical supervision and various supervision models. Second, she cut her supervisee off several times, stating "this is important" or "you need to listen." Third, she ended the session about 15 minutes early by telling her supervisee that she was done and had covered what she planned to cover. They did not discuss the supervisee's history, any goals for supervision, or expectations for their work together.

Take a few minutes to consider how you might answer each of the following questions.

1. Where is Callie now? What are her strengths? What questions would you ask her from an Appreciative Inquiry perspective?

____

____

____

____

____

____

STRENGTHS-BASED REMEDIATION CASE EXAMPLE TWO

CALLIE'S LACK OF FOCUS

2. How did Callie get here? Where do her strengths come from? How does she best learn? How has she been successful, especially regarding her identified strengths? What questions would you ask Callie?

3. Where should Callie be? What are the positive behaviors she should be demonstrating? What questions would you ask Callie?

4. How can Callie get there? Which strengths can we amplify to help her reach her remediation goals? How can we amplify them? How can we match Callie's strengths and values to her goal achievement? How will we know when remediation is complete? What questions would you ask Callie?

Strength-based Remediation Documentation

Remediation plans should be well-documented and at minimum include the following elements:

- Professional competencies to be remediated
- Specific criteria for determination of success (e.g., benchmarks)
- Time frame for completion
- Planned strategies/activities to acquire (or re-acquire) competence
- Designated supervisor of activities throughout the plan
- Responsibilities of each party
- Assessment strategies to be implemented
- Expected level of achievement for each assessment strategy at completion
- Consequences of success or failure
- Clarification of what remains confidential in the remediation process, under what circumstances the process and outcomes will be shared, and with whom they will be shared
- Signatures affirming acceptance of the plan by the trainee, director of training, and appropriate others
- Specification about who is involved in design, implementation and outcome assessment (e.g., the trainee's advisor, faculty, and/or supervisors).

When *Stuff* Happens in the Supervision Relationship: Identifying and Repairing Ruptures

Ruptures in the supervision relationship have been defined as a negative shift in the supervisory relationship that typically occurs when there is conflict or misunderstanding related to supervision tasks, goals, the roles of supervisor and supervisee, or strains in the relationship because of individual differences, lack of collaboration or other factors (Watkins, 2021). As indicated in that working definition, ruptures are most often caused by lack of agreement on goals or tasks. However, they can also result from interpersonal conflict or individual differences, including personal factors such as age, gender, cultural, or spiritual differences; or professional differences such as conflicting theoretical orientations. Regardless of the cause of the rupture, it's imperative for supervisors and trainees to have a plan in place to address ruptures *before* they happen and to act swiftly to identify, discuss, and repair ruptures as they occur.

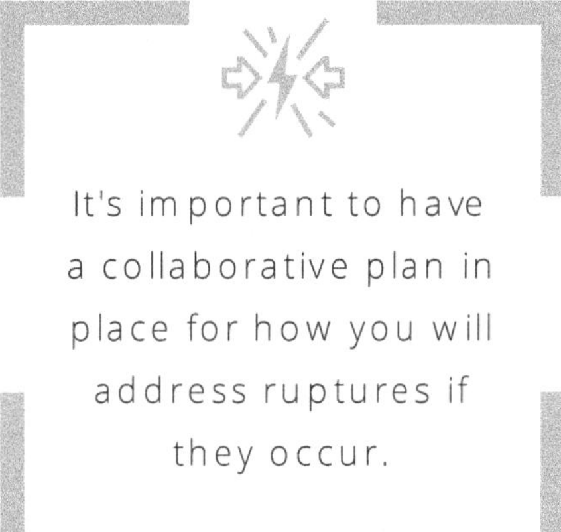

Having an action plan for addressing ruptures starts with—you guessed it—the first supervision session and the supervision contract. Setting expectations for how you both will approach ruptures can go a long way toward normalizing ruptures if they occur. Doing so also will help make both trainee and supervisor feel confident, if not comfortable, in knowing the expectations for the next steps. A conversation about this in the first session might sound something like,

> *We're going to be working closely together over this next year and it's natural for any two individuals who work together in supervision to at times experience conflict. What have you experienced in*

terms of conflict within supervision in the past? How can we use that experience to come up with a plan for how you and I will identify and address conflict if it occurs?

Even if a plan isn't in place to address ruptures, it's important that supervisors and trainees understand how to identify ruptures when they occur, as well as the best practices for rupture repair. As you read through the best practices for identifying and repairing ruptures, we'd also like you to consider the following competencies for supervisors—and we think for trainees as well:

Five Components of a Supervisor's Competency to Identify and Repair Ruptures

- Openness to examining her or his supervisory work; willingness to engage in ongoing self-reflection
- Sensitivity to signs of conflict in supervision
- Identification of the presence of a possible rupture; ability to internally process how best to proceed
- Bringing up the identified rupture in supervision for joint processing and discussion
- Working to achieve a resolution that is satisfactory to the supervisee and restores the good standing of the supervision alliance.

Identifying Ruptures

Problems in the relationship which are most often indicated by:

- Changes in behaviors. Examples might include:
  - A trainee who normally shows up early for supervision is now routinely late or often asks to reschedule.
  - A supervisor who routinely provides positive and critical feedback now seems hesitant to provide critical feedback.
  - A trainee who often brings video or audio clips to supervision for review and feedback stops doing this in favor of self-report.
- Changes in attitudes. Examples might include:
  - A supervisor who usually demonstrates enthusiasm in sessions now appears withdrawn.
  - A trainee who is generally open and curious is now often responding defensively.

Can you think of other examples, based on your experience or understanding of supervision, that might also apply? How might you talk about these indications with a trainee or supervisor *before* they occur? Think of it like flagging the minefield—another solution-focused intervention. Flagging the minefield works by identifying potential obstacles that could hinder progress and making plans to minimize or eliminate their impact by identifying and amplifying strengths, VIPs, and other resources. The approach is also useful for identifying potential contexts or behaviors that might be indicative that a previous problem is recurring or that a minefield is near.

Repairing Ruptures: The Ten Elements of Effective Apologies

When indications of changes—red flags—in the relationship occur, it most often falls to supervisors to further assess and address the problem because of the power differential. Some trainees do feel comfortable bringing up problems in the relationship, but supervisors are encouraged to be proactive as a way to demonstrate their attention and commitment as well as to model relationship skills. For both trainees and supervisors, the best practices in repairing ruptures include:

1. **Internally identifying and processing the rupture.** "John's usually on time for supervision and now this is the second week in a row that he's been late. I wonder what's going on. We had that difficult conversation about Client X a couple of weeks ago; I wonder if that's a part of it. I'll think about how to best bring it up this week."
2. **Bringing it up in supervision.** "You're usually so prompt when it comes to our sessions, but I've noticed that recently you've been late. I wanted to check in and see how things are going and if there's anything that we should talk about today. I'm wondering if this change has anything to do with that conversation we had about Client X last week. I know it was difficult and that you've been feeling frustrated."
3. **Prepare to apologize if mistakes have been made.** Supervisors and trainees make mistakes! It's normal, and for trainees it's an expected part of the process. The key is to apologize effectively by tailoring the apology to fit the context and severity of the mistake. Incorporate the following elements suggested by Watkins et al. (2015) in the graphic on p. 182.

TEN ELEMENTS OF EFFECTIVE APOLOGIES

1. Stating the apology for one's transgression (e.g., "I'm sorry. I apologize.")
2. Naming the offense (e.g., "What I did was...")
3. Taking responsibility for the offense (e.g., "I am responsible for what happened.")
4. Attempting to explain the offense, but not trying to explain it away
5. Conveying emotions (e.g., shame, remorse)
6. Addressing the emotions of and/or damage to the offended party
7. Admitting fault
8. Promising forbearance (e.g., "I want to refrain from doing that again.")
9. Offering reparation (e.g., offering something tangible to the offended party)
10. Requesting apology acceptance.

Continuing with our previous example, let's assume that John's response indicates that he felt his supervisor wasn't really listening to his ideas and opinions about what to do with Client X. Regardless of whether or not the supervisor still feels like their decision about Client X is clinically appropriate, it would be helpful to acknowledge John's experience and apologize for not fully attending to what he had to say. **Here's an example of an effective apology:**

> I'm sorry for not fully listening to what you had to say about this client. That's not OK; listening is an important part of our relationship and our work together, and I feel embarrassed that I cut you off. I think perhaps I was worried about talking about your other clients as well and felt like we were running out of time. Still, I'd like to do better next time and I'm sorry that you had that experience. Why don't we schedule some additional time this week to continue talking about that case? Does that feel like an acceptable solution?

RUPTURE IDENTIFICATION AND REPAIR ACTIVITY

Use this activity to help you proactively identify what some indicators of ruptures in your supervision relationship might be and how you can work together to address them. Notice that the examples include trainee and supervisor indicators of shifts in the relationship—both are important!

WHAT ARE SOME INTERNAL OR EXTERNAL INDICATIONS THAT THERE'S BEEN A RUPTURE IN OUR RELATIONSHIP?

Examples: I feel less excited about coming to supervision; I stop offering feedback.

____

____

____

____

____

____

WHAT WOULD BE A GOOD WAY FOR EITHER OF US TO BRING UP CHANGES THAT WE NOTICE IN THE RELATIONSHIP?

Trainee: I might feel more comfortable bringing something up over email first and then discussing it in person.
Supervisor: Maybe we can also start each session with a brief check-in about our relationship—something like "how are WE doing?"

____

____

____

____

____

____

WHAT ARE THE POTENTIAL BARRIERS TO MY BRINGING UP PROBLEMS IN THE RELATIONSHIP?

Example: Anxiety about repercussions. Unsure what to do about problems, unsure about solutions.

____

____

____

____

____

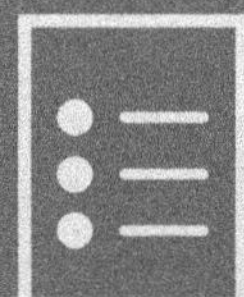

CHAPTER 11 TAKEAWAYS AND RESOURCES

TAKEAWAYS

- Remediation is a formal process that occurs when performance issues have been identified, communicated, and have not been successfully resolved even after informal feedback.
- Remediation should be as collaborative as possible.
- Strength-based approaches can help make remediation more effective by activating the trainee's strengths to help them address performance issues and increase their optimism and motivation.
- Ruptures occur within supervision relationships and are generally caused by misalignment on goals or tasks—or interpersonal differences.
- Supervisors and trainees can both take steps to repair ruptures by having a plan in place to address concerns in their relationship and being proactive in monitoring for changes in their attitudes and behaviors that might indicate that there is a problem.

RESOURCES

- Demyan, A. L., Abraham, C. M., & Bui, N. H. (2018). Trainees looking through the lens of a supervisor: remediation and gatekeeping responses to hypothetical problems of professional competency. *The American Journal of Family Therapy, 46*(1), 67–80.
- Freeman, B. J., Garner, C. M., Scherer, R., & Trachok, K. (2019). Discovering expert perspectives on dispositions and remediation: A qualitative study. *Counselor Education and Supervision 58*(3), 209–224.
- Wade, J., & Jones, J. (2014). *Strength-based clinical supervision: A positive psychology approach to clinical training*. Springer.
- Watkins Jr, C. E. (2021). Rupture and rupture repair in clinical supervision: some thoughts and steps along the way. *The Clinical Supervisor. DOI: 10.1080/07325223.2021.1890657*
- Watkins, Jr, C. E., Reyna, S. H., Ramos, M. J., & Hook, J. N. (2015). The ruptured supervisory alliance and its repair: On supervisor apology as a reparative intervention. *The Clinical Supervisor, 34*(1), 98–114.

What are your top 3 takeaways from this chapter?

1. ____________________
2. ____________________
3. ____________________

What do you wish you would have learned and how can you learn this?

- ____________________
- ____________________
- ____________________

What is one thing that you want to do differently moving forward and how will you do this?

____

____

____

____

CHAPTER 12

ENDING WELL

The Final Supervision Sessions and Stepping Into the Future

CHAPTER 12 GOALS

INFORM	ENGAGE
• Understand the essential elements of the final supervision sessions, including transitioning the relationship, reviewing and evaluating goals, caseload considerations (transfer, warm handoff, etc.), summative evaluation, and other tasks. • Understand the final two stages of appreciative inquiry (Deliver and Don't Settle) as frameworks for evaluating training goals, progress, and next steps in the trainee's development. • Learn about how termination sessions in supervision can be as impactful as termination sessions in psychotherapy. • Learn about best practices for writing and discussing summative evaluations.	• Discuss and process the experience of supervision and the transition to next steps. • Reflect on progress and best hopes for the future by completing the Deliver and Don't Settle stages of Appreciative Inquiry. • Collaborate on how to monitor and manage caseload transitions and prioritize time toward the end of supervision.

Essential Tasks and Goals of the Final Supervision Sessions

Clinicians spend a significant amount of time preparing for the end of the therapeutic relationship with their clients. Yet when it comes to supervision, the processes of ending, or termination, tend to sneak up on us, generally in the form of *Oh no! We need to do the summative*

DOI: 10.4324/9781003006558-15

evaluation paperwork this week! In this chapter we'll discuss ways that supervisors and trainees can maximize the opportunities offered by the *end* of their supervision relationship much in the same way that earlier chapters have focused on the *beginning* and foundations of the relationship. And if we think about it, much of the supervision process is focused on the end: meeting goals, progressing to next steps in training or licensure processes, and so forth.

Preparing for supervision to end well involves keeping an eye on the timeline for the course of supervision so that the end doesn't sneak up on you. It's best to always be keeping the end in mind, in order to determine at what point you should be more explicitly discussing the end of supervision and all that it entails. Using the 12-week example we outlined at the beginning of this section, here is how the focus of supervision might shift as you near the end of the 12-week term:

Weeks Eight to Nine: Continue monitoring the relationship, observing clinical work, providing formative feedback, and assessing progress on goals.

Week Nine: Start to talk about the forthcoming end of supervision. This might include asking trainees to prepare a list of recommendations for their caseload (in terms of what clients are ready to terminate treatment or need to transfer to a different clinician). Continue to observe clinical work and provide feedback.

Week Ten: By this session, supervisor and trainee should have agreed upon a plan for each client and should be able to take steps to terminate or transfer services as needed before the end of supervision in Week Twelve. Time should be set aside in this session to preview the summative evaluation form, with the goal that trainee and supervisor each complete it separately before the next session.

Week Eleven: Continue to monitor any remaining clients and clinical work. Set aside time to discuss the preliminary summative evaluation forms with a goal of finalizing the evaluation before the next and final session. Supervisor and trainee should discuss what they want to focus on in their final session, including reflecting on any lingering questions or feedback that they may have.

Week Twelve: Finalize the summative evaluation, process the experience of supervision, reinforce strengths and successes, and discuss ongoing goals and areas for growth, which may include next steps in training or professional development.

Ending Well: Preparing Trainees for Ending Work with Clients

Each clinician approaches termination or transfer of clients in a different way; in fact, Norcross et al. (2017) identified as many as 80 different techniques or approaches that therapists use in the termination process. An important component of clinical training is helping trainees learn and utilize these practices effectively and congruently within their theoretical orientation. We have summarized **termination practices** to include the following categories:

1. Process the feelings of the client and the therapist
2. Discuss client's future functioning and coping
3. Help client use new skills beyond therapy
4. Frame personal development as invariably unfinished
5. Anticipate post-therapy growth and generalization
6. Prepare explicitly for termination
7. Reflect on client's gains and consolidation
8. Express pride in client's progress and mutual relationship

Supervision can help trainees identify how and when to use these approaches. Part of the work of supervision is to help trainees design a termination plan for each client that attends to any ongoing client needs (e.g., transfer or referral), reinforces the client's progress, and allows both client and therapist to process the relationship and say goodbye. More experienced trainees may be able to do this more autonomously than newer trainees, especially those who are saying goodbye to clients for the first time. Here, we've provided some examples of initiating the conversation about termination of treatment and how to assess what goals and experiences the trainee might have, as well as any resources or learning experiences that are needed.

ENDING WELL: BEST PRACTICES FOR PREPARING TRAINEES TO END WORK WITH THEIR CLIENTS

1. *Process the feelings of the client and the therapist*
2. *Discuss client's future functioning and coping*
3. *Help client use new skills beyond therapy*
4. *Frame personal development as invariably unfinished*
5. *Anticipate post-therapy growth and generalization*
6. *Prepare explicitly for termination*
7. *Reflect on client gains and consolidation*
8. *Express pride in client's progress and mutual relationship*

Consider the trainee's developmental level and experience.

For more experienced trainees, *the conversation might sound something like this: "This is your last training placement before graduation, and I know you've experienced several transitions to new training sites and terminating treatment with clients as a part of that. Tell me how you approach ending your work with clients? Is there anything that you'd like my help with in terms of new things you want to try or existing practices that you want to refine?"*

For newer trainees it might sound differently:
"As we start preparing for your transition to your next placement, I'm hoping that we can talk about what your best hopes are for terminating with your clients? This can include your own hopes in terms of how you want to process this transition personally and professionally, as well as your hopes for the client and their experience of ending this relationship with you."

Consider the value of experiential activities within supervision.

"You mentioned that you've been working on talking more openly with clients about your experiences in the therapy relationship, but you've said that sometimes anxiety gets in the way. I'm wondering if you'd like to practice what it might be like to talk to a couple of specific clients about that during supervision today? We can take turns with who plays your role or the role of the client."

Normalize the process for trainees by utilizing self-disclosure.

"I don't know if you've experienced this, but for me, when I was in my second year of training, I was at X site and it felt harder to say goodbye than it did at the placement I was at in my first year. It felt a little different every time, but my feelings have always been a little conflicted—on one hand I'm happy to see my clients ending treatment and experiencing relief and progress; on the other it can be hard sometimes to know that I'm no longer a part of their lives and to live with the uncertainty of how they're doing."

Summative Evaluation

While feedback in all forms is a vital part of the training process, summative evaluations are uniquely important because they synthesize a trainee's development across a specific training term and lay the groundwork for their next steps. Summative evaluation formats vary from program to program and within specialty fields of mental health professionals. Most evaluations tend to follow the competency or functional requirements of the professional's governing field—for example, in psychology, training evaluations are based on APA's competency domains across each level of training (e.g., practicum, internship, post-doctoral). Summative evaluation forms usually include a rating scale with expected outcomes for each competency or performance area at the appropriate level of training.

There are several important considerations and best practices for summative evaluations:

1. **Understand the Expectations.**
   Supervisors and trainees should have a clear understanding of the summative evaluation expectations and process at their program or setting. This includes deadlines and other expectations, such as adhering to a rating range based on each trainee's expected developmental level. For example, a second-year trainee may be expected to meet but not exceed a certain rating.
2. **Make the Process Collaborative.**
   Summative evaluations should be as collaborative as possible—within reason, given the supervisor's responsibility to accurately assess and report on a trainee's development—and should be free of surprises. That is to say, after several weeks of informal feedback, a trainee should have a reasonable expectation of what their supervisor will include on the summative evaluation form.
3. **Start Early.**
   The summative evaluation is often one of the last things that trainees and supervisors do. However, we encourage you to start this process early by introducing the form during the first session(s), reviewing it again during the mid-term evaluation process, and beginning to draft the final evaluation at least two weeks before the end of supervision.
4. **Make it Personal.**
   Most forms include narrative or comment fields for each competency or performance category, in addition to a summative narrative field. These are important but often overlooked areas for supervisors to expand on their rationale for selecting specific numerical ratings. They also allow you to provide your trainee with contextualized, in-depth feedback on their strengths and next steps.

Ending Well with Appreciative Inquiry: The Final Stages

In Section II we learned about **Appreciative Inquiry (AI)** as it related to goal-setting within supervision. We called the first four stages of AI "**appreciative goal-setting**" to underline the importance of setting goals that foster competence in a strength-based manner meant to bring out the best in us. The first four stages of AI correspond to the **four intervention questions**: Where is the trainee now? What strengths and successes helped them get here? Where do they want to be? How do we work together to get them there?

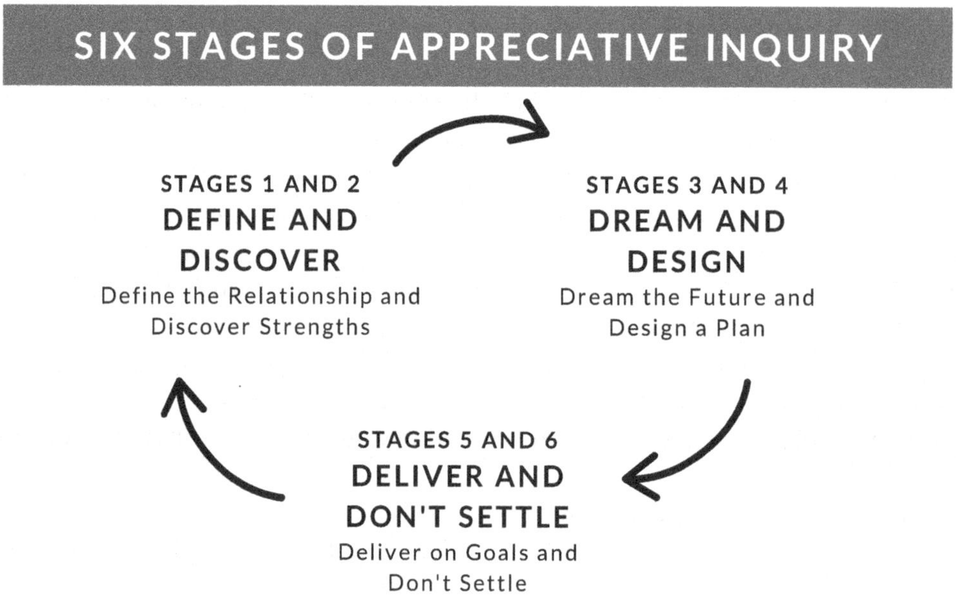

SIX STAGES OF APPRECIATIVE INQUIRY

STAGES 1 AND 2
DEFINE AND DISCOVER
Define the Relationship and Discover Strengths

STAGES 3 AND 4
DREAM AND DESIGN
Dream the Future and Design a Plan

STAGES 5 AND 6
DELIVER AND DON'T SETTLE
Deliver on Goals and Don't Settle

In Stages One and Two, the supervisor worked with the trainee to define and establish the supervision relationship and begin exploring strengths and previous successes. Stage Three involved exploring the **preferred future**, where the trainee would like to be regarding knowledge, skills, and attitudes by the end of the training experience, including collective goals aimed at achieving minimum competency as well as individual goals focused on the trainee's strengths, training, and growth. Once goals are agreed upon, Stage Four began the process of collaborating on the development of a plan to bring about these goals.

The fifth stage, "Deliver the Future," refers to the discussion of goals and progress, which has been occurring in smaller pieces throughout the supervision process through ongoing informal and formal evaluations. It typically involves a formal summative evaluation measuring the trainee's performance against minimum competencies (collective goals) and any added individual goals specific to the trainee. This process, however, is much more than just checking off boxes. It involves a discussion of strengths and resources that aided the trainee's success. This self-reflection is important for both the trainee and the supervisor.

ENDING WELL WITH APPRECIATIVE INQUIRY: THE FINAL STAGES

5. DELIVER THE FUTURE

This is often what we think of when we do summative evaluations: delivering the future is about demonstrating accomplishments compared to goals. More than merely checking off boxes, this stage is also about recognizing successes, identifying what went well and why, and working to better understand how strengths impact our successes.

SKILLS

Consider Intervention Question One: How did the trainee get here? Continue using relationship building skills and solution-focused skills. Focus on strengths and resources that were important in achieving goals. Do not ignore areas of weakness and always ensure minimum competencies have been achieved.

PROMPTS

- What progress have you made toward your goals? What else?
- How has supervision been helpful in making progress on your goals? How else?
- What has changed regarding your goals as you gain new knowledge and skill?
- What obstacles have you overcome and what obstacles remain?
- What have you learned about yourself as a therapist?
- What growth area have you found the most unexpected?
- What are you most proud of so far? What else?
- How have your strengths contributed to your successes? How else?

NOTES

The submission of all summary evaluations may mark the end of Stage Five, but it does not mark the end of clinical supervision. "Don't Settle," the final stage, represents a jumping-off point for continued growth by reexamining the strengths and resources that helped the trainee succeed and discussing how to continue their momentum. It involves a commitment to their continued growth as a counselor or psychologist in training, and it is a natural outgrowth of the **Appreciative Inquiry** sequence. The final stage implies that the growth process will continue for both the trainee and the supervisor, just not necessarily together. Ending supervision well means recognizing it as part of the supervision process, not merely the end of it.

Ending supervision well means recognizing it as part of the supervision *process*, not merely the end of it.

ENDING WELL WITH APPRECIATIVE INQUIRY: THE FINAL STAGES

6. DON'T SETTLE

This final stage serves as a jumping-off point for continued training and growth. "Don't Settle" refers to the idea that achieving goals is not an endpoint, but rather a step in our continued growth as practitioners.

SKILLS

Consider Intervention Question Two: Where should the trainee be? Continue relationship building and solution-focused skills. Begin exploring what's next, and remember that small steps lead to big steps—so discussing the next week, month, or year are all of value. Like Stage 2, the idea in this stage is to dream the future.

PROMPTS

- How can you continue your progress? How else?
- What accomplishments are you most proud of? What else?
- What have you enjoyed about your work during this experience? What else?
- Share some things you learned about yourself during this training experience. What else?
- What kept you motivated? What else?
- Who has been most helpful to you? How have they been helpful? How else?
- What resources have been useful? What else?
- What went well this year? How could you continue the momentum?
- What did you enjoy learning most? How can you continue that?

NOTES

Deliberate Practice

The cyclical pattern of Appreciative Inquiry, especially how it occurs in the developmental training of mental health practitioners, creates a **deliberate practice** of clinical supervision for both the trainee and the supervisor. The term "deliberate practice" is specific to a set of guidelines on how to purposefully improve performance (Ericsson & Pool, 2016). It is commonly used in the sports and entertainment world, where very small changes can make huge differences. One such example is from the 2016 Summer Olympics, where the American swimmer Simone Manuel won the silver medal for the 50m freestyle. Her time was 24.09 seconds. The woman who beat her, and won the gold, swam the 50m in 24.07 seconds—a difference of .02 seconds, or just 0.08%. Improving her score by less than 1/10th of one percent would have won Manuel the gold medal.

Obviously, as supervisors and trainees we are not trying to improve our performance by fractions of a second, but we do need to continually improve the work we do to maintain and improve our skills and effectiveness. We do so by incorporating new research and best practices into our work. Imagine if a therapist was practicing after 30 years of being licensed, but still using best practices from 30 years ago without ever updating their knowledge base or skill set. It would not necessarily inspire confidence.

There are several different types of **deliberate practice** that have been studied. For our purposes, we will focus on three: naïve, static, and purposeful. Using the swimming metaphor again, naïve practice would involve swimming that is not goal-directed but that uses general swimming skills without specific outcomes in mind. If a swim coach were to say, "Get in the water and get comfortable with the pool, get used to the water and then we will focus on specific techniques," that is an example of naïve practice. Static practice involves practicing a specific, identified technique but without identifying any specific goals. The coach may say, "Let's see how you do the backstroke; swim a few laps focusing on your best backstroke." That is an instance of static practice, where although they have focused the activity, they do not have an intentional goal of improvement. During a race, swimmers engage in their best static practice because they want to perform well in the moment and not be distracted by goals that go beyond the current moment.

So how do we move toward purposeful practice? Mihaly Csikszentmihalyi is best known for his work on **flow** and, along with Martin Seligman, is considered one of the founders of positive psychology. **Flow** is the mental state of full engagement (Csikszentmihalyi, 1990, 1997) in an activity that an individual is both experienced with and that fits their strengths. When a swimmer is racing to beat opponents in the 100m backstroke, they will work to get their mindset, their muscles, and their focus all in line so that they can swim at their fastest speed. While their coach may be looking for ways to improve their time, the swimmer is focused only on bringing everything together to win the race.

> When have you noticed yourself in a flow state, a time where your goals and strengths were in alignment and you felt that you were in your comfort zone?

In this sense, swimmers step in and out of **flow** in order to improve their performance. While in **flow**, they reduce resistance and put forth their best effort. When the race is over, they step out of **flow**, maybe watch the race video and talk with their coach, and work to discover ways to improve. This moves the swimmer from static practice to purposeful practice. What they learn and develop through purposeful practice can then be incorporated into the swimmer's static practice. This back-and-forth between static practice and purposeful practice is what allows us to continually improve.

What did you notice about yourself and your behaviors that allowed you to be in a flow state?

As psychotherapists and counselors, we practice statically when we see clients. We do our best to use our skills and knowledge to meet our clients' needs in the moment, and while we may consider ways to improve, we don't experiment with our clients during a session with the sole purpose of improving our own skills. Because **deliberate practice** includes naïve, static, and purposeful practice combined with expert coaching, it is an ideal structure for clinical training because the coach role is built into the role of the clinical supervisor. Finding others to serve as your coach or to coach each other (which we would likely call consultation or peer consultation) gets more difficult after you graduate and become licensed.

The back-and-forth between static practice and purposeful practice is what allows us to continually improve.

Purposeful practice involves (1) setting specific goals, (2) focusing intensely on these goals, (3) seeking immediate feedback and self-correction, and (4) operating at your peak and expanding your abilities (Ericsson & Pool, 2016). For a trainee, a specific goal may be to learn and practice new skills related to CBT. Focusing on this goal may involve reading books and journal articles, watching training videos, and role-playing with your clinical supervisor within the safety of supervision. The supervisor acts as your coach by providing immediate feedback about your performance, allowing you to self-correct quickly before bad habits settle in. You may develop a skill quickly and enjoy it immensely, but once you develop competency, **deliberate practice** means moving to the next skill or working to polish the one you are focusing on. Being in your comfort zone is great, but nothing grows there: operating at your peak means moving out of your comfort zone and expanding your knowledge, skills, and/or attitudes.

CORE COMPONENTS OF DELIBERATE PRACTICE

PURPOSEFUL PRACTICE + EXPERT COACHING

Specific Goal
Make short term goals obvious. Methods for achieving your goal should be purposeful as well.

Intense Focus
Practice tasks related to your specific goal (think successive approximations).

Immediate Feedback
Seek out immediate feedback so you can make corrections if needed.

Frequent Discomfort
Operate at your peak (edge of your abilities) then expand your comfort zone with KSAs.

Practice includes **Knowledge, Skills, and Attitudes** [Beliefs] or KSAs

Deliberately Practice **Self-Care** and **Work-Life Balance.**

Build on **strengths** and be **solution-focused.**

Find a coach to work with who can help maintain motivation and can provide feedback. **Engage others**

Appreciative Inquiry is obviously more dynamic when it is used when two people work collaboratively, one as the interviewer (supervisor or therapist) and one as the interviewee (trainee or client, respectively). The principles of **deliberate practice** necessitate a coach or a mentor to help foster continued growth. As a student and trainee, your clinical instructors and supervisors play this role.

Once you become licensed, however, you lose this structure. You can grow on your own through continuing education, but we recommend you seek out consultation groups or other means to work collaboratively with professional peers who can take on the role of coach and partner in your continued growth as a clinical supervisor and as a counselor or psychotherapist.

We hope that these strategies help you to maximize the potential for the final supervision sessions to serve as an activating, energizing stepping-off point for trainees and supervisors alike to continue their growth and development. Taking what you've learned through the Appreciative Inquiry process, combined with the other skills and strategies you've learned along the way, we encourage you to use the following worksheets to reflect on and summarize your experience of supervision and its influence on your next steps.

SUPERVISOR REFLECTION AND NEXT STEPS WORKSHEET

REFLECTION ON THE SUPERVISION EXPERIENCE

How did this experience align with my best hopes at the start of supervision?

____

____

____

____

How do I feel about this experience overall? Did I enjoy it, and am I proud of the work I did as this trainee's supervisor?

____

____

____

____

STRENGTHS AND NEXT STEPS

What strengths of mine were highlighted during this experience?

____

____

____

____

What are my takeaways from the experience, and how will this experience make me a better supervisor?

____

____

____

____

What are two goals that I've set for myself in continuing my practice of supervision?

1. ____

____

How I will meet this goal: ______________________________

2. ____

____

How I will meet this goal: ______________________________

TRAINEE REFLECTION AND NEXT STEPS WORKSHEET

REFLECTION ON THE SUPERVISION EXPERIENCE

How did this experience align with my best hopes at the start of supervision?

____

____

____

____

How do I feel about this experience overall? Did I enjoy it, and am I proud of what I accomplished and learned?

____

____

____

____

STRENGTHS AND NEXT STEPS

What strengths of mine were highlighted during this experience?

____

____

____

____

What are my takeaways from the experience, and how will this experience make me a better clinician or therapist?

____

____

____

____

What are two goals that I've set for myself in continuing my practice of supervision?

1. ____

____

How I will meet this goal: ______________________________

2. ____

____

How I will meet these goals: ______________________________

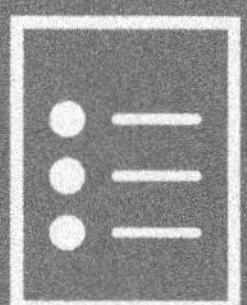

CHAPTER 12 TAKEAWAYS AND RESOURCES

TAKEAWAYS

- Preparing for supervision to end well involves keeping an eye on the timeline and recognizing it as part of the supervision process, not merely the end of it.
- The final two stages of Appreciate Inquiry look at trainee successes and involve a discussion of strengths and resources that aided the trainee's success. Since growth will continue for both the trainee and the supervisor, AI ends with a focus on maximizing momentum for continued growth.
- Deliberate practice is a purposeful approach to improving performance that involves setting specific goals, focusing intensely on these goals, seeking immediate feedback and self-correction, and operating at your peak while expanding abilities.

RESOURCES

- Csikszentmihalyi, M. (1997). Finding flow: *The psychology of engagement with everyday life*. New York, NY: Basic Books.
- Ericsson, A. & Pool, R. (2016). *Peak: Secrets from the new science of expertise.* New York: Houghton Mifflin Harcourt.
- Levendosky, A. A., & Hopwood, C. J. (2017). Terminating supervision. *Psychotherapy, 54*(1), 37.
- Norcross, J. C., Zimmerman, B. E., Greenberg, R. P., & Swift, J. K. (2017). Do all therapists do that when saying goodbye? A study of commonalities in termination behaviors. *Psychotherapy, 54*(1), 66.

What are your top 3 takeaways from this chapter?

1. ____________________
2. ____________________
3. ____________________

What do you wish you would have learned and how can you learn this?

- ____________________
- ____________________
- ____________________

What is one thing that you want to do differently moving forward and how will you do this?

____

____

____

____

CONCLUSION

Key Takeaways and Parting Thoughts

By now, you have probably picked up on the fact that we are passionate about strength-based supervision and the myriad impacts supervision has on trainees, clients, supervisors, and the various fields of mental health. We hope that some of that passion has been contagious—and that you end this workbook feeling energized, excited, and more confident about your current and future role(s) in the training process. This conclusion is our way of summarizing what we think are the most crucial takeaways from this workbook. In essence, if you only read this we believe you'll be a better supervisor and trainee, and perhaps a better clinician. We've collected these takeaways in no particular order.

- Supervision is so much more than reviewing notes, writing evaluations, and making sure that trainees avoid major ethical and clinical pitfalls. It's truly one of the highest honors of clinical work—monitoring the quality of the work of those in training to protect against harm while simultaneously shepherding new clinicians into the field through teaching, mentoring, coaching, challenging, and supporting. Our hope is that supervisors feel excited, engaged, and inspired by their work and use it as a catalyst for their own reflection and growth.
- Trainees are often not oriented in how to appropriately use and, dare we say, maximize their time in supervision. They are often not oriented to what supervision should and can be, and as a result their experiences and training may fall short. Supervisors and programs—not to mention trainees themselves—can remedy this by orienting trainees to the supervision process, setting clear expectations, and empowering trainees to be active in the process of ensuring that their training needs are met.
- Supervisors wear many hats and juggle myriad competing tasks and responsibilities—and three things should always be at the forefront: the supervision relationship, the well-being of the client, and attending to strengths.
- Observation of trainee's actual clinical work is one of the most vital and most neglected components of supervision. Time spent in video review or live supervision is never wasted and has far and wide impacts on the development of trainees and the quality of services they provide.
- Attending to what is going well and building on strengths is a powerful way to promote development and address deficits at the same time. A strength-based approach does not mean that we neglect deficits, rather that we utilize strengths to overcome them.
- Enough cannot be said about collaborative goal-setting and ensuring that training goals are well defined, behaviorally anchored, and monitored routinely. The same can be said

DOI: 10.4324/9781003006558-16

for feedback and the evidence that suggests that trainees are craving more critical and positive feedback, even as they may be anxious about receiving it.

We know that this workbook is by no means exhaustive, and for robust explorations of the content we've summarized we invite you to explore the many experts in clinical supervision—many of whom are mentioned in our reference list.

To trainees specifically—we wrote this workbook for you, in hopes that it would not only help you to receive excellent supervision, but also inspire you to become excellent supervisors—to learn from your experiences as a trainee and from the supervisors who you most admire, and to synthesize that into an approach that best fits your clinical skills, strengths, and values.

We challenge you as trainees and supervisors to look for the strengths in others, to look for exceptions and to help those with whom you work to look at negative issues as obstacles to overcome not problems that prevent us from moving forward. We hope you see competence as a minimum goal, not the end goal, and work to amplify strengths and educe what is good within yourself and those with whom you work. We encourage you to identify and amplify your own strengths and resources and to use these to continually grow as a mental health professional.

We also encourage you to practice deliberately. Move in and out of your comfort zone so you can continually grow as a mental health professional. Find someone to work with you, or to work together, on deliberately moving forward in pursuit of well-being as a clinical supervisor, as a mental health practitioner, and as a human being. We thank you for using this workbook and we hope that it helped to move you closer to your preferred future and expanded how you see yourself, your trainees or supervisors, and your clients. Finally, since we believe growth is a continual and deliberate process, we have one last question for you: ***After using this workbook, what have you learned about your strengths as a trainee or supervisor and what are your next steps to move you closer to your preferred future?***

REFERENCES

1. Abramson, A. (2021). The ethical imperative of self-care: For mental health professionals, it's not a luxury. *Monitor on Psychology*, April/May, 46–53.
2. Al Taher, R. (2021). *The 5 founding fathers and a history of positive psychology*. Retrieved from https://positivepsychology.com/founding-fathers/#:~:text=The%20Four%20Waves%20of%20Psychology,The%20Third%20Wave%3A%20Humanistic%20Psychology.
3. American Psychological Association (2012). *Building your resilience*. Retrieved from www.apa.org/topics/resilience.
4. American Psychological Association. (2014). *Guidelines for clinical supervision in health service psychology*. Retrieved from www.apa.org/about/policy/guidelines-supervision.pdf.
5. Amerikaner, M., & Rose, T. (2012). Direct observation of psychology supervisees' clinical work: A snapshot of current practice. *Clinical Supervisor, 31*(1), 61–80.
6. Barnett, J. E., & Molzon, C. H. (2014). Clinical supervision of psychotherapy: Essential ethics issues for supervisors and trainees. *Journal of Clinical Psychology, 70*(11), 1051–1061.
7. Barrett, J., Gonsalvez, C. J., & Shires, A. (2019). Evidence-based practice within supervision during psychology practitioner training: A systematic review. *The Clinical Psychologist, 5*, 88.
8. Beddoe, L., (2017). Harmful supervision: A commentary. *The Clinical Supervisor, 36*(1), 88–101.
9. Beddoe, L., Ackroyd, J., Chinnery, S.-A., & Appleton, C. (2011). Live supervision of students in field placement: More than just watching. *Social Work in Education, 30*(5), 512–528.
10. Bennett-Levy, J. (2019). Why therapists should walk the talk: The theoretical and empirical case for personal practice in therapist training and professional development. *Journal of Behavior Therapy and Experimental Psychiatry, 62*, 133–145.
11. Bernard, J., & Goodyear, R. (2019). *Fundamentals of clinical supervision* (6th ed.). Pearson.
12. Bernard, J., & Goodyear, R. (2014). *Fundamentals of clinical supervision* (5th ed.). Pearson.
13. Borders, L. D. (2014). Best practices in clinical supervision: Another step in delineating effective supervision practice. *American Journal of Psychotherapy, 68*(2), 151–162.
14. Borders, L. D., & Brown, L. L. (2006). *The new handbook of counseling supervision*. Routledge.
15. Borders, L. D. A., Welfare, L. E., Sackett, C. R., & Cashwell, C. (2017). New supervisors' struggles and successes with corrective feedback. *Counselor Education and Supervision, 56*(3), 208–224.
16. Bright, S., & Evans, A. M. (2019). Supervision development and working alliance: A survey of counseling supervisors. *The Journal of Counselor Preparation and Supervision, 12*(1), 1.
17. Brown, L. S. (2016). *Supervision essentials for the feminist psychotherapy model of supervision*. American Psychological Association.
18. Bucky, S. F., Marques, S., Daly, J., Alley, J., & Karp, A. (2010). Supervision characteristics related to the supervisory working alliance as rated by doctoral-level supervisees. *The Clinical Supervisor, 29*(2), 149–163.
19. Caldwell, J. C. & Vera, E. M. (n.d.). Critical incidents in counseling psychology professionals' and trainees' social justice orientation development. *Teaching and Education in Professional Psychology, 43*(3), 163–176.

20. Callifronas, M. D., Montaiuti, C., & Nina, E. (2017). A Common Approach for Clinical Supervision in Psychotherapy and Medicine: The person centered and experiential model. *Journal of Psychology & Psychotherapy, 7*, 1–15.
21. Campbell, J. M. (2006). *Essentials of clinical supervision.* John Wiley & Sons.
22. Campbell, J. M. (2011). *Essentials of clinical supervision* (Vol. 28). John Wiley & Sons.
23. Carroll, K.M., Nich, C., Sifry, R.L., Nuro, K.F., Frankforter, T.L., Ball, S.A., ... & Rounsaville, B. J. (2000). A general system for evaluating therapist adherence and competence in psychotherapy research in the addictions. *Drug and Alcohol Dependence, 57*(3), 225–238.
24. Carver, C. S., Scheier, M. F., & Segerstrom, S. C. (2010). Optimism. *Clinical Psychology Review, 30*, 879–889.
25. Cliffe, T., Beinart, H., & Cooper, M. (2016). Development and validation of a short version of the Supervisory Relationship Questionnaire. *Clinical Psychology & Psychotherapy, 23*(1), 77–86.
26. Codd, J. L., III, Sokol, L., Fox, M. G., Reiser, R., & Milne, D. L. (2016). Evidence-based supervisory practices in CBT. In *Teaching and supervising cognitive behavioral therapy (p. 207).* John Wiley & Sons.
27. Collins, S., Arthur, N., & Brown, C. (2013). Critical incidents in graduate student development of multicultural and social justice competency. *Academic Journal of Interdisciplinary Studies, 2*(9), 105.
28. Commission on Accreditation (2015). Standards of Accreditation for Health Service Psychology. Retrieved from https://irp-cdn.multiscreensite.com/a14f9462/files/uploaded/APA-Principles-Accreditation-SoA-AOP_200116.pdf.
29. Cooper, L. D., & Wieckowski, A. T. (2017). A structured approach to reflective practice training in a clinical practicum. *Training and Education in Professional Psychology, 11*(4), 252–259.
30. Cooperrider, D. L. (1986). Appreciative Inquiry: Toward a methodology for understanding and enhancing organizational innovation [Doctoral Dissertation, Case Western Reserve University UMI Dissertation Information Service. Retrieved from https://appreciativeinquiry.champlain.edu/wp-content/uploads/2017/09/Cooperriders-original-Dissertation-and-theory-of-Appreciative-Inquiry-1985.pdf.
31. Cooperrider, D.L. & Whitney, D. (2001). A positive revolution in change: Appreciative inquiry. In Cooperrider, D. L.; Sorenson, P.; Whitney, D. & Yeager, T. (Eds.), *Appreciative inquiry: An emerging direction for organization development* (pp. 9–29). Stipes.
32. Cook, R. M., & Sackett, C. R. (2018). Exploration of prelicensed counselors' experiences prioritizing information for clinical supervision. *Journal of Counseling & Development, 96*(4), 449–460.
33. Csikszentmihalyi, M. (1990). *Flow: The psychology of optimal experience.* Harper & Row.
34. Csikszentmihalyi, W. (1997). *Finding flow: The psychology of engagement with everyday life.* Basic Books.
35. Cummings, J. A., Ballantyne, E. C., & Scallion, L. M. (2015). Essential processes for cognitive behavioral clinical supervision: Agenda setting, problem-solving, and formative feedback. *Psychotherapy, 52*(2), 158.
36. De Shazer, S., & Dolan, Y. (2012). *More than miracles: The state of the art of solution-focused brief therapy.* Routledge.
37. Demyan, A. L., Abraham, C. M., & Bui, N. H. (2018). Trainees looking through the lens of a supervisor: Remediation and gatekeeping responses to hypothetical problems of professional competency. *The American Journal of Family Therapy, 46*(1), 67–80.
38. Dewane, C. J. (2015). Solution-focused supervision: A go-to approach. *Social Work Today*, 15(5), 24.
39. Duckworth, A. (2016). *Grit: The power of passion and perseverance.* Scribner.
40. Efstation, J. F., Patton, M. J., & Kardash, C. M. (1990). Measuring the working alliance in counselor supervision. *Journal of Counseling Psychology, 37*(3), 322.
41. El-Ghoroury, N. H., Galper, D. I., Sawaqdeh, A., & Bufka, L. F. (2012). Stress, coping, and barriers to wellness among psychology graduate students. *Training and Education in Professional Psychology, 6*(2), 122.
42. Ellis, M. V., Berger, L., Hanus, A. E., Ayala, E. E., Swords, B. A., & Siembor, M. (2015). Inadequate and harmful clinical supervision: Testing a revised framework and assessing occurrence. *The Counseling Psychologist, 42*(4), 434–472.

43. Enlow, P. T., McWhorter, L. G., Genuario, K., & Davis, A. (2019). Supervisor-trainee interactions: The importance of the supervisory working alliance. *Training and Education in Professional Psychology, 13*(3), 206–211.
44. Enns, C. Z. E., & Sinacore, A. L. (2005). *Teaching and social justice: Integrating multicultural and feminist theories in the classroom*. American Psychological Association.
45. Ericsson, A. & Pool, R. (2016). *Peak: Secrets from the new science of expertise*. Houghton Mifflin Harcourt.
46. Fairburn, C. G., & Cooper, Z. (2011). Therapist competence, therapy quality, and therapist training. *Behaviour Research and Therapy, 49*(6–7), 373–378.
47. Falender, C. A. (2018). Clinical supervision—the missing ingredient. *The American Psychologist, 73*(9), 1240–1250.
48. Falender, C. A., & Shafranske, E. P. (2004). *Clinical supervision: A competency-based approach*. American Psychological Association.
49. Falender, C. A., & Shafranske, E. P. (2012). *Getting the most out of clinical training and supervision: A guide for practicum students and interns*. American Psychological Association.
50. Falender, C. A., & Shafranske, E. P. (2012). The importance of competency-based clinical supervision and training in the twenty-first century: Why bother? *Journal of Contemporary Psychotherapy, 42*, 129–137.
51. Falender, C. A., & Shafranske, E. P. (2014). Clinical supervision: The state of the art. *Journal of Clinical Psychology, 70*(11), 1030–1041.
52. Falender, C. A., & Shafranske, E. P. (2017). *Supervision essentials for the practice of competency-based supervision*. American Psychological Association.
53. Falender, C. A., Cornish, J. A. E., Goodyear, R., Hatcher, R., Kaslow, N. J., Leventhal, G., Shafranske, E., Sigmon, S. T., Stoltenberg, C., & Grus, C. (2004). Defining competencies in psychology supervision: A consensus statement. *Journal of Clinical Psychology, 60*(7), 771–785.
54. Falender, C. A., Grus, C. A., McCutcheon, S., Goodyear, R. K., Ellis, M. V., Doll, B., Miville, M., Rey-Casserly, C., Kaslow, N. J. (2016). Guidelines for clinical supervision in health service psychology: Evidence and implementation strategies. *Psychotherapy Bulletin (Division 29), 51*(3), 6–18. Retrieved from http://societyforpsychotherapy.org/guidelines-clinical-supervision-health-service-psychology/.
55. Falender, C. A., Shafranske, E. P., & Falikov, C. J. (2014). *Multiculturalism and diversity in clinical supervision: A competency-based approach*. American Psychological Association.
56. Fialkov, C., & Haddad, D. (2012). Appreciative clinical training. *Training and Education in Professional Psychology, 6*(4), 204–210.
57. Fickling, M. J., & Tangen, J. L. (2017). A journey toward feminist supervision: A dual autoethnographic inquiry. *The Journal of Counselor Preparation and Supervision, 9*(2). https://doi.org/10.7729/92.1219
58. Fowler, J., Fenton, G., & Riley, J. (2007). Solution-focused techniques in clinical supervision. *Nursing Times, 103*(22), 30–31.
59. Freeman, B. J., Garner, C. M., Scherer, R., & Trachok, K. (2019). Discovering expert perspectives on dispositions and remediation: A qualitative study. *Counselor Education and Supervision, 58*(3), 209–224.
60. Fredrickson, B. L. (2001). The role of positive emotions in positive psychology: The broaden-and-build theory of positive emotions. *American Psychologist, 56*(3), 218–226.
61. Fredrickson, B. L. (2013). Updated thinking on positivity ratios. *American Psychologist, 68*(9), 814–822.
62. Goodyear, R., Lichtenberg, J. W., Bang, K., & Gragg, J. B. (2014). Ten changes psychotherapists typically make as they mature into the role of supervisor. *Journal of Clinical Psychology, 70*(11), 1042–1050.
63. Gonsalvez, C. J., Brockman, R., & Hill, H. R. M. (2016). Video feedback in CBT supervision: review and illustration of two specific techniques. *The Cognitive Behaviour Therapist, 9*, E24.
64. Gray, L. A., Ladany, N., Walker, J. A., & Ancis, J. R. (2001). Psychotherapy trainees' experience of counterproductive events in supervision. *Journal of Counseling Psychology, 48*(4), 371–383.
65. Gross, J. M. (2020). *Examining optimism and caregiver strain in parents with youth and young adults diagnosed with anxiety and unipolar mood disorders*. Retrieved from https://aura.antioch.edu/etds/610.
66. Hagstrom, S. L., & Maranzan, K. A. (2019). Bridging the gap between technological advance and professional psychology training: A way forward. *Canadian Psychology/Psychologie canadienne, 64*, 281.

67. Hall, J. C., & Theriot, M. T. (2016). Developing multicultural awareness, knowledge, and skills: Diversity training makes a difference? *Multicultural Perspectives, 18*(1), 35–41.
68. Hays, P. A. (2008). *Addressing cultural complexities in practice: Assessment, diagnosis, and therapy*. American Psychological Association.
69. Heffner, C. L. (2021a). *Building Psychological Capital: Hope, efficacy, resilience, optimism.* AllPsych. Retrieved from https://allpsych.com/ thrive-building-psychological-capital-hope-efficacy-resilience-optimism/.
70. Heffner, C. L. (2021b). *Well-being and the five happy lives.* AllPsych. Retrieved from https://allpsych.com/thrive-well-being-and-the-five-happy-lives/.
71. Henriksen, R. C., Jr., Henderson, S. E., Liang, Y.-W. M., Watts, R. E., & Marks, D. F. (2019). Counselor supervision: A comparison across states and jurisdictions. *Journal of Counseling & Development, 97*(2), 160–170.
72. Hladik, J. (2016). Assessing multicultural competence of helping-profession students. *Multicultural Perspectives, 18*(1), 42–47.
73. Holt, H., Beutler, L. E., Kimpara, S., Macias, S., Haug, N. A., Shiloff, N., Goldblum, P., Temkin, R. S., & Stein, M. (2015). Evidence-based supervision: Tracking outcome and teaching principles of change in clinical supervision to bring science to integrative practice. *Psychotherapy, 52*(2), 185–189.
74. Ivers, N. N., Rogers, J. L., Borders, L. D., & Turner, A. (2017). Using interpersonal process recall in clinical supervision to enhance supervisees' multicultural awareness. *The Clinical Supervisor, 36*(2), 282–303.
75. Ivey, A. E., Ivey, M. B., & Zalaquett, C. P. (2013; 9th ed. 2018). *Intentional interviewing and counseling: Facilitating client development in a multicultural society.* Cengage Learning.
76. Johnson, E. A. (2019). Recommendations to enhance psychotherapy supervision in psychology. *Canadian Psychology/Psychologie canadienne, 60*(4), 290–301.
77. Johnson, J., Corker, C., & O'Connor, D. B. (2020). Burnout in psychological therapists: A cross-sectional study investigating the role of supervisory relationship quality. *The Clinical Psychologist, 24*(3), 223–235.
78. Kaeding, A., Sougleris, C., Reid, C., van Vreeswijk, M. F., Hayes, C., Dorrian, J., & Simpson, S. (2017). Professional burnout, early maladaptive schemas, and physical health in clinical and counselling psychology trainees. *Journal of Clinical Psychology*, 73(12), 1782–1796.
79. Kangos, K. A., Ellis, M. V., Berger, L., Corp, Dylan A., Hutman, H., Gibson, A., & Nicolas, A. I. (2018). American Psychological Association guidelines for clinical supervision: Competency-based implications for trainees. *The Counseling Psychologist, 46*(7), 821–845.
80. Kassan, A., Fellner, K. D., Jones, M. I., Palandra, A. L., & Wilson, L. J. (2015). (Re)considering novice supervisor development through a social justice lens: An experiential account. *Training and Education in Professional Psychology, 9*(1), 52–60.
81. Kemer, G., Sunal, Z., Li, C., & Burgess, M. (2019). Beginning and expert supervisors' descriptions of effective and less effective supervision. *The Clinical Supervisor, 38*(1), 116–134.
82. Kim, L., Wilson, E. E., ChenFeng, J., & Knudson-Martin, C. (2017). Towards safe and equitable relationships: Sociocultural attunement in supervision. In R. Allen & S. Singh Poulsen (Eds.), *Creating cultural safety in couple and family therapy: Supervision and training* (pp. 57–70). Springer International Publishing.
83. Kuo, Hung-Jen, Trenton J. Landon, Annemarie Connor, and Roy K. Chen. 2016. Managing Anxiety in Clinical Supervision. *The Journal of Rehabilitation, 82*(3), 18–27.
84. Lambert, M. (1992). Psychotherapy outcome research. In J. C. Norcross and M. R. Goldfried (Eds.), *Handbook of psychotherapy integration* (pp. 94–129). Basic Books.
85. Lambert, M. J., Whipple, J. L., & Kleinstäuber, M. (2018). Collecting and delivering progress feedback: A meta-analysis of routine outcome monitoring. *Psychotherapy, 55*(4), 520–537.
86. Levendosky, A. J., & Hopwood, C. J. (2017). Terminating supervision. *Psychotherapy, 54*, 1, 37.
87. Loganbill, C., Hardy, E., & Delworth, U. (1982). Supervision: A conceptual model. *The Counseling Psychologist, 10*(1), 3–42.

88. Lu, D., Suetani, S., Cutbush, J., & Parker, S. (2019). Supervision contracts for mental health professionals: A systematic review and exploration of the potential relevance to psychiatry training in Australia and New Zealand. *Australasian Psychiatry: Bulletin of Royal Australian and New Zealand College of Psychiatrists, 27*(3), 225–229.
89. Lutz, A. B. (2013). *Learning solution-focused therapy: An illustrated guide*. American Psychiatric Publishing.
90. Lyubomirsky, S., Sheldon, K. M., & Schkade, D. (2005). Pursuing happiness: The architecture of sustainable change. *Review of General Psychology, 9*(2), 111–131.
91. Manring, J. M., Meszaros, Z. S., Biedrzycki, J., & Cerio, K. W. (2019). Integrating measurement-based care into supervision. In S. G. De Golia & K. M. Corcoran (Eds.), *Supervision in psychiatric practice: Practical approaches across venues and providers* (pp. 345–352). American Psychiatric Association.
92. Martin, P., Copley, J., & Tyack, Z. (2014). Twelve tips for effective clinical supervision based on a narrative literature review and expert opinion. *Medical Teacher, 36*(3), 201–207.
93. McComb, J. L., Diamond, R. M., Breunlin, D. C., Chambers, A. L., & Murray, K. S. (2019). Introducing client feedback into marriage and family therapy supervision: A qualitative study examining the transition to empirically informed supervision. *Journal of Family Therapy, 41*(2), 214–231.
94. McKibben, W. B., Borders, L. D., & Wahesh, E. (2019). Factors influencing supervisee perceptions of critical feedback validity. *Counselor Education and Supervision, 58*(4), 242–256.
95. Meara, N. M., Schmidt, L. D., & Day, J. D. (1996). Principles and virtues: A foundation for ethical decisions, policies, and character. *The Counseling Psychologist, 24*(1), 4–77.
96. Miller, S. D., Hubble, M. A., & Chow, D. (2018). The question of expertise in psychotherapy. *Journal of Expertise, 1*(2), 121–129.
97. Milne, D. L., Sheikh, A. I., Pattison, S., & Wilkinson, A. (2011). Evidence-based training for clinical supervisors: A systematic review of 11 controlled studies. *Clinical Supervisor, 30*(1), 53–71.
98. Milne, D., & Reiser, R. P. (2012). A rationale for evidence-based clinical supervision. *Journal of Contemporary Psychotherapy, 41*(3), 139–149.
99. Moore, E. C., Jeglum, S., Young, K., & Campbell, S. M. (2019). Self-care in supervision: How do we teach others to care for themselves? *Communique, 47*(8), 1–30.
100. Munson, C. (2012). *Handbook of clinical work supervision*. Routledge.
101. Neuger, C. C. (2015). Narrative therapy and supervision. In L. E. Smith (Ed.), *Reflective practice: Formation and supervision in ministry* (pp. 16–32). Moshpit Publishing.
102. Norberg, J., Axelsson, H., Barkman, N., Hamrin, M., & Carlsson, J. (2016). What psychodynamic supervisors say about supervision: Freedom within limits. *The Clinical Supervisor, 35*(2), 268–286.
103. Norcross, J. C., Zimmerman, B. E., Greenberg, R. P., & Swift, J. K. (2017). Do all therapists do that when saying goodbye? A study of commonalities in termination behaviors. *Psychotherapy, 54*(1), 66.
104. Norcross, J. C. (2011). *The therapeutic relationship, individualized treatment and other keys to successful psychotherapy*. Psychotherapy.net. www.psychotherapy.net/stream/xxx/video?vid=172.
105. Norem, K., Magnuson, S., Wilcoxon, S. A., & Arbel, O. (2006). Supervisees' contributions to stellar supervision outcomes. *Journal of Professional Counseling: Practice, Theory & Research, 34*(1–2), 33–48.
106. O'Connell, B. & Jones, C. (1997). Solution focused supervision. *Counselling*, November 1997, 289–292.
107. O'Connor, K., Neff, D. M., & Pitman, S. (2018). Burnout in mental health professionals: A systematic review and meta-analysis of prevalence and determinants. *European Psychiatry: The Journal of the Association of European Psychiatrists, 53*, 74–99.
108. Owen, J., Wampold, B. E., Kopta, M., Rousmaniere, T., & Miller, S. D. (2016). As good as it gets? Therapy outcomes of trainees over time. *Journal of Counseling Psychology, 63*(1), 12–19.
109. Peters, H. C., & Rivas, M. (2018). The self-model of humanistic supervision. *International Journal for the Advancement of Counselling, 40*(3), 237–254.
110. Peterson, C. & Seligman, M. E. P. (2004). *Character strengths and virtues: A handbook and classification*. Oxford University Press.
111. Pettifor, J., Sinclair, C., & Falender, C. A. (2014). Ethical supervision: Harmonizing rules and ideals in a globalizing world. *Training and Education in Professional Psychology, 8*(4), 201–210.
112. Polychronis, P. D., & Brown, S. G. (2016). The strict liability standard and clinical supervision. *Professional Psychology, Research and Practice, 47*(2), 139–146.

113. Presseau, C., Luu, L. P., Inman, A. G., & De Blaere, C. (2019). Trainee social justice advocacy: Investigating the roles of training factors and multicultural competence. *Counselling Psychology Quarterly, 32*(2), 260–274.
114. Remley, T. P., & Herlihy, B. (2014). *Ethical, legal, and professional issues in counseling.* Pearson.
115. Richardson, C. M., Trusty, W. T., & George, K. A. (2020). Trainee wellness: self-critical perfectionism, self-compassion, depression, and burnout among doctoral trainees in psychology. *Counselling Psychology Quarterly, 33*(2), 187–198.
116. Rieck, T., Callahan, J. L., & Edward Watkins, C. (2015). Clinical supervision: An exploration of possible mechanisms of action. *Training and Education in Professional Psychology, 9*(2), 187–194.
117. Rogers, C. R., & Skinner, B. F. (1956). Some issues concerning the control of human behavior. *Science, 124*(3231), 1057–1066.
118. Rogers, C. R. (1957). The necessary and sufficient conditions of therapeutic personality change. *Journal of Consulting Psychology, 21*(2), 95–103.
119. Rogers, J. L., Goodrich, K. M., Gilbride, D. D., & Luke, M. (2020). Preliminary validation of the feelings experience in supervision scale. *Counsellor Education and Supervision, 59*(2), 129–144.
120. Rogers, J. L., Luke, M., Gilbride, D. D., & Goodrich, K. M. (2019). Supervisee attachment, cognitive distortions, and difficulty with corrective feedback. *Counselor Education and Supervision, 58*(1), 18–32.
121. Rousmaniere, T. G., Goodyear, R. K., Miller, S. D., & Wampold, B. E. (Eds.) (2017). *The cycle of excellence: Using deliberate practice to improve supervision and training.* John Wiley & Sons.
122. Rousmaniere, T. G., Swift, J. K., Babins-Wagner, R., Whipple, J. L., & Berzins, S. (2016). Supervisor variance in psychotherapy outcome in routine practice. *Psychotherapy Research: Journal of the Society for Psychotherapy Research, 26*(2), 196–205.
123. Rumjaun A., & Narod F. (2020). Social Learning Theory—Albert Bandura. In B. Akpan & T. J. Kennedy (Eds.), *Science education in theory and practice.* Springer Texts in Education. Springer, Cham.
124. Sabella, S. A., Schultz, J. C., & Landon, T. J. (2020). Validation of a brief form of the supervisory working alliance inventory. *Rehabilitation Counseling Bulletin, 63*(2), 115–124.
125. Scheier, M. F., & Carver, C. S. (1987). Dispositional optimism and physical well-being: The influence of generalized outcome expectancies on health. *Journal of Personality, 55*, 169–210.
126. Schmidt G., & Kariuki, A. (2019). Pathways to social work supervision. *Journal of Human Behavior in the Social Environment, 29*(3), 321–332.
127. Seligman, M. E. (2004). *Authentic happiness: Using the new positive psychology to realize your potential for lasting fulfillment.* Simon & Schuster.
128. Seligman, M. E. P. (1990/1998/2006). *Learned optimism: How to change your mind and your life.* Random House.
129. Seligman, M. E., & Csikszentmihalyi, M. (2014). Positive psychology: An introduction. In M. Csikszentmihalyi (Ed.), *Flow and the foundations of positive psychology: The collected works of Mihaly Csikszentmihalyi* (pp. 279–298). Springer.
130. Shachar, R., Nasim, R., Leshem, T., Rosenberg, J., Schmidt, A., & Schmuely, V. (2012). Power hierarchy, multiple truth, and innovations in narrative supervision. *Journal of Systemic Therapies, 31*(4), 34–48.
131. Shafranske, E. P., & Falender, C. A. (2016). Clinical supervision. In J. C. Norcross, G. R. VandenBos, D. K. Freedheim, & L. F. Campbell (Eds.), APA handbooks in psychology®. *APA handbook of clinical psychology: Education and profession* (pp. 175–196). American Psychological Association.
132. Simpson-Southward, C., Waller, G., & Hardy, G. E. (2017). How do we know what makes for "best practice" in clinical supervision for psychological therapists? A content analysis of supervisory models and approaches. *Clinical Psychology & Psychotherapy, 24*(6), 1228–1245.
133. Smith, K. (2009). *A brief summary of supervision models.* www.marquette.edu/education/graduate/documents/brief-summary-of-supervision-models.pdf.
134. Snyder, C. R., Harris, C., Anderson, J. R., Holleran, S. A., Irving, L. M., Sigmon, S. T., et al. (1991). The will and the ways: Development and validation of an individual-differences measure of hope. *Journal of Personality and Social Psychology, 60*, 570–585.
135. Staples-Bradley, L. K., Duda, B., & Gettens, K. (2019). Student self-disclosure in clinical supervision. *Training and Education in Professional Psychology, 13*(3), 216–221.

136. Stark, M. D., McGhee, M. W., & Jimerson, J. B. (2017). Reclaiming instructional supervision: Using solution-focused strategies to promote teacher development. *Journal of Research on Leadership Education, 12*(3), 215–238.
137. Stoltenberg, C. D., & McNeill, B. W. (1997). Clinical supervision from a developmental perspective: Research and Practice. In C. E. Watkins, Jr. (Ed.), *Handbook of psychotherapy supervision* (pp. 184–202). John Wiley & Sons.
138. Stoltenberg, C. D., & McNeill, B. W. (2010). *IDM supervision: An integrative developmental model for supervising counselors and therapists* (3rd ed.). Routledge/Taylor & Francis.
139. Sudak, D. (2016, December 12). *Teaching and supervising CBT*. Beck Institute for Cognitive Behavior Therapy. https://beckinstitute.org/teaching-supervising-cbt/.
140. Sudak, D. M., Codd, R. T., Ludgate, J. W., Sokol, L., Fox, M. G., Reiser, R. P., & Milne, D. L. (2016). *Teaching and supervising cognitive behavioral therapy*. John Wiley & Sons.
141. Talley, L. P., & Jones, L. (2019). Person-centered supervision: A realistic approach to practice within counselor education. *Teaching and Supervision in Counseling, 1*(2), 2.
142. Tangen, J. L., DiAnne Borders, L., & Fickling, M. J. (2019). The supervision guide: Informed by theory, ready for practice. *International Journal for the Advancement of Counselling, 41*(2), 240–251.
143. Taylor, Z. E., Widaman, K. F., Robins, R. W., Jochem, R., Early, D. R., & Conger, R. D. (2012). Dispositional optimism: A psychological resource for Mexican-origin mothers experiencing economic stress. *Journal of Family Psychology, 26*(1), 133–139.
144. Thomas, J. T. (2010). *The ethics of supervision and consultation: Practical guidance for mental health professionals*. American Psychological Association.
145. Tohidian, N. B., & Quek, K. M. T. (2017). Processes that inform multicultural supervision: A qualitative meta-analysis. *Journal of Marital and Family Therapy, 43*(4), 573–590.
146. Topor, D. R., AhnAllen, C. G., Mulligan, E. A., & Dickey, C. C. (2017). Using video recordings of psychotherapy sessions in supervision: Strategies to reduce learner anxiety. *Academic Psychiatry: The Journal of the American Association of Directors of Psychiatric Residency Training and the Association for Academic Psychiatry, 41*(1), 40–43.
147. Truax, C. B. & Carkhuff, R. R. (1967). *Toward effective counseling and psychotherapy*. Aldine.
148. Tsai, M., Callaghan, G. M., Kohlenberg, R. J., Follette, W. C., Darrow, S. M. (2009). Supervision and therapist self-development. In *A guide to functional analytic psychotherapy*. Springer.
149. Tsai, M., Kohlenberg, R. J., Kanter, J. W., Holman, G. I., & Loudon, M. P. (2012). *Functional analytic psychotherapy: Distinctive features*. Routledge.
150. Tsong, Y., & Goodyear, R. K. (2014). Assessing supervision's clinical and multicultural impacts: The Supervision Outcome Scale's psychometric properties. *Training and Education in Professional Psychology, 8*(3), 189–195.
151. Tsui, M. S., O'Donoghue, K., & Ng, A. K. (2014). Culturally-competent and diversity-sensitive clinical supervision: An international perspective. *Wiley international handbook of clinical supervision* (pp. 238–254). John Wiley & Sons.
152. Vespia, K. M., Heckman-Stone, C., & Delworth, U. (2002). Describing and facilitating effective supervision behavior in counseling trainees. *Psychotherapy: Theory, Research, Practice, Training, 39*(1), 56–65.
153. Vezer, E. (2020). *Bug-in-the-eye supervision: A critical review*. Training and Education in Professional Psychology. Advance online publication. https://doi.org/10.1037/tep0000308.
154. Wade, J., & Jones, J. (2015). *Strength-based clinical supervision: A positive psychology approach to clinical training*. Springer.
155. Watkins, Jr., C. E. (2012). Psychotherapy supervision in the new millennium: Competency-based, evidence-based, particularized, and energized. *Journal of Contemporary Psychotherapy, 42*(3), 19–203.
156. Watkins Jr, C. E. (2017). How does psychotherapy supervision work? Contributions of connection, conception, allegiance, alignment, and action. *Journal of Psychotherapy Integration, 27*(2), 201.
157. Watkins Jr., C. E. (2021) Rupture and rupture repair in clinical supervision: some thoughts and steps along the way. *The Clinical Supervisor, 40*(2), 341–344.

158. Watkins Jr, C. E., & Scaturo, D. J. (2013). Toward an integrative, learning-based model of psychotherapy supervision: Supervisory alliance, educational interventions, and supervisee learning/relearning. *Journal of Psychotherapy Integration, 23*(1), 75–95.
159. Watkins, E. C., & Milne, D. L. (2014). *The Wiley international handbook of clinical supervision*. John Wiley & Sons.
160. Watkins, Jr, C. E., Reyna, S. H., Ramos, M. J., & Hook, J. N. (2015). The ruptured supervisory alliance and its repair: On supervisor apology as a reparative intervention. *The Clinical Supervisor, 34*(1), 98–114.
161. Weck, F., Kaufmann, Y. M., & Witthöft, M. (2017). Topics and techniques in clinical supervision in psychotherapy training. *The Cognitive Behaviour Therapist*, 10, E3.
162. Wilson, H. M. N., Davies, J. S., & Weatherhead, S. (2016). Trainee therapists' experiences of supervision during training: A meta-synthesis. *Clinical Psychology & Psychotherapy, 23*(4), 340–351.
163. Wrape, E. R., Callahan, J. L., Ruggero, C. J., & Edward Watkins, C. (2015). An exploration of faculty supervisor variables and their impact on client outcomes. *Training and Education in Professional Psychology, 9*(1), 35–43.

INDEX

Achievement/Accomplishment 51
ADDRESSING model in supervision 86–87, 88–89
agenda-setting 14
anxiety: feedback 164–165; observation of clinical work 142–144; supervisors and trainees 64–67
apologies, effective 181–182
Appreciative Inquiry (AI): define the relationship 108; deliver the future 190–191; design the plan 111–112; discover and reflect on strengths 109–110; don't settle 192–193; dream the future 110–111; final sessions 189–193; goal-setting 101–117; grit 113; identifying and amplifying strengths 69; mapping daily activities to goals 113; positive differences 104; preferred future 101, 103, 190; ROPES model 105, 106; sample transcript 115–117; scaling 113–115; solution-focused skills 103–104; stages of 107–112, 190–193
assessment 10, 11
attitudes and beliefs about supervision 62–63, 73
audio observation 138
autonomy 6, 10, 11
awareness 10, 11

Ballantyne, E. C. 14
Bandura, A. 51–52
Basic Listening Sequence 93
behavioral learning 71
Behaviorism 47
Bernard, J. 9
best hopes 60–61, 73, 103
best practices in supervision 21–22
broaden and build 104, 173
burnout 126–127

Campbell, J. M. 62
case presentation 139–141
character strengths 49–52, 68–69
classical conditioning 47
client conceptualization 10, 11
clinical theory based models of supervision 12–13
closed questions 95
cognitive-behavioral supervision 13–14, 17
cognitive-behavioral theory (CBT) 47
cognitive learning 71
collective goals in supervision 100
common factors model 92
competency: multicultural factors 85–87; in supervision 28–38; of trainees 6
compliments, hidden 103
confidentiality limits 40
confusion 1, 8, 11
constructivist learning 71
contract, supervision 23, 35, 40, 57, 66, 77, 81, 143
courage, virtue of 50, 69
critical pedagogy 71
Csikszentmihalyi, M. 48–49, 194
culture and cultural differences 85–87
Cummings, J. A. 14

deliberate practice 194–196
De Shazer, S. 52
developmental models of supervision 5–6; process + developmental approaches 8–11
direct observation 135–136, 137
disease model of psychology 47
documentation 40
documentation review, limitations of 138–139
domains 9, 10, 11
dual relationships 40
Duckworth, A. 49, 113

effective supervision 23–27
Ellis, M. V. 143
emotional awareness 6
Emotions, Positive 51
empathy 129
encouragers 94, 96
end of the supervision relationship: Appreciative Inquiry (AI) 189–193; deliberate practice 194–196; preparation for 185–186; reflection and next steps worksheets 197–198; summative evaluation 189
Enns, C. Z. E. 88–89
ethical and regulatory considerations 39–40
evaluation in learning cycle of supervision 123
evidence base of clinical supervision: best practices 21–22; competency in supervision 28–38; effective supervision 23–27; ethical and regulatory considerations 39–40; impact

on trainees and clients 20–21; importance of supervision 20
exceptions 104
Existentialism 47
experiential learning 71

Falender, C. A. 123, 154–155
feedback: as an intervention 157; anxiety 164–165; case examples 165–168; communication of 156; effective 154–155, 157–162, 165–169; formal/informal 153; frequency 153; implementing by trainees 163, 170; importance of 153; learning cycle of supervision 123; purpose of 152; receptiveness to, improving 165; strength-based 157–162; supervision relationship and 162–163; to supervisors from trainees 157, 159; worksheet 169
feminist supervision 14–15, 17
Fialkov, C. 68
final sessions: Appreciative Inquiry (AI) 189–193; with clients 186–188; deliberate practice 194–196; preparation for 185–186; reflection and next steps worksheets 197–198; summative evaluation 189
first supervision sessions: anxiety 64–67; attitudes and beliefs 62–63, 73; best hopes for 60–61, 73; checklist 80; contract checklist 81; identifying and amplifying strengths 68–69, 73; informed consent 82; learning styles 69–70, 71–72, 73; learning theory 69, 70–71; myths about supervision 62–63; preparation 59–83; ruptures, planning for 179–180; self-care in supervision 74–76
flagging the minefield 104
flow 48–49, 194–195
4D model *see* Appreciative Inquiry (AI)
Freud, S. 4

Give-me-five technique 145
goals in supervision: Appreciative Inquiry (AI) 101–117; collective/individual 100; developmental/deficit model 100; grit 113; intervention questions 100–101, 102; learning cycle of supervision 123; mapping daily activities to goals 113; refining and documenting goals 117; scaling 113–115; setting 99–100; solution-focused skills 103–104
Goodyear, R. 9, 60
grit 49, 51, 113

Haddad, D. 68
happiness 51
Hays, P. A. 86
HERO acronym 51–52
history of clinical supervision and training 4
hope 51
Humanism 47
humanistic supervision 13, 16
humanity, virtue of 50
humility, virtue of 69

individual differences 10, 11
individual goals in supervision 100
informed consent 40, 57, 82, 136–137, 143
Integrated Developmental Model (IDM) 5–6, 8–11
Integrated Social Justice Model (ISJ) 88–89
integration 8
interpersonal assessment 10, 11
Interpersonal Process Recall (IPR) 145
interventions 10, 11; feedback 157; questions 100–101, 102, 140–141, 172–176, 189; solution-focused 46–47, 52–53
I-spy technique 145

Johnson, E. A. 153
justice, virtue of 50, 69

Kangos, K. A. 30

Lambert, M. 92
learning cycle of supervision 123
learning styles 69–70, 71–72
learning theory 69, 70–71
liability standards 40
live observation 138
Loganbill, C. 6, 8

Manring, J. M. 142
Maslow, A. 47
Meaning 51
miracle question 52–53, 103
models of supervision: benefits of 5; clinical theory based 12–13; cognitive-behavioral supervision 13–14, 17; developmental 5–6; feminist supervision 14–15, 17; humanistic supervision 13, 16; individual 5; narrative supervision 15, 17; person-centered approach 13; process-based approaches 6–8; process + developmental approaches 8–11; psychodynamic supervision 12, 16
monitoring of clinical work: anxiety 142–144; audio observation 138; case presentation 139–141; categories of 135–136; direct observation 135–136, 137; documentation review, limitations of 138–139; Give-me-five technique 145; importance of 134–135; informed consent 136–137; integrating methods 147; Interpersonal Process Recall (IPR) 145; I-spy technique 145; limited occurrence of 134–135; live observation 138; methods 137–139, 145–147; progress and outcome measures 141–142; questions to consider during 146; role induction 143–144; self-report, limitations of 138–139; video observation 138, 148–149; worksheet 148–149
Moore, E. C. 74, 127
motivation 10, 11
multicultural factors in supervision 85–87
myths about supervision 62–63

naïve practice 194
narrative supervision 15, 17

Neuger, C. C. 15
next steps worksheets 197–198
Norcross, J. C. 93, 186

observation of clinical work: anxiety 142–144; audio observation 138; case presentation 139–141; categories of 135–136; direct observation 135–136, 137; documentation review, limitations of 138–139; Give-me-five technique 145; importance of 134–135; informed consent 136–137; integrating methods 147; Interpersonal Process Recall (IPR) 145; I-spy technique 145; learning cycle of supervision 123; limited occurrence of 134–135; live observation 138; methods 137–139, 145–147; progress and outcome measures 141–142; questions to consider during 146; role induction 143–144; self-report, limitations of 138–139; video observation 138, 148–149; worksheet 148–149
ongoing supervision sessions: checklist 132; essential tasks 124; learning cycle of supervision 123; relationships, supervision 130–131; remediation 173–179; responsibilities 122; ruptures in supervision relationships 179–183; self-care 126–129; 12-week timeline 125–126 *see also* feedback; observation of clinical work
open questions 95
operant conditioning 47
optimism 52
outcome measures 141–142

parallel processes 12, 13–14
paraphrases 94, 96
patient-centered category of psychodynamic supervision 12
performance in learning cycle of supervision 123
permission, asking 103
personal motivation 6, 7
person-centered approach 13
person-centered learning 71
Peterson, C. 49–50
planning: final sessions 185–186; first supervision sessions 59–83; learning cycle of supervision 123; for ruptures 179–180; treatment 10, 11
positive differences 104
Positive Emotions 51
Positive Psychology 47–52
Positive Relationships 51
preferred future 46, 51, 99, 101, 103, 190
presuppositions, positive 104
principle ethics 39
problem-solving 14, 40
process-based approaches 6–8
process + developmental approaches 8–11
professional ethics 6, 7, 10, 11
professional identity 6
progress and outcome measures 141–142
progress questions 95
psychodynamic supervision 12, 16
psychological capital 51–52
purpose and direction 6
purposeful practice 194–196

Quek, K. M. T. 85
questions: intervention 100–101, 102, 140–141, 172–176, 189; during observation of clinical work 146; supervision relationship and 93, 95, 97

reflection and next steps worksheets 197–198
reflection in learning cycle of supervision 123
reflective listening 93–94, 96
regulatory considerations 39–40
Relationships, Positive 51
relationships, supervision: common factors model 92; feedback and 162–163; final sessions 185–186; healthy, factors in 92; ongoing supervision sessions 130–131; remediation 173–179; role of 92; ruptures in 179–183; skills in building 93–97; therapeutic outcomes and 92
remediation 173–179
resilience 52
respect for individual difference 6
Rogers, C. 13, 92, 93
role induction 143–144
ROPES model 105, 106
rules and guidelines, ethical 40
ruptures in supervision relationships 179–183

scaling 113–115
Scallion, L. M. 14
self-care in supervision 74–76, 126–129
self-disclosure 127, 129
self-efficacy 51–52
self-report, limitations of 138–139
Seligman, M. 47, 49–50, 51, 101, 194
Shafranske, E. P. 123, 154–155
shared goals in supervision 100
Simpson-Southward, C. 88
Sinacore, A. L. 88–89
social justice 88–89
solution-focused interventions 46–47, 52–53
solution-focused skills 103–104
solution-focused therapy 15, 17
stages in development 9
stagnation 8, 11
static practice 194
strict liability standards 40
summarizations 94, 96
summative evaluation 189
supervisory-matrix-centered category of psychodynamic supervision 12

Tangen, J. L. 71
temperance, virtue of 50, 69
termination practices 186–188
theoretical orientation 10, 11
theories/techniques of strength-based supervision: character strengths 49–52; flow 48–49; grit 49; individuals, models for 53–54; Positive Psychology 47–52; present/future focus 46;

solution-focused interventions 46–47, 52–53
see also models of supervision
therapy, key components of 4
Tohidian, N. B. 85
Topor, D. R. 142
trainee-centered category of psychodynamic supervision 12
trainees: anxiety 66; competency in supervision 30, 34–36; effective 27; evidence base of clinical supervision 20–21; feedback to supervisors from 157, 159; implementing feedback 163, 170
transcendence, virtue of 50, 69
treatment planning 10, 11
12-week timeline 125–126

using this workbook 2

VARK questionnaire 72
video observation 138
virtue ethics 39
virtues 50

well-being 51
wisdom, virtue of 50, 69